Corporate Diplomacy

# Corporate Diplomacy

## The Strategy for a Volatile, Fragmented Business Environment

Ulrich Steger
International Institute for Management Development (IMD)

with a foreword by

**Antony Burgmans**
CEO, Unilever

**WILEY**

*Other Wiley Editorial Offices*

John Wiley & Sons Inc., 111 River Street, Hoboken, NJ 07030, USA

Jossey-Bass, 989 Market Street, San Francisco, CA 94103-1741, USA

Wiley-VCH Verlag GmbH, Boschstr. 12, D-69469 Weinheim, Germany

John Wiley & Sons Australia Ltd, 33 Park Road, Milton, Queensland 4064, Australia

John Wiley & Sons (Asia) Pte Ltd, 2 Clementi Loop #02-01, Jin Xing Distripark, Singapore
129809

John Wiley & Sons Canada Ltd, 22 Worcester Road, Etobicoke, Ontario, Canada M9W 1L1

**British Library Cataloguing in Publication Data**
A catalogue record for this book is available from the British Library

ISBN 0-470-84890-1

Project management by Originator, Gt Yarmouth, Norfolk (typeset in 12/15pt Garamond)
Printed and bound in Great Britain by Biddles Ltd, Guildford and King's Lynn
This book is printed on acid-free paper responsibly manufactured from sustainable forestry
in which at least two trees are planted for each one used for paper production.

# Contents

# Acknowledgments

As always, in this book I have collected, processed and framed the ideas, experiences and sometimes the suffering of other people, taking advantage of the unique position that the International Institute for Management Development (IMD) occupies – being close enough to business to see what is happening but still detached enough to observe. So my first thanks go to the literally scores of executives from global companies who, in the constant stream of interviews, discussions, dinner conversations and questions, moulded my concepts and thinking to flow like a river shaping its bed as it goes along. Most influential among them were the "standard bearers" in IMD's Learning Network, my role models for Corporate Diplomacy: Hans Adams, Dow Chemical Co.; Ruth Blumer, Sulzer Ltd.; Jeroen A. Bordewijk, Unilever BestFoods; Peter Hughes, Philip Morris Int'l SA; Bart Jan Krouwel, Rabobank; Teresa Presas, Tetra Pak Int'l; Michael Robertson, ABB Group; Shawqi Hamdan Sajwani, Dubai Aluminium Co. Ltd.; Michael Schemmer, Bombardier Transportation GmbH; Thomas Streiff, Swiss Reinsurance; and Pierre Trauffler, De Pont de Nemours Int'l SA. The intimate sharing of experience was the real litmus test for the conceptual thinking outlined in this book.

Next in line is the great team of the Forum for Corporate Sustainability Management at IMD who supported my research in many ways: Aileen Ionescu-Somers, Kay Richiger, and especially Oliver Salzmann who participated in the literature and case research (as did

Benjamin Bieber) and took care of the final shape of the manuscript. Debbi Brunettin improved my Teutonic English with patience and competence. My colleagues Derek Abell, Joe DiStefano, Jay Galbraith, George Haour, Jan Kubes, Jean-Pierre Lehmann and Piero Morosini were conspicuous in their readiness to give me feedback, encouragement, and trails to follow.

The academic literature was less relevant than I had originally hoped. Nevertheless, I owe a lot to my discussions with, among others, Stuart Hart, Forest L. Reinhardt, Paschen von Flotow and Jan-Olaf Willums. Being closer to the corporate side, it was helpful that Thilo Bode (formerly with Greenpeace, now with Food Watch), Chris Hails, and Paul Steele (World Wide Fund for Nature [WWF]) and especially Heike Leitschuh-Fecht with her "go-between" experience, challenged me along the way and helped me to better understand how NGOs (non-governmental organizations) are evolving and how they perceive the issues. In the same category I should like to include John Elkington, the most wonderful person to disagree with, and his team from Sustain-Ability.

However, in the end it is a very personal book that reflects my own experiences and shows how my views and thinking have developed through observation, research, and constant exposure to global managers. Consequently, I take sole responsibility for any errors, shortcomings and flaws that may be found in the book.

# Foreword

We operate in a global business environment in which the rate and scale of change can be perplexing. While profit may appear to be the one and only reason that we are in business there is more to business than just profitable growth.

Some people are suspicious of any association between society and companies. But, as Ulrich Steger points out, "Companies are intertwined with the surrounding society." At Unilever we believe this and live this. Corporate Social Responsibility is integral to our operating tradition. We also have a system of ethical principles, the Code of Business Principles. There is nothing new in this, it has always been the way our company runs its business – though it is now reassuringly fashionable.

The reasons are simple enough. Millions of people put their trust in us each day for their food, their household hygiene and grooming. We must retain that trust. People expect us to be accountable for what we do. That is why we have been engaged in making our operations more transparent through stakeholder dialogue and reporting.

Running a business that meets the needs of stakeholders (consumers, customers, suppliers, shareholders, etc.) can also release social value. In this book, Ulrich Steger cites the example of the Marine Stewardship Council (MSC). Unilever founded the MSC together with the World Wide Fund for Nature to establish sustainable fishing. As of 2005, Unilever aims only to buy and process fish from sustainable sources. We will inform the consumer of this decision and are certain that the consumer will prefer fish products obtained according to sustainable methods. If our colleagues in the industry do the same, this will be a tremendous impulse for the entire project.

In addition, it is easy for managers and people in corporations to underestimate the potential impact of their skills. Unilever is a manufacturer of branded products and we are good at communicating with people and training them. We are using those skills, for instance, in Africa to boost awareness of the risks of Aids.

Corporate social responsibility lies at the heart of the CEO's job. It is not an obscure programme or initiative. It is personal. I am called to account by consumers, employees, shareholders, and many more. And many of our senior managers have to be involved as well. Instead of being bland or non-committal they need to know what is going on. They need to find out for themselves how their company is touching people's lives, and they have to lead the way. They must be responsible and their responsibility must shine like a beacon over the entire organization. So we believe that if a company meets its consumer or customer needs on a sustained basis it will also be able to generate prosperity for employees and shareholders.

Corporations must make it clear that they have nothing to hide. Corporate Diplomacy is not the art of spin, but the practice of being upfront and communicative with a wide variety of people directly and successfully. The reality explored by Ulrich Steger is that companies have to be transparent if they are to succeed in an age when scrutiny is global and unrelenting.

Perhaps this sounds impossible. But I think it is not only possible but a commercial imperative. Ulrich Steger's book makes this abundantly clear. Companies must deliver to the expectations of their stakeholders. If companies are responsible they can not only change the world but create prosperity for those whose lives they touch. No one can ask for more.

*Antony Burgmans*, (CEO, Unilever), November 2002

# Preface

Sometimes it hurts to see companies hitting the wall because they ignored the basics in managing their business environment, which includes customers, regulators, the media, environmental or social activists, or even all of them together, including their own employees. Companies readily go to war with the rest of the world without knowing how to end the war successfully and are often forced into a hasty retreat, losing more than money in the process.

*Corporate Diplomacy* summarizes and conceptualizes the wealth of experience that can be found in every industry and country, and develops a strategic approach and complementary toolkit that can help companies to deal responsibly and strategically with a fragmented, volatile, and, to some extent, hostile business environment. Responsibility and strategy are interdependent; in today's world, a global company does not act strategically if it is not responsible – basically, there have to be acceptable and communicable reasons for its behaviour. This does not mean being everybody's darling, but rather being enlightened about the way in which a company is pursuing its interests, anticipating conflicts, and understanding interdependency and "goldfish bowl" transparency. The alternative should be obvious: if companies do not act responsibly, a return to the heavy-handed regulation of the 1970s and 1980s is lurking in the wings because a democratic society does not, in the long run, accept the irresponsible use of power. The current struggle of US corporations to regain legitimacy after the excesses of the stockmarket bubble is only the most recent example.

## A ROADMAP FOR THE BOOK

After the Introduction, and a definition in *Chapter 1* of Corporate Diplomacy together with a summary of the research results, *Chapter 2* begins with a more general review of the world of today and tomorrow. It endeavours to cut through a great deal of rhetoric about globalization by focusing on the question of what really is new on the subject. Central to this is the observation about the erosion of boundaries that leads to both much greater interaction and higher complexity. However, globalization is not without contradictions and we are very far from a "world society", let alone a trend towards homogeneity in general. But the concerns, sometimes even fear, regarding the largely unknown and uncontrollable impact of globalization lead to a predictable countertrend: in short, "anti-globalization" or, more precisely, a political and powerful critique of current globalization trends. The "honeymoon" for global companies is over – instead, maintaining their "licence-to-operate" without old-fashioned, heavy-handed regulations now depends greatly on "Corporate Diplomacy".

To understand this confusing world, one has to look at the players in the global village, which is covered in *Chapter 3*. The often-heard claim of the "powerless (national) state" is discussed, especially in the light of 11 September 2001: security, now back and a priority on the agenda, can only be guaranteed by governments. Global companies, on the other hand, are often regarded as faceless, footloose, yet mighty organizations that are now ruling the world. However, not only competition but also the narrow focus on markets and the internal contradictions of decentralized organizations lead to many dilemmas and ambiguities in corporate decision-making and actions, a fact that is often exploited by the organizations of the emergent "civic society", all lumped together under the wobbly expression of "non-governmental organizations" (NGOs). They have powerful leverage to press for change – if they play by the rules of 30-second attention spans and ever-fresh "dramas" afforded to them by the global media.

*Chapter 4* looks at the "status quo" of Corporate Diplomacy. Using Monsanto and Genetic Modified Organism (GMO) clashes as a template, it can be seen that there is a set of "typical" mistakes that companies make: not really understanding the issue, the core of the controversy; underestimating the adversary; and moving too slowly, too little and too late. This is partly, and not least, caused by the low emphasis that companies put on relevant stakeholders when specific issues came up. However, not all (or even the majority of) companies have got it wrong. Many have learned over the years to survive public pressure by adapting. Four generic corporate strategies (explained by caselets) can be observed in this context: "nice guy", "good citizen", "lonely fighter" and "stealth bomber". But, in addition, one has to understand what constitutes the "transmission belt" that can transform stakeholders' expectations, or even anger, into corporate relevance. The new role of brands, and their promises, is an additional driver that makes companies more vulnerable.

To identify relevant issues, a company first needs an early awareness system (covered in *Chapter 5*). This is not so much about huge resources or systems, but more about having an enquiring attitude or being open-minded, and can be exercised by some simple tools that are introduced. Second, two (tested) checklists for assessing the relevance of an issue for a company are explained: one from the corporate perspective and the other from the adversary's point of view (because NGOs do not choose their campaigns at random). Only very few clashes occur "out of the blue" and understanding the characteristics of issues helps to clarify a company's position and how defendable it is.

*Chapter 6* discusses the critical elements for making Corporate Diplomacy happen. Being economic entities, companies have to build a business case for what they are doing (otherwise it remains rhetoric) and overcome seven specific barriers to achieving potential benefits or risk reductions. However, with some exceptions, those institutions that were built to deal with the business environment – the industry associations – are probably the least helpful in supporting Corporate Diplomacy because of their structural deficits. Therefore, new organizations have now sprung up – from the World Business Council for Sustainable Development (WBCSD) to the Global Reporting Initiative – that allow companies to share experiences and find support in development of tools. In addition, new developments in capital markets may also support "good corporate citizenship".

A lot depends on communication in the global "goldfish bowl transparency" that is analysed in *Chapter 7*. Starting with the difference between today's and future communication needs and patterns, relative to "the good old days" when far more happened quite naturally in stable social structures, it continues with an explanation of the needs of different target groups and their requirements. Although this is a book on crisis prevention, I have nevertheless defined "Seven Golden Rules for Crisis Management", just in case . . .

*Chapter 8* looks specifically at the relationship between NGOs and companies. Both types of organization legitimately have different goals and pursue different interests. Therefore one can expect varying degrees of conflict as well as co-operation, depending on the circumstances, the issues and the goals, or even the pressure to come up with a common solution. Managing an alliance with NGOs, as the Marine Stewardship Council indicates, is a learning laboratory – you can probably manage any business alliance if you can manage the co-operation of such different players. But a company can also enjoy confrontation with NGOs, as for example Exxon is doing. In any case, you have to be clear in your goals and consistent and professional in your action and communication.

*Chapter 9* looks at three examples of companies that have succeeded in finding a sustainable balance, and their experience is analysed using three different criteria: how to learn and develop organizational competencies (ABB), what processes you need to have in place (DaimlerChrysler) and the issues that are confronting the company (Shell). These more in-depth case studies of reference companies complement the many smaller cases that highlight the findings in each chapter.


## RESEARCH METHODOLOGY

The findings of the book are based on a plurality of applied research methods. The least important source was, unfortunately, academic literature. Too much is either "preaching" to companies encouraging them to behave nicely, well-meant advice from an ivory tower, or pretty meaningless correlations of two variables that fit well into the US "publish or perish" system as the "least publishable unit". (I well remember the sight of Henry Minkberg reviewing the strategy literature; he would be happy if, as in gold-mining, he found 3% gold in the vast amount of rock.) More relevant were empirical investigations and surveys on a broader scale, not just opinion polls (but, remember, behind every survey there is a hidden agenda . . .), and case studies that we partly carried out ourselves (see "Further Reading" on p. 293 and "IMD Case Studies" on p. 291). Reviewing professional journals and economic newspapers was more revealing – for example, a couple of cases were written from public sources because few companies were ready to "sign off" their disasters.

But most valuable were the many interviews and discussions I was able to conduct with approximately 250 executives over the past three years. Having personally been through many similar dilemmas and stresses, I believe I am better able to detect patterns, general learning points, and what worked and what did not. I conducted formal interviews, which I have treated in the same way as quotes from public sources, and undertook many informal interviews, including lunch and dinner discussions; in doing so, I have respected the confidentiality of the conversation and disguised the source. Not being under pressure to come up with an academic "apparatus" for this book, I decided not to miss the real-life insights that these discussions permitted, hoping that the reader would trust my methodological rigour and judgment.

# Introduction and Overview 1

## 1.1 YES, YOU CAN GET AWAY WITH IT

On 21 September 2001, an explosion rocked the Total Fina Elf plant in Toulouse, leaving 30 dead, approximately 2,500 injured, and destroying many properties in the surrounding neighbourhood – it had all the ingredients of an accident to be mentioned in the same breath as Seveso, Bhopal, Schweizerhalle ... In addition, some of the merged company's predecessors were embroiled in high-profile corruption trials and investigations.

However, some 10 days earlier the tragedy at the World Trade Center in New York had occurred and public attention was directed elsewhere. At the beginning, Total Fina Elf played the "terrorist card", managing to keep matters low-key, setting up an emergency fund for the victims, meeting with the French environment minister to outline "the foundations of the safety issues concerning industrial facilities and their coexistence in highly-urbanized areas".

The company's critics claimed this to be a "smoke screen", a cover-up by the French elite to ensure that public attention would soon turn away. Although the official report stated that it was due to a number of factors, one seasoned safety executive maintained, "the explosion was due to a flaw in the safety design of the process. And, based on previous experience, you do not survive for long in our competitive industry if your environmental and safety processes are not state-of-the-art. They determine your productivity." So justice may come via a different route, because public punishment in a market economy is an effective way of correcting corporate inefficiency.

## Box 1-1   The long battle on PVC

Since the mid-1980s, "chlorine chemistry" has come under intense scrutiny from environmentalists and public authorities. However, although approximately 60% of the chemical industry deals with chlorine at one stage in the value creation process, many end products do not contain chlorine at all. This, coupled with the increased safety standards achieved on chemical sites (especially those based in Europe following the so-called "Seveso Guidelines"), plus industry's own actions under the Responsible Care Programme, has encouraged environmentalists to turn their attention to the "outlets" where products containing chlorine are entering the environment. These products are certain agro-chemicals (the most well-known being DDT) or chemicals for wood preservation (for example, Unidan) and PVC – the most important of all. PVC absorbs by volume two-thirds of the chlorine used. In the course of time, most of the toxic chlorinated compounds (most of them chlorinated hydrocarbons), bio-accumulative and persistent, have been banned, restricted in use or voluntarily phased out by the chemical industry and therefore no longer offer environmentalists an interesting campaign.

This was not the case with PVC, however. Due to its importance, the chemical industry (and in a show of solidarity from even those companies that did not produce PVC) stood its ground. A protracted war evolved, a real dogfight, and, more often than not, industry lost. PVC is no longer used in most packaging materials, but the important construction industry holds its ground (window frames, roofing systems) because it is so hard to find viable alternatives to PVC; for example, wood is environmentally questionable due to its need to be treated with preserving chemicals every other year and environmentalists hesitate to recommend aluminium as an alternative. In some countries, the chemical industry was forced into organizing expensive collecting and recycling measures, narrowing the economic advantage over substitutes to avoid the ever-present accusation that, otherwise, dioxins are generated (for example, in waste incinerators). Those who like a sophisticated debate will point out that there are approximately 240 different kinds of dioxin with a wide range of chemical properties, but, of course, for the public dioxin is simply an ugly poison.

Anti-chlorine activists began to link the PVC debate to another debate, one which was difficult for them to handle: endocrine disrupters and oestrogen mimicking. This debate concerned a wide range of chemicals (amongst which, of course, chlorinated compounds were prominent) that influence the functions of the body because they behave like oestrogen produced by the human body.

The controversial scientific debate has not yet produced clear evidence as to whether accusations of a rise in the incidence of cancer or reduced repro-duction capabilities (low sperm count, for example) are plausible or not. (It would, of course, be easier to become involved in the debate if we knew whether man was more like monkeys or rodents in his reaction to these chemicals.) Yet, because the sources are so varied and the effects not visually obvious (it would be difficult to prove that a man's impotency has been caused by a particular chemical), the campaigns have not led very far.

So, the next step was to look for a link between PVC and endocrine inter-rupters. This was easy: phthalates, used to give PVC special features and particularly to make it soft. Most adults do not consume PVC products though, so it is difficult to establish a path to link phthalates in PVC to any effects on the human body. However, there are exceptions: babies and small children. As soon as Greenpeace discovered that teething rings made from soft PVC had a greater share of phthalates than normal, a European-wide campaign was launched.

There were no standards for measuring the exposure of babies biting their teething rings to phthalates, and the European Union (EU) refused to impose a ban due to a lack of scientific evidence. Although questionable, numerous EU countries nonetheless imposed a national ban. Toy-makers too, for example LEGO, were concerned about negative publicity and substituted PVC in their toys for small children. In the event, a standard protocol was put in place and things have now calmed down. However, PVC has lost another market application – perhaps small, but nevertheless a stepping stone towards the next battle: PVC use in medical products, where an especially high amount of softeners are used.

Although the industry dismissed Greenpeace's latest "anti-PVC fusillade" as being "rife with many tell-tale features of junk science: fear, specious logic and misleading information", market leader Baxter preferred to play it safe. The company announced that it was researching alternatives to PVC, which is used among other things in the manufacture of intravenous blood bags.

Other companies were less lucky: Talisman Energy, the largest Canadian independent oil producer, published a comprehensive report with the help of experts in business ethics and social auditing, to evaluate its progress in human and employee rights, community involvement, its record in environmental protection and so on. PricewaterhouseCoopers verified the report – to no avail. Critics remained unmoved and pressed ahead in the attempt to force Talisman out of a Sudan oil production joint venture with state-owned oil companies from China, Malaysia and Sudan.

Unfortunately, a civil war has been raging since 1956 in Sudan, mainly the Muslim north against the non-Muslim south, and the Khartoum government has allegedly been a host to Bin Laden. After a series of hearings in the US Congress and being pitched against Amnesty International, church clerics and academics, eventually Talisman decided that the toll was too high and withdrew from Sudan.

Talisman's surrender added to the long list of victims who have suffered from public pressure, been haunted by the media, defeated by environmental organizations, and finally pushed down the slippery slope that can lead to commercial turmoil. The list includes Nike, Coca-Cola, McDonald's, General Electric, Mitsubishi, Ford, Pfizer, Shell, BP and prominently Exxon – but also includes less famous names such as New Zealand Milk, Animex SA (a meat packer conglomerate), and Birkel (noodles) – to name but a few.

Some attempts have been made by companies to avoid potential trouble. For example, when Lufthansa negotiated an agreement with Pro Wildlife on the handling of wild animals, restricting among other things the transport of endangered species. But even having Green credentials does not always help: when Ford donated money to the US conservation group, the National Audubon Society, it was confronted with boycott threats from cattle ranchers in the Midwest who regarded this conservation organization specifically as a threat to their business, because the Society tried to impose restrictions on intensive cattle-grazing, subsidized by the low rent of federal land.

So, yes, there is the possibility that as a manager you may have to face public pressure or attacks from non-market forces like non-governmental organizations (NGOs) such as Friends of the Earth or Amnesty International (see Chapter 3). What makes every manager increasingly nervous is the uncertainty as to who will be the target and the increasing probability that the threat can come from every corner of the global world.

It is not understood when, why and how you might be hit, nor how one could prevent it. What has changed is the business environment; it now covers everything, not just markets, and includes government agencies and activist movements and everything is conducted in the full glare of the media.

Political advice for salvation abounds. For example, the European Commission (EC), published a green paper, "Corporate Social Responsibility"; the Organization for Economic Cooperation and Development (OECD) and national governments, political parties, all kinds of associations and – last but not least – academics are joining in. There is an overwhelming trend to follow the new "trinity" of social, ecological and economic criteria, advising corporations that "Sustainable Development" should be your goal; be nice to your stakeholders and eternal prosperity is just around the corner ... (I admit this description is somewhat oversimplified – but only a little ...) In Appendix I interested readers will find a more elaborate discussion.

If life in management was that easy, probably more would follow this wealth of advice, but "socially-responsible companies" are a small minority. Always the same names crop up: the Body Shop, Levi Strauss jeans and various co-operatives; and sometimes companies such as Shell, Otto, Novo Nordisk, or Unilever are mentioned as role models – as are family- or founder-owned businesses. Even state-owned companies are monopolies have been known to jump on the bandwagon, as have consultancies of all kinds. However, the vast bulk of mainstream companies are out of the loop (which does not help prevent them from being hit by activists or aggressive regulators) and it is not only Exxon that demonstrates that a company can be continuously successful by swimming against the tide.

## 1.2   WHAT CORPORATE DIPLOMACY IS ALL ABOUT

This book takes a different approach: first, let us agree that corporations are, above all, economic entities. In the centuries-long evolution and differentiation of societal institutions, corporations were not charged with the task of care for the common good, but rather for customers – that is, those willing to pay a price for the products and services on offer. In this role, then, the corporations are, hopefully, not wasting resources but adding more economic value through their activities.

So markets are dominant for companies. Secondly, however, companies are intertwined with surrounding society in several ways. For example, governments influence business in many dimensions – from the definition and enforcement of the legal infrastructure, without which no market could function, to specific regulations – and employees and customers are not only economic agents, but play multiple roles as parents, citizens, lobbyists and so on. In addition, a large part of the population work in public services or the not-for-profit sector (sometimes up to one-third of the workforce, depending on the country concerned and organization of government services). Economic goals are only one facet of what people often wish to achieve. And, as we see later (in Chapter 3), some individuals have dedicated their lives to fighting what they see as the evil consequences of corporate dominance.

Whether companies like it or not, they cannot avoid (and mostly not afford) dealing with interests, institutions, ideas and rules that are ouside the market domain. In this book, I use the expression "non-market" for such a business environment. And, as explained in Chapters 2 and 3, globalization makes this relevant part of the business much more fragmented, partly hostile, unpredictable, opportunistic, demanding, notably media-driven, and more diffuse than it used to be in the "good old days" of industrial feudalism.

The *Oxford English Dictionary* explains diplomacy as "art of, skill in dealing with people so that business is done smoothly". Therefore, "Corporate Diplomacy" is an attempt to manage systematically and professionally the business environment in such a way as to ensure that "business is done smoothly" – basically with an unquestioned "licence to operate" and an interaction that leads to mutual adaptation between corporations and society (in a sense a co-evolution). This does not exclude – on the contrary – free expression and conflicts of interest and values, different priorities and disagreements about facts. After all, this is the core of a democratic society. But the companies who engage in "Corporate Diplomacy" understand what the issues are and respond both reasonably and professionally, even to adverse activists, and use the expressions "activist" or "pressure group" – important parts of the pluralistic society as they are – without any negative connotations.

The central theme of *Corporate Diplomacy* focuses therefore on the question of how companies can understand this diffuse business environment. Can companies meet the social and ecological expectations of society without sacrificing their mission – which is to generate a profit by satisfying market demands? If so, how? What are the strategic implications and organizational consequences? What if the expectations are conflicting, unreasonable or contrary to most (if not all) advice? I do not want to convince anybody about a normative concept, or even lure companies into specific decisions. The strategy for *Corporate Diplomacy* is highly contextual, industry- and company-specific. All I can (and want to) do is create more transparency, transfer insight, document experience and provide some hopefully useful tools for executives, so that they can better manage the job in hand. After the stockmarket crash this seems to be more necessary than during the bubble.

## 1.3  A SUMMARY OF THE RESEARCH FINDINGS

### Beyond the buzzword: what's new about globalization?

In Chapter 2, I have tried to explain what's really new about globalization, arguing that it is a "changed change", its impact similar to the Industrial Revolution of some 200 years ago. This can be seen if one looks at the characteristics of globalization. I have listed six below.

- "Eroding boundaries" in every dimension: economics, society, politics, culture, etc. Of these, the economic impact is the most visible and most heatedly debated. Previously, boundaries between states or within society defined identities, allowed protection from the "evil outside" and limited impacts (for example, on national monetary policy). Today's world is more fluid, volatile, densely interactive and speedy.
- Higher mobility is a factor, notably capital and information, leaving behind less mobile workers.
- A move from hierarchy to "heterarchy", which means a mutual, horizontal interdependence (even if this is asymmetric: exercising power has higher costs than in the traditional hierarchy).
- Erosion of legitimacy, because responsibilities can no longer be defined in this complex world: national governments, for example, cannot be held accountable for economic well-being, but are the only institutions frustrated voters can turn to.
- Past–future asymmetry: many more "breakpoints" than linear progression of any development, which discounts experience as a guidance for decisions.
- Allocation of more responsibilities to each individual – to the point of overburdening – than was the case in previous, more "structured" and immobile societies. This offers freedom and opportunities, but also creates uncertainty, ambivalence and even anxiety.

These new conditions have far-reaching implications for states, regions, organizations and the individual. And for companies too, who must have an understanding of the changed business environment they now have to deal with. Multinational companies have increased their power to a degree not seen since the early days of capitalism because they can adapt more easily to the new conditions, being both driver and driven at the same time. Competition is everywhere, and new competitors are coming from all sides, technology and economic dynamics uprooting even entrenched market positions. But, when compared with other organizations and institutions, such companies appear to "rule the world" – and for some people this is accompanied by an expectation of their being the "problem-solver", beyond their commercial mission.

But now the "honeymoon" of globalization is over. A powerful alliance is fighting back against what it calls the "neo-liberal world order", which has created in its view only a few winners (for example, investment bankers), many losers (for example, workers and Third World peoples) and set a vicious "race-to-the-bottom" in motion – using low-paid labour and destroying the environment, social standards and national cultures in the process. Although this might seem to be a caricature of the measurable facts, perception is reality. A lot will depend, for future development, on how companies manage the new task of "corporate diplomacy". This requires an understanding of the players in the "global village".

### The players in the global village

Chapter 3 looks at the players that companies need to understand if they are to successfully manage their business environment. This understanding includes their own role in the process.

First, after years of declining importance due to globalization, the state is back. National security after 11 September 2001 is now a top priority. Security can only be delivered by governments. This does not only mean by the use of police or military force, but also by taking more control of technology and financial flow. As can be seen in the US, it also means more government interaction in trying to jump-start the economy and intervene in specific sectors (airlines, steel, agriculture, etc.). In times of war, domestic consensus is more important than market efficiency.

But the leading role the US has taken (unavoidably, because the Europeans are so weak) in the war against terror and rogue governments is aggravating many who are opposed to globalization: they see the cultural and economic hegemony of the US shaping the world. They resent mass-consumer ideals, represented by McDonald's and Coca-Cola. Sometimes this makes life more difficult for US companies abroad.

Beyond this more spectacular multinational development, nation states have fought against their own decline by forming "strategic alliances" (no mergers or acquisitions!). The European Union is probably the most advanced of these alliances. Governments pool their resources to solve specific problems that they cannot tackle on a national level: from global safety standards in shipping to cross-border waste management policies (Germany, for example, has signed more than 380 international treaties of this kind, which are now national laws). So, while it would be premature to write off the nation states, the EU is the only dominant player of the last decades to come onto the global political stage. Even the US is tied in a heterarchy relationship: without allies, it can achieve little and then only at a much higher cost.

Multinationals cannot expect to have an easy life, as the myth of a "footloose" enterprise – that is, one that always relocates with ease to the most convenient place in the world – suggests. The reality is that they require an in-depth understanding of the wide variety of market and non-market conditions they are faced with – not an easy job in organizations with high job rotation, a shift of power to "vertical" product lines following a global logic, and many outsourcing and alliance partners. But any mistake or failure they make, even in a remote area, can have dramatic repercussions in today's global goldfish bowl.

Responsible for this are, not least, the many NGOs. They encompass a wide range of causes and traditions: from millennium-old organizations such as the Catholic Church, to special purpose initiatives – literally nothing is uncovered (there are some 70 different NGOs for an issue such as "sustainable tea"!).

While some NGOs fight multinational corporations with dedication, skill and professionalism, others are ready to co-operate with business to further their cause. Even contradictory interests (for example, a vegetarian and a cattle rancher) may join together to protest, possibly connected by the Internet. And they have their victories: from an anti-trade-liberalization majority in the US Congress to the sinking of the planned World Trade Organization (WTO) agreement on Multilateral Agreements on Investment (MAI).

Other NGOs are at work in the less developed part of the world for humanitarian reasons, or serve as a substitute for government. This fluid, extremely fragmented scene is hard for corporations to monitor – and is therefore an area of many, mostly unpleasant, surprises. So, globalization has significantly changed the business environment in which companies have to operate.

Terrorism and organized crime have used the same infrastructure for globalization as have companies: easy travel, telecommunications, open financial markets, etc. It is no small wonder that they have prospered. Up to a couple of years ago, organized crime as terrorism was only a local issue, occurring in the less developed spots of the world, where multinational companies had to routinely deal with kidnappings for ransom, blackmail and widespread corruption.

In most cases, the companies themselves were left alone to handle matters; this may have meant giving up the market or failing to resource exploitation. Local government was either unable to help or was part of the mafia-like structure itself, so that support or intervention from the home country government to the host country government was of little use. But over the years money-laundering, especially from drugs trafficking or prostitution, penetrated the legal economy as mafia-controlled companies expanded into new markets, prompting OECD nations to react, albeit often half-heartedly. The US government, for example, did not sign the United Nations Convention for the Suppression of Financing Terrorism, because Wall Street objected – although it was pretty clear that the securities industry was a "weak spot" (as the US General Accounting Office put it).

However, global "goldfish bowl transparency" and actions by NGOs (for example, "Transparency International") have had the effect of making corporations steer clear of close relations with corrupt dictators or rogue business partners. Countries such as Myanmar (Burma) found it hard to encourage premier league oil companies to invest in their oil industry, despite attractive tax conditions. And 11 September 2001 marked the beginning of a dramatically changed political landscape. Most nations made new commitments and established restrictions designed to fight corruption, money-laundering and illegal trade with new vigour, as an indispensable precondition for fighting global terrorism. But there is a price tag: the preconditions for globalization and the eroding of boundaries are now re-established to some extent, impeding the free flow of information and technology as the restrictions take effect.

An important role, which global companies must understand and appreciate, is that played by the media. Today's media is dominated by global conglomerates, which fight 24 hours a day and seven days a week for the attention of readers/viewers/listeners, and for the advertising revenues thereby generated. The media is not so successful at telling people what to think, but rather what to think about, in effect establishing the agenda of the day. And, of course, good news is never going to make major headlines – harassing mighty companies is a far better story, especially if the issue can be visualized (for example, smashed windows at McDonald's). NGOs have become extremely skilful at playing by the rules of this game and its never-ending hunger for "breaking news".

### *Managing outside pressure: where do we stand today?*

In Chapter 4 we look at the empirical evidence on how companies have so far managed their business environment and the pressures with which they are confronted. One can learn more from failures than from straightforward success stories. Therefore the "classic" case of Monsanto and its "fight for hearts and shopping aisles" in the battle surrounding genetically modified organisms (GMOs) is used as a "template" to establish a pattern of typical mistakes in such confrontations:

● Monsanto did not understand the "real" issue (as it was perceived by the public and the media) – that is, the public's concerns regarding food safety, following a series of high-profile controversies and scandals. Instead, Monsanto's arguments were mainly scientifically-based. The company did not realize that the benefits of its innovation were on the producer side, with no advantage for the consumer who would be the one ultimately shouldering the "residual" (unknown) risk (such a risk/benefit ratio has been a sure recipe for disaster on many other occasions).

- Underestimating the adversary, not only misunderstanding how media-savvy the Greenpeace-led hunt was, but also how easily protesters could block permission at national level. By trying to overwhelm them with arguments that GMOs were "unavoidable", no different from non-GMO seed, and could not to be labelled as such for the consumer, Monsanto fuelled resistance further.
- Monsanto reacted too little and too late. This was demonstrated by failing to build European alliances first (choosing instead to bring in the US government, which made the mistake of setting up a David-vs.-Goliath conflict with the protesters) and giving in to pressure (for example, on the labelling issue), when everybody else had already jumped on the bandwagon.

In addition to these key points, the confrontation revealed (but did not create) the risk of a business model that put "all eggs into one basket". And yet this pattern can be seen time and again.

Underestimating the importance of stakeholders never pays off. But research for this book reveals that companies take a position somewhere in between – they see the emerging pressure, but it is not reflected in their priority list. It is not that companies pay no heed to the players in their business environment, they just display the "economic principle" in its minimum version – do something, but not too much; appear responsive, but not soft; be proactive, but only a little ...

Depending on the amount of pressure and a company's attitude, shaped by culture, recent experience, dependence on stakeholders, etc., four distinct clusters of generic strategies can be observed (and illustrated by cases).

- The "nice guy" (often in fast-moving, branded consumer goods) who invests in sponsoring, or positive public relations, and tries to avoid all risks or negative experiences which could upset customers.
- The "good citizen" (often in risk-exposed industries like energy, chemicals or car manufacturing) who demonstrates responsible behaviour through comprehensive reporting, life cycle assessments, public dialogue (even with adversaries), trying to convince the public and politicians alike that risk is being managed.
- The "lonely fighter" (probably not a position of choice, but rather one into which a company is pushed or has cornered itself – for example, as has happened in the nuclear and tobacco industries) who cannot build alliances, but circles wagons, rallies supporters, and defends himself vigorously.
- The "stealth bomber" (often heavily subsidized industries such as agri-industry, coal, etc.) who shies away from the limelight – because he always has to hide something, but does not want to change.

In addition, the research reviewed the "transmission belts" through which activists or protest groups exert pressure on companies to induce change (just having a bad image is not reason enough to change – as long as it does not hurt the bottom line). Direct action has somewhat gone out of fashion, but lobbying regulators and governments has definitely increased. There is a growing influence on capital markets – and very effectively one involving customers. Organizing a boycott is a powerful threat, but it only works under certain preconditions: the base line here is really unacceptable corporate behaviour has upset people – but the boycott should not mean consumers having to make too many sacrifices.

For companies with a household name brand, especially those whose brands promise more than quality – a better lifestyle, carefree fun or positive attitudes – the exposure to risk is higher. The more successful marketeers become in establishing a positive well-known brand, the more vulnerable the company will be to any (perceived) mismatch of brand promise and actual behaviour.

The lives of executives become even more complicated when the claims made by stakeholders (or even shareholders) contradict each other – as is often the case – or if potential adversaries or stakeholders are not identified in the fast-moving, complex business environment. But the way out is clear: do not target stakeholders, but rather look at issues and the characteristics of an issue. This calls for an "Early Awareness System".

## Detecting and preventing trouble ahead

As with every management system, an early awareness system needs processes and an information technology (IT) infrastructure. But this is the easy part. The real challenge relates to a company's attitude – its ability for open-mindedness, its inclination to observe and not be blind-folded by its own prejudices, filters or biases towards what it would like to see or hear.

A couple of simple tools (for example, the diffusion curve and cross-impact analysis) are presented. An outline of some of the general characteristics of an early awareness system, used to capture any weak signals that indicate an approaching issue for the company, are explained. Nobody can monitor the thousands of issues that are "cooking" out there, but companies should endeavour to capture them once they start to take off.

As most issues do not come out of the blue, but can be detected through weak signals emitted, companies can then rigorously test the relevance of an issue. Can this lead to a confrontation? How strong is our position? Based on observation of more than 120 conflicts between corporations and society (or segments of society), the research for this book came up with (and tested) the following checklist:

1 Are the arguments against the issue plausible?
2 Does the issue evoke emotion? Is it understandable – visual, touching – by the public?

**3** Is the issue media-friendly?

**4** Are there connections to other issues concerning the company or other companies?

**5** How strong is the activist group?

**6** How isolated is the company?

**7** How far have the dynamics of the crisis already evolved?

**8** How easy is the solution?

The use of the checklist is intuitively plausible (as can be seen from the explanation and the test case), but by no means sufficient: one has to put oneself into the shoes of the other side, too. Activist groups do not choose their campaigns at random – this would by far exceed their resources and diffuse their activities. Based on the research, the checklist from the "other side" could be as follows:

**1** The campaign has a clear aim or goal.

**2** The issue is easily understood by the general public.

**3** The issue has high symbolic value.

**4** The issue has the potential to damage the image of the company.

**5** The opponent is strong enough (no "underdog" effect).

**6** The issue can be "packaged" in a campaign in which the public can get involved.

**7** There are solutions that are confrontational, not gradual (political concepts, management concepts, product or process concepts that are competitive in price and quality).

**8** There is perhaps a dramatic element in the campaign that will engage media interest.

Only once managers work open-mindedly through both these checklists will it become clear what risks lie ahead, what could be the dynamics and how managers should best prepare. When a company decides to see the battle through, it must be aware of the "why's" and "how's". Far too often, companies embark on wars, only to find themselves shortly afterwards in a difficult retreat (mostly leading to a disorderly rout). The art lies not in starting a war, but in ending it successfully.

### Making corporate diplomacy happen

The most important action for any executive responsible in one way or other for managing the non-market environment is to build a company-specific, robust business case. It is only when companies have economic reasons that they will embark on an integrated strategy that comprises all three dimensions of Sustainable Development and an interactive approach to stakeholder dialogue.

General statistics or nice success stories in the media are not sufficient: the business case has to be industry- and company-specific, and look at the economic incentives (or disincentives). However, this does not mean (similar to other strategic decisions) that everything has to be quantified into detailed numbers (but as always some compelling figures do help). The main economic benefits can normally be detected through better risk management, both in the short and long term, a better understanding about newly-emerging business opportunities, and employee motivation. Risk management involves both political and regulatory impacts, as well as direct economic consequences – for example, on the brand itself or even declining demand through consumer boycotts. An early awareness system normally helps in all circumstances.

However, there are some obstacles to overcome – as in any change programme: the mindset and values of top management might blind them as, too, might a science-driven, inward-looking corporate culture. Regulatory barriers or the need to drive issues through the whole value creation process, getting the buy-in from suppliers and customers, could also be obstacles.

But pioneers also face a "first-mover disadvantage". When they move into uncharted territory they may have to deal with additional up-front investments in terms of acquiring knowledge and developing tools, processes, etc. Followers can easily profit from these efforts.

These costs have to be compensated by higher incentives. To overcome internal resistance, a "power promoter" – in an ideal case the chief executive officer (CEO) – is also needed to support the "professional promoter" in the implementation of the strategy. Six requirements can be defined here:

1  The attention and support of top management is an absolute must.
2  Even if companies do not develop a comprehensive strategy, but settle for a "case-by-case" approach (due for low incentives or risk exposure), an early awareness system (in a minimum version) is needed.
3  To get "your voice heard in the flood of information", clearly-defined target groups, with tailored messages, are essential.
4  The company has to speak globally, with one voice – not a trivial task, given the many different business environments and product markets in which global companies operate (not to mention internal politics). But this, together with the presence of a credible spokesperson (with operational credentials) is essential – keeping in mind the realistic assumption that a global company cannot be "everybody's darling".
5  Given today's global "goldfish bowl transparency", the possibility that the public will have to ask for confidential business information is normally pretty low. One just has to accept that emission data or working conditions in developing countries are no longer regarded as legitimate corporate secrets in today's "show me" world.
6  "Structure follows strategy" is a wise motto here, too. And any organization for managing the non-business environment has to be in line with the overall corporate organization: the more integrated the management of the issues, the better.

In endeavouring to build alliances (for example, to create an industry standard), industry associations are normally a mixed blessing. They serve predominantly as a "rearguard" due to the high consensus needed, which makes it easy to block any innovation. And it is always easier to organize (immediate) losers of structural change than it is to organize (future or potential) winners. This defensive attitude costs industry a good deal of credibility. Therefore, it is pretty clear that lobbying efforts will also come under greater scrutiny by NGOs, which will test whether a corporation "walks the talk" or misuses its power and its privileged access to decision-makers.

More progressive companies therefore have three options: to ignore the industry association and its message altogether; to split the association so that it becomes paralyzed and cannot do harm; or to push the association into an alliance, in the event that industry standards are needed.

Luckily, a number of initiatives have been created (for example, the WBCSD), which can serve as a platform for exchange of experience and benchmarking, joint research or common standards for reporting. In addition, there is now a small but growing segment of the capital market that wants to promote "corporate social responsibility" by investing in companies that perform well in all three dimensions: economic, ecological and social. A whole rating industry is growing up around this, and law-makers are pushing pension funds to reveal the social and ecological criteria of their investment policies.

Although this is a book on crisis prevention, some principled advice is provided as to what to do and how to behave when something has gone very wrong in some part of the world (and remember Murphy's Law: what can go wrong, will go wrong). It boils down to the ability to see a crisis in human terms, and to see the values that have been – unintentionally – violated. It is better to say "We apologize" in time, than to be sorry to have missed the slot were it could calm down a crisis.

## Corporate communication on a global scale

The difference between previous communication strategies and today's global requirements can be summed up in the following points:

- Erosion of local roots. In today's mobile world, with job rotation and commuting, there has to be a deliberate communication effort to establish earlier what has happened, and to ensure stable local interactions.
- Erosion of political importance. This has led to higher expectations for corporate behaviour, which has resulted in the appearance of "celebrity CEOs" and convenience promises: if a CEO shakes up an industry with multi-billion euro deals, why can he or she not save an indigenous tribe from a corrupt government?
- A new type of regulation, based on voluntary, negotiated agreement and a code of conduct; this also increases expectations for good corporate behaviour.
- The global "agenda" of nations and the different rules (from political correctness in the US to Japanese taboos) have to be recognized in order to get the corporate message across. Again, clear target groups and a thorough content are needed to cut through the usual "noise" level.

The target groups are first and foremost customers (especially where there are strong brands), who want to see a company in line with their own values, transparent, credible and tolerant. Other target groups will include: financial analysts, who always need a "story" to tell to the investors; those who need to be convinced by senior executives at "road shows" that the strategy will deliver in all aspects ("no surprises and only good news" is their expectation); people in the administrative/political environment and the regulatory community, who need scientific data and hard facts for their work, which can only be delivered by corporations; and last but not least all the players in the global village with their diverse interests, which shape the lens through which they view companies (for example, for a bird protection society, the most important corporate aspect could be that birds get caught in refinery smoke stacks and die).

As far as the content of the relevant issues is concerned, the ingredients and indicators for credibility are as follows:

- The involvement and commitment of top management, who "walk the talk".
- An understandable and practical vision and strategy (not expecting to save the world, but to do the utmost within the framework of the business case).
- The policy formulated to implement the strategy (for example, by environmental management systems and third-party verification).
- The transparency of performance indicators and results achieved over time, covering not only the industrial, but also the developing, world.
- Going beyond the obvious (for example, climate change) and "politically correct", and addressing emerging issues, dilemmas or challenges with which the business is confronted.

### "Suits" and "Sandals": balancing conflict and co-operation

Business and NGOs and activist groups have one thing in common: they are all "single issue" organizations (as opposed to political organizations). Yet they follow very different agendas: "making money by satisfying market demand" on the one hand and "promoting the chosen issue to satisfy members and donators" on the other. Despite the "partnership" rhetoric, expect more tension and conflict than harmony in the relationship. (In my estimate: in approximately 25% of all relevant issues, NGOs will run and try to win a campaign; in approximately 50% we can expect a confrontational debate, pitching lobbyists from each side against each other; and approximately 20% will have a more constructive, problem-solving-oriented dialogue; finally, in less than 5% of issues, co-operation is tried). Nobody is to blame: free expression and organization of interests is the core of any democratic society, and innovation comes out of conflict or dissatisfaction – not out of harmony.

Therefore, any company should have reason to establish stakeholder dialogue or even try co-operation. One has to realize that there are different games with different rules, by players with different agendas –

but when it works, the outcome is more than that resulting from "business as usual".

Depending on the commitment of business and NGOs, four options exist:

1   Opportunistic, *ad hoc* coalition on specific issues (for example, the EU regulation on clean fuel, where the auto industry and environmentalists teamed up to beat the oil industry).
2   Lending credibility (for example, allowing the use of the NGO logo to support environmentally-friendly products without a recognized brand).
3   Teaming up with outsiders to harass the industry mainstream (a preferred and successful Greenpeace strategy).
4   Joint problem-solving by the two partners as in the example of the Marine Stewardship Council (MSC).

Given the options, one has to be careful to map the territory, not along the for-or-against-me model, but much more looking at the interests certain groups pursue, and the cross-pressures they are under (for example, workers may support a factory extension for reasons of job security, but are uneasy with the increased traffic in their street). The key to this is: Don't try to convince an adversary, convince the audience instead.

Based on this analysis, the preconditions for co-operation become clear (as can be seen from the MSC):

●   Shared and important interest, with a win–win potential.
●   Top management involvement and entrepreneurial implementers.
●   Managing a balance between pushing forward and involving many stakeholders to build consensus.
●   Isolating the project from other conflicts (for example, by a separate organization).
●   Instead of being perfect, a readiness to experiment and pick the "low-hanging fruits" is needed first.

But you can also enjoy a confrontation (as Exxon is demonstrating). Confrontation can sharpen your (internal) corporate identity, your sense of mission (for example, "prudent science" vs. the "stampede of public opinion") and pride in your own achievements and excellence. You only have to have an outstanding performance record, harmony with some important stakeholders (in Exxon's case: the current US Administration) and a more centralized, culturally more homogenous organization than most global companies have today.

### Learning from three reference examples

For this study three companies were selected with an outstanding track record in managing their broader business environment over the last five years: ABB, DaimlerChrysler and Shell.

History was key in the analysis of ABB, indicating the process of going step-by-step from modest beginnings to becoming a frontrunner. Continuity of priorities, especially through a succession of CEOs, matters – as does an openness to be challenged by emerging issues, integrating everything into the business, learning continuously from experience and mistakes, testing building blocks, and never resting on one's laurels.

With DaimlerChrysler (DC) the focus is on the processes needed to comprehensively manage the business environment and anything that may affect the brand. The efficient design of global processes, and their back-up with a tailored IT infrastructure, is as important as its "fit" with the organizational structure and its alignment with corporate strategy.

Shell is a telling example of the range of issues a global company is confronted with (at the time of the research there were over 120, all of which could "flare up" at any time). However, there are strategic "make-it-or-break-it-issues" (in the long run probably climate change and the move to renewables are the most prominent), issues with high public attention (for example, Nigeria and biodiversity, which breaks down to local conflict) and local issues (for example, protest by

Right-wing religious groups in the USA about sales of girlie magazines at Shell stations). How to build a business case for dealing with these issues and how to monitor them are decisive questions to be addressed.

But all these three examples indicate that nothing prevents a business from being commercially successful while at the same time operating a global "Corporate Diplomacy" strategy.

# The Tangled World – Trends and Countertrends    2

This chapter begins with a more general review about the world of today and tomorrow. It tries to cut through a lot of rhetoric about "globalization" by focusing on the question: What is really *new* about globalization? Central to this question is the observation about the erosion of boundaries, which leads to both much greater interaction and higher complexity, more "break-up points", mobility of factors, reduced hierarchy and a rise in global economies. However, globalization is not without contradictions and we are much removed from a "world society", let alone a trend towards homogeneity in general. But the concerns about, and sometimes even fear of, the largely unknown, largely uncontrollable impacts of globalization – "legitimacy erosion" – lead to a predictable countertrend. In short, "anti-globalization", or more precisely a political, powerful critique of current globalization trends. The "honeymoon" for multinationals is over; now it will depend upon "Corporate Diplomacy". Whether they can maintain their "licence-to-operate" without old-fashioned, heavy-handed regulation is the problem multinationals cannot yet answer.

Throughout history, society has changed continuously, either at given moments or at a more steady pace, sometimes faster, sometimes slower. We describe different epochs and ages using suitable terms: for example, "the nuclear age", "the information age" or "the age of extremes".

What has also changed is that the former privilege of historians, to name such ages in retrospect, has today been usurped by politicians and the media. How quick they are to label epochs with terms such as "the age of [...]".

Indeed, for our present time, a term has been found that is very appropriate – "the age of globalization". In this chapter, what this catchword stands for, what lies behind the phenomenon of today's social, political and economic change and what this means for corporations are analysed.

## 2.1 WHAT'S NEW ABOUT GLOBALIZATION?

Globalization – and the newly added prefix "anti" – seems to be one of the most utilized buzzwords of our present world: few intellectual, economic, political discussions fail to refer to it. The man in the street often uses the term as a scapegoat for his personal needs and failures.

The problem that occurs in the use of "globalization" is that the definition seems to vary according to the people who use it. Globalization means internationalization, no doubt. But globalization also means a condensation of interdependencies in economic as well as in political or cultural areas. Internationalization could also mean bilateral co-operations, while globalization means more than just these bilateral relationships. Globalization describes a process, and not just simply a state.

Similar to what occurred during the Industrial Revolution of some 200 years ago, we can observe that the traditional roles played by institutions like the nation state and governments, as well as that of the public, the media and, last but not least, the economy, are changing dramatically and rapidly. But it is hard to find globalization in the statistics: there is no significant change, for example, in the export and import share of OECD countries, with percentages remaining close to those before the First World War.

This begs the question of what are the new, relevant, lasting features of globalization? (See also Box 2-1.)

## Box 2-1   Central Characteristics of Globalization

In approaching the phenomenon of globalization, one must first ask: What is specifically new about it? In what way does it break with the previous trend of development? Globalization is understood here as a new kind of change – a "changed change", affecting not only economic structures, but also the entire social and institutional make-up of our society. The phenomena concerned can be subsumed analytically under six central characteristics of globalization and these are discussed below.

### Boundary erosion

As a central feature of globalization, boundary erosion refers to the blurring of existing boundaries, the increasing permeability or even the dissolution of frontiers. This development affects not only state frontiers, but also boundaries within society and between economic units and cultures. Many problems connected with globalization are decisively influenced by the fact that boundary erosion is proceeding at very different speeds in different spheres.

The dissolution of boundaries is least advanced in politics and between states, especially as developments here are very contradictory. For example, although cross-frontier policies are now more frequent as a result of agreements, international treaties, and arrangements between states, the immigration policies of many nation states are more restrictive now than they were in the late 19th century.

By contrast, boundaries within society and cultures are disintegrating more rapidly. The biographies of people today evolve in conjunction with very diverse religious, social and cultural influences. Cultural boundary erosion thus has far-reaching effects on the identities of individuals.

Boundary erosion is undoubtedly most advanced in the economic sphere. It is seen in the liberalization and expansion of worldwide availability of information and the splitting of the commercial value-creation chain into activities distributed throughout the world.

One of the motors of boundary erosion is technical progress. For example, the development of the communications industry has meant that the effects of individual actions extend much further than before. The cause–effect chains of social, political and economic actions are therefore extended at the same time; an overview of the world is made more difficult.

## Heterarchy

Heterarchy refers to the transformation of hierarchical structures, characterized by clear relationships of dominance and subordination, into co-operative organizational forms, marked by reciprocal and asymmetrical dependency.

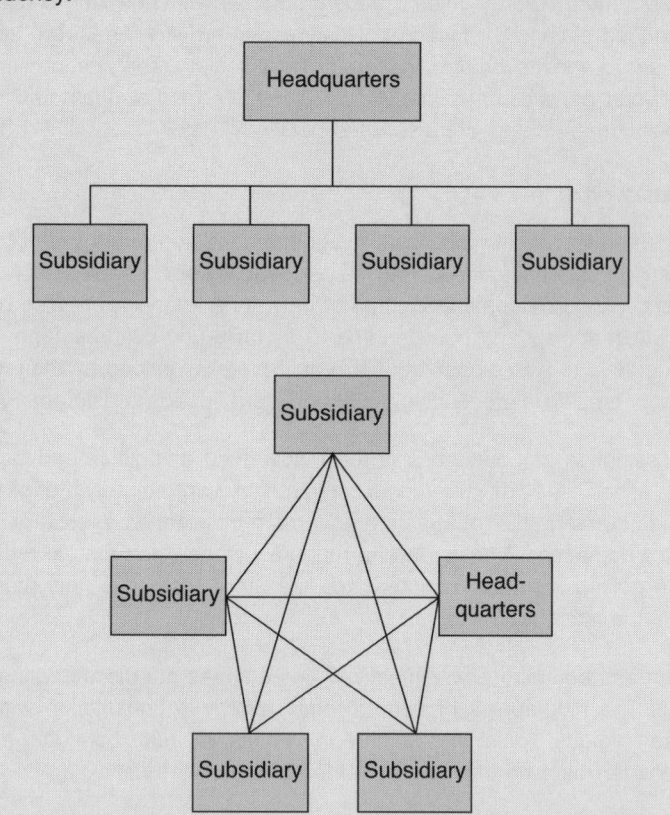

It is hardly possible for any actor today to attain his or her goals without the support of, or co-ordination with, other actors. In a frequently self-organizing network, individuals and institutions have a higher degree of autonomy and a greater number of behaviour options. At the same time, the newly created structures are more flexible and, therefore, less stable.

## Factor mobility

A direct consequence of boundary erosion is *high and increasing mobility*, not only of raw materials, goods and services, but of capital and knowledge

as factors of production. This factor mobility heightens competitive pressures and thus promotes market efficiency. However, the worldwide integration of markets for capital and labour, for example, has advanced to very
different degrees. This difference contributes to the problems resulting from
globalization: states compete for the elusive production factor – capital. As a
result, the position of the far less mobile factor – labour – and, above all, the
position of groups excluded from the labour process, is deteriorating.

### Legitimacy erosion

In the age of globalization, responsibilities often cannot be allocated clearly.
This results both from increasing boundary erosion and from the form in
which heterarchy is organized. This phenomenon, referred to as *legitimacy
erosion*, can be detected at all levels of society: the weakened role of nation
states reduces the general acceptance of laws and regulations, corporations
are both hunters and hunted in the global competition, and the same
individuals in their different roles are often both "agents" and "victims" of
globalization.

### Past–future asymmetry

Under the heading of *past–future asymmetry*, it is observed that the future
can no longer be regarded as a linear continuation of the past. In highly
complex, dynamic interaction systems, change takes place discontinuously,
while developments are becoming less predictable in all areas of society.
Connections unrecognized yesterday can become dominant influences
today, and ruptures may occur unexpectedly, even in trends that have
been stable for many years.

### Variety of options

One consequence of the numerous changes, and especially of past–future
asymmetry, is the variety of options open to both institutions and individuals.
The spectrum of possible futures prompts a diverse range of responses. But
with the gain in choice comes the pain of indecision: fields of action are
increasingly marked by ambivalence and ambiguity, so that flexible behaviour and variable reactions to the continuously changing context of decision-
making are called for. The disappearance of all certainties gives rise to
individual anxieties and collective extremisms – the more so as opportunities
and risks are unevenly distributed in global, boundary-eroded society. For
highly qualified people there is a much higher probability that the diverse
opportunities will work to their advantage than for unqualified people.

*Source:* Steger, U. (ed.) *Discovering the New Pattern of Globalization*.

## Impact of eroding boundaries

Globalization means erosion of boundaries. That erosion takes place on several dimensions: one can identify erosion of the time axis as well as of the space axis. Erosion of the time axis means that this dimension will accelerate in the economic sense as well as in information exchange, decision-making, trade and tourism. The space axis is eroding in the sense that it is condensed by technological and informational development; space is contracted by such developments because people, information and goods are a great deal more mobile than they were in former times.

A very prominent field of eroding boundaries is migration – refugees, brain drains, immigrants. The United Nations estimates that hundreds of millions of people are presently on the move – without counting the number of internal migrations within borders, mostly from rural areas to cities.

But this also indicates that a border's openness is not without restrictions: today, more nationals require a visa to enter the EU than was the case in the early 1970s. Globalization is not without contradiction.

As already mentioned, boundaries have been eroded in several ways; but it would be practically impossible to live without borders, to live a life without limitations and boundaries. We should, for a moment, take a step back: normally, we think of the geographic and political type of limitations, the frontiers and the borders. But in a broader sense they also mark social and cultural identity and personal identity and character. Living suddenly within a much more diverse, multicultural environment challenges a society's identity and makes people feel insecure.

Luckily, the EU has not denied local, regional and national cultures, identities, and languages; it is a conglomerate of several of these and represents not only one direction of interests but also a strategic alliance of conflicting interests. And this ability is the key for ongoing success. Every grand strategy would otherwise have failed somewhere along the road.

Erosion of boundaries takes place in many – if not all – ways. Probably one of the most important ways is that of communication, and the manner in which information is exchanged. Economic and political globalization depend on information and communication networks. It can be seen in the condensing and acceleration of such processes.

Just observe the development of today's Internet technology, a spin-off product originating in military R&D. Almost overnight it changed its original function for decentralized military communication in the event of nuclear war to a (mostly) civilian-used information platform that permits communications within seconds all over the world. Rare is the university, government, company or individual in Western cities today without access to an Internet link. And it opens up new opportunities to confront companies and organize protests.

But only some 5–10% of the global population will have easy access to the Internet over the next 10 years; it has an ambivalent effect – on the one hand it makes it easy to cross boundaries while strengthening these same boundaries on the other. Concretely, this means that the Internet contrasts the gap between the "info-elite" and the "have-nots" on the one hand, while it overcomes the boundaries of time and space on the other.

The biggest impact of all this has been seen in the economies of nation states. The flow of goods and services has been complemented, and partly substituted, by the flow of direct investment and capital after the borders of former communist or state-run developing countries were opened. The number of global companies – not only exporting to but operating in several countries – multiplied by a factor of five within two decades.

## 2.2 GLOBALIZATION AND ITS FEARS

The term "globalization" evokes (and provokes) fear – and not only for the economic consequences. It also deals with the fear of standardization and loss of identity. It may be a fear of subjection to the "American

Way of Life", often used as a synonym for globalization. Perhaps a new generation has grown up in the meantime for whom the blessings of a democratic form of government, free market economy, free press and a free mind are not satisfactory. As these become taken for granted, new horizons, a vision for the future and a purpose in life for some may appear to be absent.

Often, globalization seems to be a lightning conductor for different fears. One of the most prominent misgivings, but not often explicitly articulated, is that of losing control. "Frontiers" also define identities; frontiers and borders protect identities, create identities. In a world with no borders, nobody knows which identity has meaning.

The founding of numerous international, political, economic and military institutions, the increase of international conventions and the trans-boundary codifications to solve problems does provoke fear. Individuals fear the loss of personal sovereignty and nation states fear losing their ability to solve such problems. The antipathy shown by US citizens toward the UN is an example – even if you belong to the most powerful nation, you are still fearful.

The erosion of boundaries is often identified as a process that takes place everywhere, all the time. This is absolutely wrong: the erosion of boundaries develops asymmetrically – and is often contradictory, as we have seen. Probably, the erosion of economic boundaries means the locking in and closing down of cultures. German sociologist Karl Otto Hondrich points out that the collapse of political borders and frontiers (for example, in Europe) will not lead to an erosion of cultural boundaries – quite the contrary. The more one gets to know others, the more one will realize the difference.

## More flexibility – social decline?

Eroding boundaries result in the liberalization of decision-making for the individual, freeing him or her from institutions and their social control, which have been imposed for centuries by churches, local nobility, families, etc.

In the past, these institutions guaranteed the answer to "Where do you come from?" as well as to "Where do you eventually want to go?" Such institutions seem to guarantee whole biographies, whole lives. And today? What about the individual in a world between "New world order" (former US President George Bush) and "New complexity" (German philosopher Juergen Habermas)? Again, many myths cloud the facts.

American sociologist Richard Sennett is a popular (and perhaps populist) but typical example. In his well-known book *Corrosion of Character*, Sennett describes the flexible (American) man who has to change his job more than ten times in his life. Families suffer, social loyalty degenerates as (geographic) mobility increases.

But German sociologist Hans Bertram recently presented some very important facts on empirical reality: today's world of labour does not call for any more flexibility than the industrial society of former times. Bertram's team carried out research into the number of job changes made over different lifetime periods. Those who were born between 1910 and 1917 had changed their job as often as today's young men do – that is, five times. The only exception was during the period following the Second World War, between 1952 and 1970, when positive industrial development guaranteed more stability, meaning job changes of only one to three times.

## Facts of social dynamics

Probably the most important findings of Bertram's analysis are that social networks and loyalties do not suffer if conditions decline. Insecurity does not necessarily cause a loss of social relationships. This follows along the lines of what early sociologists, such as the French scientist Emile Durkheim, said – in periods of crisis and chaos, the number of suicides decline.

The point of view of many individualization theorists is that participation and solidarity decline – but again the data show the opposite: since the beginning of the 1980s, people have wanted to become more involved in political processes and decisions, and have participated in citizens' action committees – such as in Germany. The scenario of the free fall of the individual is empirically nothing other than a "bugbear" for some sceptic intellectuals.

Those who criticize globalization often argue that it causes people to lose their links to traditional institutions – family, church, unions. These institutions are weakened and therefore lose their attraction as well as their integrative power. Without any doubt, such institutions are all involved in far-reaching social change – and compared with corporations, their change is slower and more stable.

## Box 2-2

Just look at the relevance of the church: in the United States between 1952 and 1993, apart from some smaller fluctuations, the relevance of the church on a ranking between 1 (= not very important) and 3 (= very important) always could be allotted between 2 and 3 (a similar situation could be observed in western European countries). But relevance does not mean that the personal ties are as strong as they have been to guide patterns of behaviour (for example, going to church).

### Engagement without organizations

Disaffection with established political parties and organizations is widespread. Other forms of engagement and a need to be more involved are signs of a society that defends general – not individual – interests. Human rights and environmentalism, Amnesty and Greenpeace: every case is of general concern. Or think of the Red Cross and its members. The Austrian Red Cross points out that the belief that there are no more helpers and volunteers in the Red Cross and similar organizations is completely wrong: "Never before, have so many people volunteered in charity organizations." In Germany, since the beginning of the 1960s, the number of volunteers increased by a factor of 5. One of the possible mistakes in analysis lies in the concentration of memberships in large organizations, parties, trade unions and their like. It is support for spontaneous, often single-issue engagement that has grown rapidly and could make corporate life more difficult (see Chapter 3).

The focus has tended to be on general social behaviour rather than on the organization. What has changed is not the character of the people (from altruist to egoist, for example) – it is the form of action that has changed.

When we think of the conditions in which individuals acted at the beginning of the 21st century, we can conclude that in some (not all!) dimensions the options to act have increased. We now no longer live in a system of global bi-polarity; we live in a multi-factorial world system. This can cause stress, uncertainty, even "angst" – but it offers new opportunities, and less social and political control by organizations. Companies have to take this into account, not only in terms of understanding the new breed of employees they hire, but also with regard to the attitudes of citizens, which are changing.

But even more importantly, companies have to take into account why a large part of the public has turned against globalization.

## 2.3  THE PREDICTABLE COUNTERTREND: GLOBALIZATION CRITIQUE

Are you familiar with the organization "ATTAC"? Perhaps you should be if you do business in France. With its 26,000 members and even more supporters, it is bigger than the French Green Party. Its charismatic leader, José Bové, an organic farmer and shepherd, and leader of the "Confédération Paysanne", rose to prominence when he smashed McDonald's windows to protest against globalization. Some 50,000 people supported him when he stood trial. Now every European country has its own, rapidly growing chapter of ATTAC.

Due to the influence of its president, the French thinker Bernard Cassen, the dominance of ATTAC is increasing rapidly. It has set up many "people colleges" across the country to teach what is wrong with globalization and what to do about it. The key idea is the "Tobin Tax" on the movement of speculative money – an idea to which even former prime minister Jospin was sympathetic.

"Anti-global" organizations like ATTAC abound around the globe. But the "anti" label is not always fair. They are critical of the current economically driven form of globalization, despite the fact that they themselves are a global movement. What is happening is that the "Seattle" men are fighting back against the "Davos" men, as Rüdiger Dombusch has put it. That is, the anti-WTO protesters in Seattle, who kick-started the protest against the rich-and-famous crowd who used to meet every year for the Global Forum in Davos, Switzerland, but now do so in New York.

### Globalization as a rallying cause

"Who elected the WTO?" could be read on large posters at the demonstrations against the WTO's annual meeting held in Seattle 1999, in which nearly 50,000 protesters participated. And others soon followed. It always had the ambience of a protest at a county fair – multi-generational, multi-class, multi-issue and multinational. The protectionist cattle farmers walked next to the peace movement vegetarians, both shocked by the violence of the "black bloc" – anarchists for direct action.

As a consequence of the mass demonstration, the Seattle Conference was interrupted, and large segments of the population appeared – at least tacitly – to agree, forcing politicians to make sweeping statements about the need to "put a human face to globalization" on any similar event. But it didn't help much to prevent further demonstrations.

No doubt there is no direct democratic election for membership of the WTO. But is it really necessary to elect a body that national governments have delegated to rule on trade? There *is* a democratic feedback to national governments. The object of the protestors' aggression was the – supposed – goal of the WTO to build a neo-liberal world economic order in the interest of global companies, leaving out everybody else.

So what are the critics of global capitalism asking for? In their eyes, globalization has a destructive impact; their intention is to develop controls on global financial transactions as well as on institutions like the WTO and the World Bank. They want to urge governments to control global markets much more effectively. And they believe that globalization (in the form of multinational companies, international free trade, open borders for goods, services and finances) is responsible for local social cleavages and inequalities.

Most economists disagree with such causality: the empirical data indicates that international trade plays only a minor part in the problems found in job markets and income inequality in industrial countries. But economists agree that there could be some cases where international trade undermines national politics – for example, when child labour in the clothing industry in India means the dismissal of textile workers in North Carolina. But this is clearly the exception, not the rule.

The anti-global trend has been easily predictable, assisted by media-hyped globalization being referred to as "inevitable". It is only surprising that the anti-movement gained ground even before the US stock market crashed (true, one can also wonder – as the *Economist* always does – that the US stock market lasted for so long at its "exuberant" height). But, for companies, tougher times ahead are not only on the macro-level. In this day and age, you can be sure that the countertrend is gaining strength, when the media – and all those contributing to it and enhancing its message – declares something has "won" or is "inevitable". Monsanto learned the hard way that growth of "Green food" is not inevitable, as did Thyssen Krupp, the main developer of the innovative Maglev train. Its test drive project from Hamburg to Berlin was abolished despite being enshrined in law.

The underlying theory of "countervailing power" is as old as mankind's philosophers. Karl Marx was a powerful proponent and John Kenneth Galbraith formulated the principle for the democratic, pluralistic and capitalistic societies after the Second World War. The dynamic of market-driven value creation has many benefits, but still has its downside. In a cycle of trial and error, we try to reap the benefit and avoid the costs. The stability of democracy and the market economy lays in its permanent change: once you've reaped the benefits of being up, you must surely go down – and then struggle to recover.

## Globalization's honeymoon is over

Where do we stand in the cycle today? After several "revolutions" (for example, information, knowledge, global, environmental, consumer – you name it!) and a time of unprecedented change, it seems that we are over the peak of the free market cycle: too many are disenchanted and many more will be, particularly after being stuck in a slow growth period. With the stockmarket in the doldrums, the misdeeds of the bubble are an additional shock. After all, in several major countries, pensions depend on the capital market and people trust in the honesty, transparency and fairness of the system. Companies may have to fight to regain corporate legitimacy. Even if this assumption is wrong, nobody will deny that the "honeymoon" period is over for globalization, deregulation and shareholder value strategies. The war against terrorism will confirm this development, as does the stockmarket decline.

But, still, globalization has led to a major shift in the balance of power between companies and governments as well as traditional organizations such as churches and unions. Companies are perceived to be the most powerful institutions – with sheer size exceeding status – and are thus held increasingly responsible for employment, environment, welfare, innovation and growth, replacing the government as the guardians of economic well-being. "Sustainability" is the buzzword under which all these expectations rally: putting wider corporate responsibilities and shareholder value back on a par.

But, obviously, too many people across the globe believe that global growth means jobless growth and increasing inequality, like a tide that lifts a few lucky ships, but leaves the rest aground. Because of this, resistance to globalization has become pre-programmed – all it needed were some triggers and advocates to start hounding the "merciless profiteers" in efforts to make them understand or at least consider the "human cause" of economic, social and environmental criteria.

Certainly, the trends are not the same in the United States, Japan and Europe but they point in the same direction, identified as described below.

- In the US, the only world power left and the main beneficiary of globalization, the resistance against free trade has developed to a new dimension. At the peak of the business cycle, which can only be compared with the "Golden Sixties" (which, incidentally, globally created the famous 1968 revolution), there was no majority in the US Congress for any major global trade initiative. What would happen in a recession? And the threat of trade wars loomed large, from bananas to steel between Europe and the US, and from "sweat labour" to whaling between the US and Asia, especially Japan. (See Box 2-3.)

- Even in the US, the inequality of distribution is increasingly becoming the focus of many political (campaign) debates. Whereas the top 20% have gained, "middle America" struggles even more to make ends meet (the poor have lost out, but they are not politically powerful); their small gains are due to more women in the workforce and overtime – gains that could easily be lost in the slow growth of the US economy.

- In Continental Europe, though, the resistance against "shareholder value" capitalism has been higher – politicians, unions and the public at large have grudgingly adjusted to the new realities as far as necessary (and did an even better job in the deregulation of energy and telecommunication markets than the US Congress, where special-interest groups were much more powerful, as can be seen by the blockage of WAP technology applications by local TV stations). But there is concern that companies are indulging in shareholder value and disengaging from their former responsibility toward communities, their workforce and other stakeholders (whether this is more rhetoric than action, as some critics argue, does not matter; it is perceived in that way, as opinion polls indicate). As indicated by the example of the closure of Rover plants in the UK, the British seem to have caught on to the Continental mood.

• In Asia, there is also a mixed picture: Malaysia was successful in the short term because it embarked on a protectionist policy. Indonesia is in a difficult transition, Japan is stagnating and outsiders like Vietnam are still sitting on the fence. In China, the ruling elite made it clear that economic progress would never be allowed to challenge Communist Party rule. Nationalism is on the rise in India, as is religious tension – two tendencies that are often the symbol for the underlying conflict between the "haves" and "have-nots". Of course, China joining the WTO is a reason to celebrate – but one should remember that in China signing a contract is just the beginning of a negotiation . . .

## 2.4  BACKLASH AGAINST CORPORATIONS

*Globalization: what does it mean for corporations?*

The globally active, technology-intensive (big) businesses are already more advanced in the transformation process of globalization than are other social institutions. Even though they have been active for a long time in a number of countries, it is no longer the local market *per se* or commodity production that is important today, but the distribution of the value-added chain across different regions according to comparative benefits. This is reflected in the huge increase in direct investment.

Even major functions such as marketing, research and development are being relocated from their original "headquarters". Yet not only are internal processes losing their boundaries, the external boundaries of a company are also becoming blurred due to joint ventures, strategic alliances, development partnerships, and so on. What is left at the very end of the process is the "virtual company", in which the competences and resources required on a project basis are drawn together from the most favourable suppliers.

Rapidly changing, differentiated markets and technologies require strong decentralization and decision-making autonomy, which in turn increases the organization's complexity, thereby hampering the use of joint resources, especially knowledge. The still-existent hierarchy is supplemented by the heterarchy, which makes it harder for decision-making authority and responsibility to be allocated (the "internal legitimacy" dilemma). Management today means living with contradictions.

Globalizing companies must choose from a variety of options so that an overall "fit" of strategy, organization and resources can be achieved – at least temporarily. The necessary creation of "cultural" co-ordination mechanisms is made more difficult due to the broad spectrum of national cultures and the constant change in business fields and organizational structures. Hence, management is employed more to balance conflicting goals and relatively incompatible demands than to maximize a single objective. As discussed later, this employment is required by the changing business environment, which requires a more sophisticated management – a "Corporate Diplomacy".

Will we therefore see a backlash towards corporate power and independence as was seen in the late 1960s, with massive regulation, expansion of the welfare state and a public rejection of capitalists?

The answer to this question is both "Yes" and "No". "No", because people, especially the younger generation, are more individualistic and do not want a return of the "nanny state". The cost of reversing globalization and reinstalling barriers would be tremendous, and the IT connecting the global village would not disappear. "Yes", because trends for re-regulation are clearly visible. For example, nation states form strategic alliances to regain some of their lost powers, and new players, such as NGOs, abound and form a countervailing power. The latter exploit the downside of jobless growth, environmental destruction and social inequalities. The former seek priority for security, which strengthens the role of governments once more.

Go a step further: What about the opposite process – that of de-globalization? It *is* possible to turn back, or rather to change direction. Again, we should turn our attention to the period after the First World War when the world economy was in total shock. Political, social and economic crises can result when events become national rather than global. Nonetheless, today, national economies can no longer be restricted and closed. Technological development as well as the organization of production and finances prevents such isolation. Globalization, it appears, depends on good times . . .

---

### Box 2-3   The US–EU Banana War – Does a Corporate Vendetta against Governments Pay Off?

The "Banana War" of some eight years' duration is on the radar screen of every US politician. Lambasting the EU for violating WTO rules and discriminating against US companies follows a rhetorical pattern, loved not only in Washington. "Right and Wrong" can be clearly distinguished, and the US are the "good guys".

And in this case they are right: driven by both protectionist instincts and the colonial legacy, the EU set up a Banana Import Policy in 1993, which replaced the patchwork of national regulation. In this case Germany is the lone free trader (having lost its colonies during the First World War).

The new import regime privileged more expensive (and as some claim – less tasty) banana imports from former (French and British) colonies, especially in Africa, and this left Latin America (except the Caribbean) – and with that US exporters – in the cold.

Chiquita (a US printing company) was instrumental in ensuring this violation of WTO rules stayed at the top of the US trade representative's agenda over the years. Chiquita had invested heavily in European markets, and in the supporting logistics, and enjoyed a pre-import restriction market share of approximately 40%, with an even higher share of corporate profits. Due to the protectionist rules, bananas sold at 50% higher prices than in the USA, whereas transportation costs were only 15% higher (the case once again indicates that protectionism is a rip-off for consumers).

Chiquita felt that these investments, for which it had piled up debt, were illegally expropriated. None of the US banana exporters had lobbyists in Brussels, so the EU legislation took them by surprise and especially since Chiquita's recourse was to the US government.

The aggressive and permanent lobbying on Capital Hill soon became a "best practice example", but commercially Chiquita went downhill. In early 2001, it announced that it had to seek bankruptcy protection, stopped paying debts and asked bondholders to restructure US$862 million in damages from the banana import regulation since 1993, rejecting in addition the new EU import scheme (on a "first-come, first-served" basis), which was introduced – after lengthy wrangling – as a result of the latest WTO ruling.

As the *Wall Street Journal* noted (23.01.01), "The nastiest, longest and biggest trade war in recent memory ... has Chiquita buffeted by a combination of politically ambitious EU trade commissioners, restive bondholders, and angry activists" (who claimed that Chiquita violated human rights in Latin America, caused a lot of environmental damage there, and attempted to force the company into a transformational "Better Banana Project"). However, the strong dollar, high oil prices and weather conditions also had to be factored into the equation.

But one question remains: Why are Chiquita's US competitors – especially Dole Food Co. and Del Monte Food – so much better off after eight years of banana war with the EU? The answer is that, unlike Chiquita, they did not fight against the EU system, but worked around and with it. They bought banana plantations in Africa (instead of expanding in Latin America), diversified in additional tropical fruits (for example, Del Monte is the EU leader in pineapples) and bought importers to obtain the necessary licences (for example, Dole bought a majority holding in the large Swedish fruit, vegetable and flower importer Saba Trade).

Now doing well in Europe, both Del Monte and Dole are concerned that Chiquita is asking for a "guaranteed market share" to their detriment, and urge the US trade representative to accept the latest EU Banana Import Regime.

Although trade lawyers argue endlessly about WTO compatibility, Dole and Del Monte want to stop the controversy and uncertainty it is creating, and get down to business "under the rules of the game" (as Milton Friedmann has put it).

The lesson to be learnt here is that brilliance in lobbying is not a substitute for smart business decisions in local markets. And, obviously, one has to know when to stop fighting – when one gets so embroiled that managers take their eye off the ball in business decision-making and become politicians or – even worse – crusaders.

Life is not always fair and that remains so even in the age of globalization: government can hurt companies – and consumers! – by turning protectionist, not only in the EU ...

Although there will be no return to the status quo ante, current trends are not likely to continue. Unless there is a massive crisis, globalization is going to continue – but with different agendas. And much will depend on the question of how companies master the challenge of Corporate Diplomacy, being economically successful, contributing to the well-being of communities, communicating with more stakeholders – and thus perceived more as problem-solvers than as trouble-makers.

The main questions arising from this analysis of globalization dynamics – and the dominant research focus of this book – will be: What does this mean for corporations? How can they thrive in the volatile and fragmented new business environment? And how can they avoid being punished like Monsanto, beaten like Coca-Cola, Ford and the Pharma Industry – to name but a few of the recent victims? Therefore "corporate diplomacy" is about dealing successfully with a fragmented, volatile, "fluid", unpredictable, hostile, opportunistic, wobbly media-driven business environment. In short: preventing a crisis you do not want to manage. First, this task needs an understanding of the players currently within the global village.

# The Players in       **3**
# the Global Village

---

To understand the confusing global world, one has to look at the players in the global village. In this chapter the often-heard claim of the "powerless (nation) state" is investigated. But, especially after 11 September 2001, this means that security is now back high on the agenda and can only be guaranteed by governments, which are now more inclined to intervene in the internal "grey war" consensus (the war on terrorism post-11 September).

On the other hand, global companies are often regarded as faceless and footloose, but nonetheless seen to be mighty organizations, over-riding the world. However, it is not only competition but also the limits on market focus and the internal contradictions of decentralized organizations that lead to many dilemmas and ambiguities in corporate decision-making and actions in trying to meet changed expectations. These facts are often exploited by the activist organizations of the emerging "civic society", as emphasized by the media.

## 3.1  BACK TO THE "SECURITY STATE"?

The global village (as H. Marshall McLuhan called it) is inhabited by many colourful players. In this chapter some of the most important are discussed, beginning with the nation state, whose death knell has been ringing according to such globalists as ex-McKinsey guru Kenichi Ohmae.

Since the French Revolution in 1789, the nation state as we know it – and probably the most successful export of Europe – has fulfilled three main functions:

1   Security against "evil", both from outside and within.
2   Ensured welfare for its citizens.
3   Self-determination of its government.


In the "Golden Decade" following the fall of the Berlin Wall – *the* symbol of the most significant of political borders – all three functions seem to have fallen victim to the erosion of what a state defines: its borders.

The most hotly debated of these functions is welfare. After the Second World War, all Western democracies built, in varying degrees but not different in principle, a "welfare state". This assured the population of care in meeting the main risks (health, pension and unemployment) of life in one way or another, through a collective insurance. The labour markets were regulated, as were many industries, and public services extended.

In a global economy, so the argument goes, this is no longer affordable. Reality bears this out: deficit spending has stored up huge liabilities for future generations, so most citizens welcome the fact that capital markets often discipline government spending more rigorously than parliaments.

Deregulation has had as much to do with technological development, which made previous monopolies unnecessary, as has the cut in welfare to do with demographics, the rapidly growing number of old people in all rich countries, and the wealth accumulated over a long period of peace.

Furthermore, globalization puts pressure on inefficiencies, be they in the global supply chain or ineffective government, because the global market has given the customer better comparison and choices than in previous, more closed economies. And globalization, too, has shifted the balance of power from more immobile factors to more mobile ones.

Capital is more mobile than labour and within labour, skilled labour is more mobile than unskilled labour. Forgetting all the controversy about statistics: the only trend that seems pretty clear with regard to globalization is that unskilled labour is, relatively speaking, always the loser, both within nations and between nations (still, growth might overcompensate the relative losses, but in many cases income stagnates or declines).

Not only in the US but also in Europe has there been a tendency to tolerate – albeit sometimes reluctantly – income distribution tilted toward capital owners and skilled labour as a price for more rapid growth and global effectiveness.

But, clearly, people recognize that (economic) welfare cannot be achieved nationally. Key instruments – monetary and fiscal policy, exchange rates or import barriers – can no longer be exerted by national governments, or only at high cost in a more borderless economy. This is one reason why, in all Western democracies, trust in politicians and government is declining (the erosion of legitimacy).

## Globalization = US dominance?

The third function, self-determination, is often discussed when talking about the symbols of culture. But here – as pointed out in Chapter 1 – the problem is ill-labelled: it is not globalization, but US dominance in certain sectors. Be it Hollywood movies with their stereotypes, McDonald's and other fast-food chains, or Nike and other brands, worship of the American way is "new religion". For sure, globalization depends economically on a certain homogeneity, which was always disguised by elitists. But has today's globalization not led to an explosion of choices? Or, more precisely, international available choice, while smaller regional specialties either decline or become products of the global market. After all, French cuisine still persists and is exported to the US, as was the French movie *Asterix*, which attracted eight million US filmgoers (but did not beat – as was hoped – *Titanic* at 21 million). And even Coca-Cola, the ultimate indicator of global homogeneity, is bowing to regional differences with various marketing campaigns and tastes . . .

The first function of the nation state was the need for security, which has clearly reduced after the crumbling of the Soviet Empire. Yes, civil wars continue, but they no longer involve a "hair-trigger" confrontation of nuclear superpowers. Some terrorist movements persist in Europe (Northern Ireland, the Basque Country, Corsica), and also in some Latin American countries. But the "domino theory" that, due to communist insurgents, one state after another would fall into the communist camp (which triggered the US involvement in the Vietnam war), no longer prevails.

Yes, there were think-tank scenarios about new, unconventional threats, but more political attention was absorbed by the repercussions of the disintegration of the Soviet Empire, notably in Yugoslavia. But it was argued that, for example, "environmental security" – the dwindling ozone layer, climate change or water scarcity – were much more important than traditional "state security" and should be achieved globally.

## Number of nation states growing

But does this all lead to the predictions of the end of the nation state? Hardly, though there is a requirement to argue and differentiate between the time before 11 September 2001 and after (admitting that 11 September was more a crystallizing event of previously emerging trends).

First, a look at the empirical evidence might be sobering: between 1900 and 1950, the annual rate of generation of new nation states was 1.2; between 1950 and 1990 it was 2.2; and in the 1990s, the decade of accelerated globalization, it amounted to 3.1. And the demand is still strong: from the Kurds to the Kosovo Albanians, the Saharans (exiled from their home land is what was Spanish Sahara) in the western Sahara, to the Tamils in Sri Lanka – all are fighting for their own nation state. Why?

The conduct of and the context for a state has changed – but it remains the key political player in the world arena. Two significant changes, however, have occurred. First, the nation state has formed "strategic alliances" with other states to cope with trans-boundary problems. Second, security is back high on the agenda and increases the importance of nation states. The first change illustrates that there is a host of such alliances (no merger!) from the Organization for Security and Cooperation in Europe (OSCE), to issue-specific bodies for the standards of waste crossing borders.

In some cases, nation states even "outsource" some of their authority and delegate sovereignty "upward". The WTO is a case in point, where nations agree to obey its ruling on trade issues.

The EU is probably the most extended model in this direction. Member states transfer specific responsibilities to the community level and take – in an often-complicated process – decisions together in this area. This gives them more weight than one individual member can provide. In some areas, this means they can co-operate on an equal footing with the US: for example, in antitrust negotiations (as Jack Welsh learned the hard way – see Box 3-1). Nevertheless, co-operation is not equal in all areas (for example, the military).

In addition, a nation state like Germany is today bound by over 380 international treaties with legal implications for its citizens, as a result of these problem-solving strategic alliances.

But there is also "downward-outsourcing" of competences and tasks. "Devolution", "federalizing", "subsidiary principle" are some of the buzzwords with which France, the UK, Japan or even Mexico are decentralizing their juggernaut governments and moving relevant decision-making power to local or regional authorities. The process doesn't stop at the public sector: to an increasing degree, former state activities are outsourced to a variety of "private" organizations: not-for-profit foundations, associations and churches, grouped under the title of NGOs (see next chapter). As a "public–private partnership", these run development aid programmes for minority education or infrastructure investments.

All this is a classic example of "boundary erosion", contributing to today's political complexity and interdependence, which sometimes makes the decision process so slow. But it clearly marks an adjustment process of the nation state to cope with globalization. By no means is this adjustment process perfect – there are control deficiencies (for example, global environmental problems). But it does explain why the nation state survived – and not only because there is no realistic alternative in sight. This could be a far-fetched statement, given the UN – and other multinational – peace-keeping missions around the world. But here clearly the member nations of the UN or any other state federation, for example, the Organization for African Unity (OAU), do not only have the final say on the specific details of a specific mission but also implement the commonly agreed mission with their troops.

It is not the type of international "upward delegation" that is seen, for example, in the WTO. It is a case-by-case approach, given a specific context, where the international community or neighbouring countries have a specific interest to intervene and override in this case the otherwise sacrosanct sovereignty of nations.

### Box 3-1   Global Antitrust Busters: When Even Jack Welch Got It Wrong

The media saga and the political uproar in the US surrounding the aborted acquisition of Honeywell by General Electric (GE) in summer 2001 teaches two very different lessons: how easily even brilliant managers can botch a global process and how close the co-operation of competing national agencies, especially between the EU and the US, has become.

The uproar in the GE/Honeywell case disguised the fact that it was very much the exception, although not the only one. A year earlier, US antitrust concerns sunk the acquisition of British Oxygen by (French) Air Liquide, two European companies. Sometimes, the US hurdles are higher (for example, in the case of AOL–Time Warner). And sometimes the Europeans are more sceptical (for example, in the case of Boeing–McDonnell Douglas). But more often than not the EU Commission and the US Department of Justice and the Federal Trade Commission have worked together "hand in glove".

This alliance wrung major concessions out of the Exxon–Mobil and the

BP–Amoco merger, before they waved it through, by unanimously blocking the proposed merger between the now-bankrupt Worldcom and Sprint at the peak of the telecom bubble (to mention the more spectacular cases of the last three years).

But, also, below the level of those cases that have made news headlines, the co-operation is daily and close. At least during the Clinton administration there was a strong belief on both sides of the Atlantic that globalization required an active global response to antitrust matters, because the impacts of mergers and acquisitions no longer stop at the borders.

The EU and the US authorities claim the right to look at any merger and acquisition (M&A) activity, regardless of the nationalities of the companies involved, as long as it is significant in its respective market. Both authorities no longer look predominantly at statistical indicators such as market share, except for an early screening indicator. More relevant are impacts on open market access and the customer/consumer.

Both authorities struggle with new "phenomena": for example, the "network effect". That is, the larger a network the higher the benefit for the individual member, but also the more likelihood that one standard company is dominating the network – Microsoft is the key example of such a case.

However, legal procedures are different: whereas the EU Commission can block a deal directly (and the company can appeal to the European Court in Luxembourg), US agencies have to bring their case to court. The practical difference, however, is minor. Who wants to live for years with a legal struggle that jeopardizes a major strategic decision? But clearly the EU Commission has more room to listen to competitors' arguments (which is widely used by US companies), because they are more concerned with maintaining the competitive dynamic within the industry than is their US counterpart, which looks more at customer impact.

So, why was the Honeywell acquisition by GE the exception to the rule? Why did the European antitrust busters come to a different conclusion than did their US counterparts? First, it should be noted that the deal – the largest industrial transaction to date – was negotiated in 72 hours – a record even for Jack Welch in terms of decision speed, dictated by the need to crack the already existing merger agreement between Honeywell and United Technology. So the usual pre-check with antitrust authorities could not be conducted.

But the real mistake – according to the research for this book – happened when the US Department of Justice waved the merger through with only minor modifications (for example, the sale of Honeywell's helicopter engine business), and the GE executives obviously believed the EU would follow suit, not daring to block a deal between two US companies. Clearly the "writing on the wall" was not seen: the Boeing–McDonnell Douglas deal; here, the EU's objections were very strong – that further concentration in the aerospace industry might impede competition.

The "bundling theory" applied by the EU, that is, the assumption that GE could bundle its dominance in aircraft leasing and other services and could therefore direct sales to the other GE affiliates, discriminating against the competition, clearly reflects that concern.

Once Jack Welch saw how the cards were stacked, he started to mobilize his allies in the Bush administration and the US Senate to put pressure on the EU Commission – especially Mr Monti, the EU commissioner in charge of antitrust. This mobilization immediately backfired, because it made any compromise impossible once political intervention became known to the public (and some had an interest that it did indeed become public).

First, it is probably less acceptable in Europe to intervene politically in a legally defined antitrust case – in any event, it hardened Mr Monti's resolve. And, second, it is even more counterproductive when it is carried out in Europe by an unpopular US administration, which already has the image of being too "pro-big business" (rightly or wrongly, remember: perception is reality). After this US intervention, no EU commissioner would have been able to support the GE case without committing political suicide.

It is hypothetical whether there could have been sufficient room for a compromise anyhow, because it could never have really been tested (different from the Boeing–McDonnell Douglas case). And pundits can therefore argue endlessly as to whether it was or was not a wise move to let the merger fail and blame the EU Commission, and how this will affect the memorial of Jack Welch in the Hall of Fame for Management (relative to corporate perks after retirement . . .).

More of a practical nature is the question as to whether the GE/Honeywell case reflects a shift in the attitudes of US antitrust busters, indicating more conflicts to come, or whether this will remain the exception to the rule.

## War on terrorism

The second reason for the resurgence of the nation state is that the "clash of cultures" could be even more "bloody" than Samuel P. Huntington had envisioned in his famous book with the same title.

When it comes to national security, states prefer a cautious, risk-averse, no-nonsense approach and act according to their interests (the interesting question, however, is: How do they define their interests?). Or, to put UN peace-keeping missions into perspective: the former UN Secretary General once complained that the UN budget for peace-keeping missions is smaller than that of the New York fire brigade.

The "war on terrorism" has tipped the balance of power again a bit in the favour of the state. Security can ultimately only be guaranteed by accountable governments, who are the ultimate source of power, using military and police. (Even the most market-minded pundits have not yet proposed to sell security – and with that armed forces – through markets, although it was usual in earlier centuries. With the exception of anarchistic libertarians, everybody seems to agree that the power monopoly of the state in security was a cultural and democratic progress.) And if security is moving up on the public agenda, so is the importance of governments. As a result, not only personal freedom but also economic freedom is at least supervised more closely by governments. Literally, within hours of the attacks on 11 September, the US government had changed its views on illegal arms trades, enforcement of international actions against tax havens and non-transparent banking (see Section 3.4).

Decisions in multinational organizations (for example, the IMF, the World Bank) are again – as in the Cold War – driven by political considerations: bailout of Turkey by the IMF had more to do with Turkey's crucial role in the war against terror than with the economic merits of the reform package Turkey promised (again) to the IMF. However, in the days when the war was "cold", the world map was simpler: the communist versus the capitalist bloc – and a third party, the neutral and non-aligned states, who made a political and financial venture out of their neutrality. After 11 September 2001, the question once again is: "Are you with us or with the terrorists?" But, with the exception of some rogue states, nearly everybody is against the terrorist, and therefore the differences within this broadest possible coalition – between nations and within nations – will probably not go away.

Internally, 11 September was followed by a remarkable policy shift. Economic "pump-priming", which had been politically incorrect for more than two decades, subsidizing of industries (for a start airlines, soon followed by agriculture and energy) and a protectionist move in the steel industry. Although some were speechless at this U-turn in politics, nobody should doubt: if security is top, stability and consensus – not market efficiency – are also top. The state is back. Does this mean a reverse of corporate dominance? Or just a need to manage more complexities, ambiguities and contradictions in the policy framework?

## 3.2   GLOBAL COMPANIES

German sociologist Karl Otto Hondrich described today's world as more Marxist than ever before, captured in Bill Clinton's maxim: "It's the economy – stupid" – and the economy is the global corporations. Whatever happens (or rather, what fails), companies are held responsible – environmental degradation, cultural ill-feeling, social inequality, to name but a few. Often mentioned is the fact that, of the 100 largest economic entities, the majority are global companies, not states (which is based on crude accounting: whereas states are measured by value-added GNP, companies' turnover is compared. As every student knows, in an economy the turnover is several times GNP).

But, so far, these are not really global companies: after all, they are incorporated in one state, have – in most cases – a dominant cultural orientation toward their home base, and very few of their boards of directors reflect today's world's diversity. But they can easily get in the way of local politics and have recourse to their national governments. (See Box 3-2.)

## Box 3.2   Enron Corp: The War of Attrition in Maharashtra

Texas-based Enron became a classic case study in nearly every business school the world over, when it finally had to file for a most spectacular bankruptcy after a takeover by rival Dynegg failed. Its transformation from a stodgy, regional gas pipeline company into one of the hottest global innovators in gas and electricity trading, hedging and e-based clearance systems demonstrates American entrepreneurship at its best, and the forces unleashed when competition substitutes heavy-handed regulation.

Now this is seen completely differently. But even at the peak of (perceived) success, Enron executives were always hounded by the ghost of Enron's first major foreign investments in 1993: its 2.184 MW gas-fired power station in Dabhol, 100 miles south of Bombay in the Indian state of Maharashtra.

For all anti-globalists this investment became a symbol of "winners and losers" in the global market place: innocent locals are exploited by shareholder, value-driven, global energy companies who sold naive politicians an unneeded power plant at horrendous prices. And – unavoidably in India's major infrastructure projects (but in this case never proven in court) – was there a whiff of corruption in the air.

For more well-meaning people, the joint venture (60% Enron, 10% Bechtel, 10% GEF and 15% State of Maharashtra), which proposed probably the world's largest gas-fired power station, is an example of American naiveté when going abroad.

Maharashtra is an industrial centre in India, its state-owned power company is like any other India power company: inefficient, heavily subsidized and often corrupt, with a notoriously unreliable power distribution system. One-third of the electricity is stolen, often by well-connected companies, or gets lost; bills more often than not remain uncollected, although nine out of ten people pay only a marginal amount due to subsidies that can easily reach 80% of the cost of electricity. Small wonder that the World Bank refused in 1993 to finance the Dabhol project, due to the assessment that it never would work economically.

The core of the problem is that electricity in India did not grow as rapidly as expected in the early 1990s. The state power company is obliged to buy cheap power sources first – which was not the case at Enron's Dabhol plant because of the high capital cost (also a result of the weak rupee) and its use of costly naphtha. So the state uses only 10–20% of the power station's capacity, while it has to pay the full fixed cost (including a profit margin for investors) under the 20-year contract.

"Free us from Enron," has therefore become the battle cry of state politicians – but all attempts to sell the plant to other states or power companies have ended in "nirvana". For six years, the state government has been seeking re-negotiation of the contract (already carried out once in 1998) and is refusing payments, issuing claims of unreliable power run-up and waging a hostile PR campaign against Enron. Crisis and short-term compromises are woven into a never-ending story.

For India's central government Dabhol has become a dilemma, too. The finance minister guaranteed the payments by the State of Maharashtra and has already been held liable for refused state payments. But, as the US ambassador to India pointed out, Enron's Dabhol plant has also become a symbol for how India is treating foreign direct investment and honouring contracted obligations. After all, democratically governed India received only 5% more foreign investment than communist-ruled China.

Torn between an extremely unpopular project and the need to attract foreign investment, so far the finance minister has paid Enron's bill. Enron's desperate attempts to pull out of the project in summer 2001 failed: the expected price was too high for the two Indian bidders. Now, with Enron in bankruptcy, Dabhol might become a fire sale.

But beyond these misperceptions (which companies have to deal with), the role and importance of global companies has increased, not only because their number has – according to the UN – increased five-fold since the 1970s. Being under severe pressure from competition – more so than governments – multinationals have probably adapted best to the new global business environment. Their investment decisions contribute significantly to the economic developments of countries and their know-how transfer can accelerate competence-building. China is a role model: 50% of its recent growth is owed to foreign direct investment and the exports this has triggered (although much of the investment emanates from expatriate Chinese).

However, and contrary to financial portfolio investors, most multi-nationals cannot exit a country in a second, once they are locked in by big investments. Any retreat can only be made gradually. And, as discussed later, few big companies can afford not to be a role model in terms of social and environmental conditions. The host country expects this, but so does the public at home; and all empirical evidence points in this direction, with some unavoidable exceptions. The fact that the often-proclaimed "race to the bottom" did not happen has sound economic reasons: if a company is producing, for example, chemical compounds for global distribution, then the quality has to be the same across all its facilities and would require very similar technologies. Therefore, the environmental standards of locations within a company across the world do not differ much either (and it would be counter-productive to adjust to lower local standards).

Although the public regards multinationals as homogeneous powers, their internal politics are often much more complicated and decision-making is fragmented. Such companies have tried to reduce complexity by means of decentralization into business units, profit centres, product lines, etc. This has created a heterarchy (as described earlier), where subsidiaries or product areas exert some influence over the head-quarters and enjoy varying degrees of autonomy. For example, Tetra Pak is very committed to recycling their packages. Whereas this works in Europe, in Asia most of the preconditions are missing: Tetra Pak does not have a high enough market share to start their own collection system; nor do service companies exist to pick up the post-consumer waste (because recycling is not the key problem, collecting is – this applies not only in packaging). So the Asia region is reluctant to follow the corporate strategy.

This "multi-axial" organization – where decisions are taken about functions, country, products, customer and product at the same time – is not only slow, but sometimes inconsistent. This opens up a can of worms – criticism by the many observers a global company is exposed to: journalists, followed by politicians, financial analysts, etc. – in other words, what this book is all about.

And the new players that companies are confronted with – in addition to governments and other established players – are the NGOs in the so-called "civic society".


## 3.3   THE EMERGENT "CIVIC SOCIETY"

If one is to heed the message from, for example, Harvard sociologist Amitai Etzioni, a new type of society is emerging, in which the economy and competition are less important. Standard-bearers of this civic society are the NGOs, a title which obviously disguises a certain perplexity, because these organizations are only defined in terms of what they are *not* (and even this line is blurred, as we shall see).

But the reason for this "non-definition" is that this segment is so hugely diverse that it defies any simple categorization of what these organizations are: from centuries-old, international organizations like the churches or the Red Cross and Red Crescent, to local, single-purpose civil initiatives (such as campaigning against construction on a greenfield site). The US National Rifle Association is an NGO like any organized peace movement. Organizations that fight each other are clustered under the same label . . . unions and employers, Greenpeace and the Global Climate Coalition, the industry lobby against climate protection. What makes NGOs the hope of communitarians is their rapid growth in recent years. The UN has now registered 29,000 international NGOs – up from approximately 2,000 two decades ago. It is not only in rich democracies that there are literally hundreds of thousands – Russia counts 65,000 and Bangladesh 12,000. There are several dozen for every single issue: 70 NGOs deal with "sustainable tea growing".

To make sense of this huge diversity, the *Economist* clustered NGOs into three categories:

1   The "Rengos" – the religious NGOs, which one finds everywhere (even nowadays in Afghanistan) and which are indispensable in delivering humanitarian relief aid, operating hospitals in the rougher

parts of the world, implementing development aid programmes, and so on.

2 The "Gringos" – the government-dependent NGOs, either through money or affiliation, today mostly from authoritarian or religious-governed states (if you see a Saudi delegation at the UN Conference for Women's Rights, you know what this means – and can imagine how frustrated the "real" NGOs are . . .).

3 The "Bingos" – which understand how to turn their cause into a good business, which allows them independence and freedom of action, similar to a profitable company in a market economy.

This last type of NGO is the most interesting for corporations, because it is either an enemy or a partner. As will be argued later in more detail, the tangled, complex nature of NGOs, their purposes, attitudes, strategies and actions not only make it impossible to scan all movements or map all stakeholders but also to look at the characteristics of an issue (see Chapter 5). To give the reader a better understanding of how NGOs act – and act together like a school of fish – here we should look at anti-globalization protests and that most powerful weapon: the organization of a boycott.

As seen in Seattle in 1999, Prague in 2000 and Geneva in 2001, nothing more technical than a personal computer is needed to disturb a meeting of 15,000 bankers and politicians, to mobilize 15,000 police-men and 20,000 activists from all over the world. All that is needed in addition is the right event, the right network and the ability to define a specific crystallizing, rallying cause. (See Box 3-3.)

## Box 3-3 Professionalizing Protest – the Ruckus Society

The Ruckus Society (www.ruckus.org) is an, let's say, academy for activists against globalization. In the Californian woods selected participants are trained in civil disobedience and effective public relations methods. Those who organize the camps and those who take part in the courses want to act as professionally as their enemies do – and without any violence.

The Ruckus Society was founded in 1995 by Mike Roselle, located in Oakland. Roselle is not an unknown; he set up the Greenpeace so-called "Action Team" where he was the first coordinator. Most of the Ruckus Society founders were activists in the peace and human rights or environmental movements in the 1970s. They include, for example, Anita Roddick, who founded The Body Shop International.

Scenes are played out as they might occur in reality; policemen rush at protesters, throw them to the ground – and what happens? The activists began to sing peace songs! Not only the songs but the whole scene recalls the anti-Vietnam War or anti-nuclear movement. After a short moment a film crew is on the scene, their cameras filming policemen and protesters, and within 30 minutes probably half of the worldwide TV public between Alaska and Patagonia, Vancouver and Vladivostok knows what has happened during the protest of X against Y in Z.

An official statement gives an insight into the goals of the Society: "In addition to providing training and support, Ruckus also aids and abets a growing number of organizations in action-planning, logistics and tactics, preparing staff and volunteers for high-profile direct actions. Ruckus helps to create actions and images that penetrate the fog of media blackouts, draw public attention and get a positive reaction. Ruckus actions for organized labour, human rights and environmental battles are covered by media worldwide and have been featured on NBC World News Tonight, CNN, the *Washington Post*, *Mademoiselle* and *The Times* of London."

Protesters have also learned to employ rags soaked in kerosene or vinegar against tear gas, and caused police horses to slip on marbles.

Modern information techniques have transformed the activists into modem warriors or network guerrillas enabling them to say, "Our resistance is as global as capital." The very best example for the role of the political use of electronics is the action against the Multilateral Agreement on Investment (MAI). In 1998, this agreement should have been passed by the member states of the OECD. A mixture of trade unions, environmentalists, human rights activists, etc. protested, but the problem for them was that nobody really knew what was or should be written into the agreement. This very same problem also became a problem for the OECD: it looked as if the OECD wanted to keep the agreement secret from the public.

Through a porous means, a copy of the preliminary document was given to the activists. Within minutes the paper was published by the activists on the World Wide Web. The storm of protest triggered an internal disagreement at the MAI negotiations. The activists had won another public relations battle, because the blockade of an "investor-friendly" agreement was attributed to NGO activism.

Some like it, some do not – but the time of classic diplomacy behind closed doors seems to be over. *In former times, diplomats and governments "only" needed the agreement of a parliament; nowadays, they also need a minimum agreement of non-governmental activists and organizations as well as the public at large.*

Transparency and responsibility, democracy and legitimization – these are the attributes that NGOs see as absent within companies and multinationals as well as at international organizations. Such exceptions are enough to trigger calls for "boycotts", a term first coined in Ireland in 1875, when the Irish Landliga called – successfully – to stop all business with the British landowner Charles Boycott. Nowadays, the term "boycott" has become the word for any action of refusal and denial against companies and states.

And, to change the behaviour of their opponents, activists are ready to fight with different tools and actions (but always with a high media profile): the oldest form is direct action – occupying plants or chimneys, blocking ships or trucks carrying dangerous material, demonstrating in front of headquarters, etc.

But, as effective as NGOs are at pushing their specific issues, it is a far cry from substituting governments or dominating the organization of society. This is also seen by the activists themselves. "The idea that Greenpeace could rule like a government is ridiculous," stated Thilo Bode, former head of Greenpeace International, brushing such ideas aside. "We are watchdogs, and try to balance recklessly used power.

We step in when governments and companies despise environmental or social concerns." This is probably a more adequate description of today's and tomorrow's world than the idea of a "civic society" – not the least because, for any environmental and social NGO, there is an opposing industry association (or vice versa), so a lot is about counter-vailing power.

---

### Box 3-4   Mitsubishi and the Rainforest Action Network – RAN

The Mitsubishi Group is one of the largest Japanese "Keiretsu" (an inter-woven business group), consisting of 190 interlinked companies and hundreds of related firms, with an estimated turnover approaching US$200 billion.

It is active in mining, nuclear power, aircraft, a wide range of investment goods, cars, electrical appliances, beer, cameras, as well as timber-logging, processing and trading. Its activities are spread across Bolivia, Brazil, Burma (Myanmar), Chile, Indonesia, Malaysia, Papua New Guinea, the Philippines and Siberia.

Executives in Mitsubishi's US operations were surprised when, in 1993, a full-page advertisement in the *New York Times* specifically accused them of destroying the rainforest. There had been some "ban Japan from the rainforest" activities in the past, but nothing that specifically targeted their company.

Those responsible for the advertisement were unknown to Mitsubishi – the "Rainforest Action Network" (RAN), which set about co-ordinating a wide range of environmental organizations from Greenpeace to the Japanese Tropical Forest Action Network (JATAN), in their activities against Mitsubishi. As well as media-campaigning, RAN showed up at dealer outlets and do-it-yourself shops every week, posting huge banners and an inflatable 35-foot-long chainsaw emblazoned with "Mitsubishi, Stop the Chainsaw Massacre". They produced a video documenting the destruction of the rainforest by Mitsubishi companies. This and other educational material was distributed widely in schools and colleges, resulting in more than 30 US colleges banning Mitsubishi products and recruiters from their campuses.

The heat increased for Mitsubishi when the US Environmental Protection Agency listed its Alaska Pulp Company as one of the ten worst polluters in the American West. Within Mitsubishi Motors' US facilities, prosecutors were involved in the biggest-ever sexual harassment case, drawing the attention of the powerful National Organization for Women (NOW) to the company.

In the meantime, RAN was assembling scientists and experts to develop proposals for more sustainable logging at Mitsubishi. Their high-profile actions continued, with activists chaining themselves to a raw log export ship in a US west coast harbour, preventing it from embarking.

Mitsubishi reacted slowly, and not always successfully. Although they increased their environmental communication efforts, including advertising, they had to withdraw a comic brochure in which they had tried to explain their logging operations. Only after five years of RAN actions were some very junior managers able to speak to RAN for the first time.

However, when retail chains took Mitsubishi products off their lists and the company lost a previously signed contract with San Francisco Airport for US$137 million (the official reason was, of course, unrelated to logging), the company started in 2000 to negotiate an agreement with RAN that cost them an estimated total of US$500 million – a top-to-bottom environmental review, the development of an environmental accounting system in conjunction with RAN, a pledge to end the use of old-growth forest and phase out the use of virgin paper and packaging by 2002, the creation of a "Forest Community Support Program" to provide funding in order to actively restore and preserve the world's remaining ancient forests and support the indigenous people who inhabit them.

In return, RAN ceased all boycott actions against Mitsubishi in the US. Ralph Nader, the prominent consumer rights advocate, hailed the agreement as "a testament to the efficiency of consumer boycotts."

But a lot has been hidden, since the 1990s, behind both public and corporate radar screens, which exceeds every democratic principle and is just plain crime, but on a global scale.

## 3.4   ORGANIZED CRIME AND TERRORISM

It is not only business that has "globalized", so has terrorism and organized crime, too, using the same infrastructure – easy travel, sophisticated telecommunication and open markets – that drives globalization.

Up until a couple of years ago, organized crime and terrorism was a local affair, and, especially in developing countries, was hard to separate. "Liberation movements" financed their activities, for example, by kidnapping expatriate managers or drug-trafficking (only history will tell what will be classed as terrorism and what will be classed as liberation).

For the most part, the governments of these countries (including the security forces) were corrupt, or even part of the mafia structure. So companies were left alone to handle the issue or give up the market or resource exploitation, because any support or intervention from the home country government was of little use. Partly, companies decided to pay a "support fee" to continue their operation with minimal interruption. But, over the years, money-laundering, especially from drugs or prostitution, penetrated the legal economy, and mafia-controlled companies expanded into new markets. As explained in Section 3.1, 11 September changed this dramatically. "Clean up" is the battle cry – although not without some success, the war has still yet to be one.

One of the more notorious examples was YBM Magnex International, which amassed one billion Canadian dollars in market capitalization on the Toronto stock exchange, before trading was halted. An FBI raid on YBM Magnex offices in the US revealed strong links to the Russian mafia, which is said to control some 25–40% of Russia's GDP (and 80% of the banks) through 5,000–8,000 criminal organizations. And in Russia they continue to prosper.

When it comes to money-laundering, terrorism and organized crime become inseparable – especially as radical and criminal organizations draw their financing from the same sources: drug-trafficking, the slave and prostitute trade, large-scale insurance fraud, extortion, illegal weapons trade, etc.

As a reaction, national governments and international organizations have stepped up the co-ordination of their policing activities, introduced new laws and reinforced existing ones. But many loopholes remain (for example, hedge funds that accept anonymous money) and many measures were only half-heartedly implemented from the beginning. A telling example is the OECD's conduct against bribery: tailored along the lines of the US Foreign Corrupt Practices Act, it should forbid all kinds of bribery by multinational companies (notorious among corrupt countries, public procurement or construction contracts). But not much changed in practice – the incentives for the involved management to circumvent the rules, for example by third-party involvement ("facilitation payments") were too high, and the likelihood of getting caught too low.

Even in the US, in the first 20 years of the Foreign Corrupt Practices Act, on average only 1.5 cases per year were prosecuted. Often this was reported by the companies themselves (for example, IBM) and the fines were low, provided companies took "corrective measures".

But then the "Grey War" started on 11 September 2001 – a war without armies, rules or a specific battlefield. It impacts not only macro-policies (see Section 3.1), but specifically the rules and regulations under which companies are operating. One example among many: in December 1999, the UN Assembly adopted the "Convention for the Suppression of Financing Terrorism", and invited member states to ratify the Convention. The US, however, was dragging its feet, confronted with heavy resistance from Wall Street, which was concerned about restricting regulation. In the light of 11 September, this resistance melted like the steel girders in the World Trade Center. It became clear that the securities industry was a "weak link" in the war against terrorism and money-laundering, as the US General Accounting Office put it.

The hastily conceived "Patriot Law" imposed the same regulations that applied to banks on broker dealers and mutual funds: due diligence of account holders, reporting suspicious transactions to the Treasury, cessation of all dealings with correspondent banks, for example, in tax havens ("shell banks"). Even the secretive "hedge fund" had to stop accepting anonymous money.

The financial services industry will not be the only industry affected by this legislation. Increased concerns that terrorists may acquire weapons of mass destruction will lead to a stricter control of technology in diverse industries. The pharmaceutical industry in the US (and not only there) has now positioned itself as part of the national defence system, fighting "bio-terrorism". Companies such as BMS, Pfizer and Aventis have promised to accelerate the development of new "anti-terror" drugs, happy to steer the focus away from the unpleasant discussions surrounding their pricing of AIDS and other patented drugs in developing countries, which had tainted the image of the industry.

Beyond that, much information and "dual technologies" (that is, technologies that have a civil as well as a military application) will come under new "Cocom" rules, which regulate the transfer of sensitive technology to "rogue" states. "Old-hands" remember the time of the Cold War, when the US and its European allies often clashed about the interpretation of these rules. In particular, the US "extraterritoriality" approach will gain in importance again (and lead to additional conflicts): the US expects, for example, in the case of an embargo, foreign companies to follow US legislation – or face sanctions in the US. Recent examples of this were European oil companies drilling in Libya, declared by the US to be a "rogue state", supporting terrorism (among other types of misbehaviour).

And the US Government is currently withdrawing more than 6,000 public documents that could give potential terrorists the know-how for weapons construction – amidst concern from scientists, who fear for the free flow of information, which they believe is a basic need for research.

A further dimension has been added with the new, still somewhat "informal" Securities and Exchange Commission (SEC) disclosure rule, which regulates the US stock exchange. NGOs and think tanks have long lobbied to ensure that national security issues or investments in countries with, for example, poor human rights records, should be disclosed to investors as a specific risk – similar to, for example, environmental liabilities. In the summer of 2000, the SEC announced that it would follow that logic. One of the first victims was PetroChina, the world's largest oil company (at least in terms of its more than one million employees), which happens to have exploration interests in Sudan (another Muslim rogue state, also accused of persecuting Christians). PetroChina intended to raise US$10 billion in the capital market, but, due to opposition, investors only put up US$3 billion.

Other industries simply have to write off the US market. The European aerospace industry had high hopes of penetrating the US market for military equipment, using alliances and joint ventures as an entrance. "Forget it" was the brief answer from a European Space and Defence Corporation (EADS) executive, when asked about the plans for the US.

Yet, another target will be the civil nuclear industry. All non-proliferation controls (outside the US) will be stepped up, not only for nuclear power operators but also those industries that store radioactive material, including that used for medical purposes. A main concern is the psychological impact of a "dirty bomb", a conventional explosive wrapped in radioactive material. Given today's skilful use of the media by terrorists, it could easily trigger the public to panic.

Something which will benefit from the "Grey War" will be the fight against corruption. Note, incidentally, those countries in which corruption is endemic are also those that harbour terrorists or offer a fertile ground for terrorist movements. Transparency International (TI), the global anti-corruption NGO, publishes an annual "Corruption Perception Index", which lists the same nations as those on the US list of rogue states. TI praises companies with a strong anti-corruption policy, who "walk the talk": Unilever, for example, recently withdrew from Myanmar (Burma) and Bulgaria, because in these countries no business could be conducted without bribery.

Other companies, however, have suffered from a non-effective, corporate, anti-corruption policy: for example, Siemens was banned from all public purchasing in Singapore for five years, because its local management allegedly "channelled" US$19 million over several years into the pockets of the city state's officials. A new and tougher anti-corruption policy by Siemens came swiftly, but nevertheless too late.

Expect more clean-ups to come . . .

## 3.5  MEDIA

In the 2001 SustainAbility Report *Good News and Bad* on the media, corporate social responsibility and sustainable development, the bottom line of the research was straightforward: "the media is one of the most powerful – yet least trusted and least accountable – institutions in the world." Let's take these descriptions one-by-one.

The "least accountable" description becomes immediately clear if one looks at the empires of Murdoch, Kirch, Berlusconi or Summer, and their mixed reputations. Other examples are the huge and non-transparent conglomerates; for example, AOL Time Warner, Disney or Vivideni Universal. And the consolidation of the industry has led to six players dominating an increasingly global industry.

But why "most powerful"? Because the media determine which topics will receive attention, how problems are structured and perceived, and only in exceptional cases how they are or should be solved. So it is the "agenda-setting", to which the other players – politicians, companies, NGOs – happily respond, that feeds the frenzy further: the media are less inclined to change perceptions or educate their readers/viewers, because this might create cognitive dissonance with their audience.

Or, as sociologist B. C. Cohen has put it: "The press may not be successful much of the time in telling people what to think, but is stunningly successful at telling its readers what to think about."

And there is much choice when it comes to what to think about: just one example will suffice here. The Institute for International Mediation and Conflict Resolution in Washington, DC alone counted 126 high-intensity conflicts worldwide (characterized by more than 1,000 deaths from mid-1999 to mid-2000), 78 low-intensity conflicts (less than 1,000 deaths) and 178 violent political conflicts (less than 100 deaths). It would be almost impossible for the media to cover them all. So, the media have to choose and select – otherwise they drown their readers/ viewers in information instead of attracting them. Typically, Americans are today more interested in Christian persecution, whereas some European countries are more interested in former colonies.

And that is the name of the game: much more depends on advertising revenues than reader/viewer subscriptions; the numbers count – every 24 hours of each day of the week (24/7). Gone are the days where you had "deadlines" in the media world. A lot of observers argue that such breathless competition with no "time-out" has taken its toll on quality. Dramatic images are favoured, with 30-second soundbites. A colourful, emotional language is needed for the "story line" – not the traditional differentiation between reporting and commentary – to beat the competitor. And the person is the message – people probably know more intimate details about the management hero Jack Welch than they do about the wide range of products and services sold by General Electric.

But it is not only celebrity CEOs who are in the limelight – companies find themselves much more exposed, too. More intensive reporting has partly to do with the increase in stock ownership, but also because much more corporate information is easily available – and people are eager to comment on this: the chatting class in business is the (sell side) financial analysts, who are eager to offer their dedicated opinions on every corporate aspect to every media outlet – happy to aggravate opinions into headlines.

The noise of the corporate fair is today as loud as on the political playground – with the same rules. The politicians have been written down, now it is the turn of the corporations. Companies – with or without their CEOs – are as long written down as they have been written up. You only need to look at all the Telecoms, Vivivendis and DaimlerChryslers of this world to understand the pattern (in Chapter 6 we address the question of how companies can deal with this situation).

Aware of the rules of the game, others have jumped on the bandwagon. The Ogoni Movement in Nigeria, for example, rose from obscurity as one of the many suppressed minorities in a multi-ethnic developing country by "streamlining" their message on "ecological warfare" against Shell.

And even terrorists play by the rules and take the media impact into account when they make their plans, because their effectiveness also depends on global media coverage. And media coverage can easily have far-reaching consequences. In today's goldfish bowl transparency, events at the remotest of places are instantly disseminated to the centres. Moreover, the channels that use and process this information are plentiful. When SGS, the world's largest inspection and certification company, was accused of corruption in order to get custom inspection contracts in Asian and African countries, it did not make headline news other than in the company's hometown *Tribune de Genève* newspaper. The successful anti-corruption watchdog, TI, used this case for promoting OECD guidelines, and the US government took a special interest in the SGS subsidiary in the US, under the Foreign Corrupt Practices Act.

However, there is bad news for well-known companies: harassing mighty corporations always makes a good story. Smash a couple of windows in McDonald's and you are guaranteed to be selected for an interesting feature about anti-globalization ... and so on (I will come back to this in greater detail in Chapter 5). Good news, which many companies in between try to spread through a sophisticated Sustainability Reporting system (see Chapter 6), does not find a similar resonance. It is not because the media are biased toward companies; it is more that they are biased against good news, and the more long-term, complicated-to-understand issues in general. In the 24-hour fight for readers and viewers, many journalists have stopped looking beyond the "breaking news" for prime time.

This selective process is exactly what makes people suspicious and the media less trustworthy. Instinctively, most people are aware that the media do not fairly represent real life. Even UK Greenpeace campaigner Chris Rose observed that the news on business was "The equivalent of covering the economy by only reporting bank robberies." And John Jennings, the Chairman of Shell Transport and Trading

UK, and probably one of the managers who suffered most from the Brent Spar incident, came to this conclusion: "It's a CNN world. And that means it's a 'show me' world, and not the 'trust me' world of the past" – because people don't trust anybody, *per se*, any longer: not the media, nor the corporations, nor the politicians. Everybody has to earn trust through their actions. And for the media, the question is looming large as to whether they have gone beyond the reasonable, and that it is now time to bounce back. But this does not exclude companies from putting their own house in order: the media represent outside pressure – they do not create it.

After reviewing the players in the global village, let us now review how companies have managed corporate diplomacy so far.

# How Business Has Managed $4$
# Non-Market Interactions up to
# the Present Day

Using Monsanto and its fight for hearts and shopping aisles in the case of genetically modified organisms (GMOs) as a template, this chapter describes what industry is typically doing wrong in managing conflicts with its business environment: not understanding what the real issue is for the public (and the media), underestimating the adversary and reacting too late and too little. This is partly caused not least by the low emphasis that companies put on relevant stakeholders when specific issues arise. However, not all (nor even most) companies get it wrong: many have learned over the years to survive public pressure by adapting. Four generic corporate strategies could be observed in this context: "nice guy", "good citizen", "lonely fighter" and "stealth bomber" (explained in caselets). But what also needs to be understood is the "transmission belt" transforming anger from stakeholders into corporate relevance (including the role of brands) and why therefore companies should not "map" stakeholders, but look at issues instead.

## 4.1  WHERE INDUSTRY FAILED? THE LESSONS OF MONSANTO

The question as to how corporations have so far managed their fragmented, partly hostile and volatile business environments depends – as usual – on the benchmark chosen. Look daily at every business and you will see numerous cases popping up.

Some examples. The chocolate industry is a classic for its use of the "language of denial" when it comes to child labour on plantations.

While the confectionery industry comes under pressure, the carpet industry has – so far – managed to avoid this, although the use of child slaves in the "carpet belt" of Uttar Pradesh in India is widespread. Nike is – again – in the midst of a controversy because some of its advertisements are accused of being "disgusting" and "repelling". While Benetton, for the time being, however, is surrounded by calm. In August 2001, United Airlines was busy buying airtime to apologize for mistakes, assuming that a "sorry CEO" would harness some goodwill.

Instead of going through literally hundreds of happenings, in this chapter one specific drama is able to represent where industry has failed so far. It fits the often-observed pattern of not understanding the real issue, underestimating the adversary and reacting too late and too little. In one way or the other, this could have happened to any global company – and this particular company was far from incompetent. The story here is told and analysed without gloating – but rather in the context that one can learn more from a disaster than from a success story.

We are talking about Monsanto, the once high-flying genetic engineering company. In a video-linked speech on 6 October 1999, Robert Shapiro, the then CEO of Monsanto, told a Greenpeace conference:

> There's no question in my mind, nor I suspect in yours, that the public discussion of biotechnology up to this point has had all the characteristics of a debate. [...] Our confidence in biotechnology and our enthusiasm for it has been widely seen as condescension or arrogance. [...] We're committed to engage openly, honestly and non-defensively in the kind of dialogue that can produce good answers for all of us. Monsanto and I personally have to bear our share of responsibility for that situation. We believed that biotechnology is a good technology and because of that I think we've tended to see it as our task to convince people that we are right and that by extension people who have different points of view are wrong. The unintended result [...] has been that we have probably irritated and antagonized more people than we have persuaded. Because we thought it was our job to persuade, too often we forgot to listen.

This was a far-reaching confession by an executive who ambitiously regarded himself as a standard-bearer for the new management paradigm of "Sustainable Development", contributing to the fight against hunger and poverty. (This interview in the *Harvard Business Review* in January/February 1997 is a "classic".) Shapiro invented the "life science" concept – the separation of agro-chemistry and pharmacy based on biotechnology from the chemical core business, which was followed globally, from Aventis to Zeneca. Formerly, chemical companies were "integrated", covering all basic and pharmaceutical chemicals.

Shortly after the speech, the Swedish-American Pharmacy bought Monsanto, kept the drug division and started to spin off the agrochemical business. Previous merger intentions had failed to materialize. In the end, Monsanto's ambitious strategy led to a dramatic drop in the share price, so that it switched from being an acquirer to an acquired.

The ambivalent market prospects and the heavy, protracted resistance of consumer and environmental groups contributed significantly to Monsanto's downfall. As Thilo Bode, former President of Greenpeace International, pointed out: "Monsanto was the first company wrecked by the civic society."

Pundits often blame Monsanto's "misdirected PR" for its thwarted ambition – but perhaps this is not a convincing explanation. It was the strategy itself, and a faulty misreading of the business environment, that led Monsanto into the "hot pot".

### Pioneering genetically modified seed

Monsanto was a "typical", integrated, mid-sized US chemical company, located in St Louis, Missouri. The agro-chemical division was relatively strong; the "Roundup" herbicide being one of its few better known (and more profitable) branded products. The product had advanced environmental properties, but could only be sprayed before sowing. And its patents expired worldwide around the turn of the millennium.

In the early 1990s an idea was developed to design genetically engineered crops (especially soy beans, corn, cotton and rape), which were resistant to Roundup. Roundup could be sprayed later in the season, thus only affecting weed, and not the cash crop. Fewer herbicides would be needed – a benefit for the farmer and the environment – but also a benefit for the company, since it would protect Roundup's market position.

When Shapiro took over in 1995, the genetic engineering development was dramatically accelerated. The chemical division, as well as other divisions (except pharmaceuticals) were spun off and Wall Street was enthusiastic: the share price skyrocketed from US$14 to US$55 between the end of 1994 and 1998. Investments into the new business model were huge. Not only did R&D reach 8% of turnover, but also new distribution channels had to be developed.

The traditional means of selling Roundup – via distributors to farmers – was no longer valid. To capture the value of its biotech investments, Monsanto now needed direct access to farmers – and seeds. Therefore, Monsanto acquired, between 1996 and 1998, seed companies worth approximately US$8 billion.

Competitors such as DuPont and Novartis followed a similar strategy, so the acquisitions did not come cheap (in one case 123 times the acquired company's annual profit). Contrary to its more diversified competitors, which developed this new area more slowly, Monsanto focused on the new area and was the most aggressive in terms of acquisitions. As a result, debt rose to 60% of its market capitalization. The pressure for a quick return on biotechnology investments grew in parallel.

### A new business model

Monsanto offered farmers a "Crop Protection Package" (CPP) which consisted of the genetically modified seed, "Roundup Ready", the herbicide Roundup and an Internet-based consulting service, which provided advice as to the most effective application suited to specific soil and weather conditions. The higher price of the GMOs was compensated – according to Monsanto's calculation – by the lower herbicide intake and the consulting service.

However, every contract contained complicated legal provisions regarding Monsanto's intellectual property rights for the seeds. The farmer was obliged to buy a new CPP every year, thus no saving was made for next year's harvest. Monsanto was entitled to inspect the farmer's field without any prior warning, up to three years after the CPP had expired.

Monsanto saw this provision as a necessity, to protect its GMO seeds and to capture the value out of its biotech investment. Part of the logic of this business model was to manipulate the genes of the seed in a way that the seed was sterile (the "Terminator Gene"). This would have rendered any controls obsolete. Monsanto aggressively patented its own technology, especially seeds, and was often sued for infringing other patent rights. The licensing process for the new seed was complicated in detail, but overall ran smoothly.

Critics claim today that Monsanto had laid down the rules due to its heavy lobbying power, and the influential ex-politicians on its board. But several times the US Federal Food and Drug Administration (FDA) came to the conclusion that there was no difference between GMOs and "natural" seed – therefore GMOs contained no risk for the consumer. The US Ministry of Agriculture was actively promoting GMOs and sponsoring research, because it saw biotech as a new competitive advantage for US agro-chemical businesses (the Terminator Gene among them).

Monsanto's aggressive strategy seemed to pay off. It was estimated that in 1998 Monsanto had a market share of about 50% in soy beans and 40% in cotton – the two cash crops where GMO seed was widely used (in soy bean approximately one-half of the fields). In other countries, too, Monsanto was the clear market leader, employing half its assets for biotech.

Despite this impressive market gain, in August 1998 the stock market lost confidence in Monsanto. Contrary to booming Wall

Street, Monsanto's shares crashed. The trigger was resistance to GMO in Europe.

## Europe: the battle for hearts and shopping aisles

Whereas in the US political support for GMO soy beans was relatively unanimous, their first arrival in Europe in 1996 stirred widespread protest, resistance and alarm. Being the market leader, and with Shapiro's missionary zeal, Monsanto was always at the centre of the controversy, with high media attention. At different times and with different priorities, five issues were debated throughout the various European countries:

### Ethical issues

Although not only relevant for agriculture, ethical issues about tampering with nature were frequently raised or played an important part in fueling the opposition. Whereas analogies between GMOs and human cloning were often made, the use of Genetic Engineering for pharmaceuticals was often, interestingly, left out (probably due to the visible benefits).

### Food safety and quality in BSE-torn Europe

The issue of food safety was a top political issue. Although all scientific evidence still supports the assumption that GMOs do not cause any health problems, a "residual risk" (due to long incubation times, unknown synergies, for example, with allergies, etc.) could probably never be excluded – enough to scare most customers away from GMOs that do not offer any benefits for them (for example, better taste).

Elitists pointed out the difference between European cuisine and the US fast-food culture. Future environmental impacts were more controversially discussed. This debate ranged from GMO-accelerated trends to monocultures, "super-seeds" and impacts on species (for example, the Monarch butterfly), with contradicting evidence and interpretation, and all parties not hesitating to use their perception of scientific results as a "weapon" for their cause.

### The dependence of farmers

The European mythos of farmers is still centred around the independent entrepeneur as the foundation for society. The more visible dependence of farmers as sub-suppliers to the agro-industrial complex in Monsanto's business model was violating deep-rooted "Leitbilder" (although they appear outdated and unrealistic today, many food advertisements suggestively promote a kind of 19th-century agriculture). This additional dependence of farmers explained why support for GMOs from the powerful farm lobby was muted.

### The new North–South divide

It was argued that the farmers in developing countries were further exploited by expensive CPPs, which did not fit into their conditions. The moral right of withholding the millennium-old rights of farmers to secure seed from their harvests was questioned. In addition, developing countries opposed the patenting of genes and the use of their bio-diversity heritage.

### Regulation for GMOs

Just months after the controversy started, Europe was a patchwork of inconsistent, partly contradictory national regulations, with the EU Commission struggling to contain this. However, the "revision" of the relevant EU directive led to a multi-annual moratorium for any commercial application. The US government saw all this as a new example of European agro-protectionism, and pressured governments to open up markets.

## Box 4-1    The Palmstroem Phenomenon and the Thomas Theorem

Everybody knows the legendary statue of the three monkeys that would not see, speak or hear anything. Volker Leichsering, a Swiss management consultant, wrote about companies' reactions in such situations, describing their behaviour as the *"Palmstroem* effect". "Palmstroem" is a famous, fictitious character (created by German lyricist Christian Morgenstern) who says *it could not be what should not be.*

Even hard-nosed businessmen often do not believe how "unfair" life can be, and therefore assume it will not happen that the public misread their intentions, the media misrepresent their arguments, and that politicians jump on the bandwagon.

The Palmstroem phenomenon could be contrasted with the theorem of American sociologist William Isaac Thomas – the so-called "Thomas Theorem": *If men define situations as real they are real in their consequences.* This means that companies often fail because they underestimate the dynamics of collective emotions that may often appear irrational in the light of economic logic – but not in the light of other value-based logic.

Companies are often surprised by criticism of their decision-making processes as being structured purely rationally. Their mostly scientific and technical way of thinking, also their own ethical dimensions, prevent companies adapting to the emotional variant of the public and other audiences.

But as the battle for Europe continued, the home front was collapsing too. Monsanto triggered a public outcry in the US when it inspected and sued farmers across the country, according to conditions in the CPP contracts. The controversy of the "Terminator Gene" haunted Monsanto in every public debate. Although Monsanto never legally owned any patent rights to the research sponsored by the US Ministry of Agriculture (the acquisition of the company that owned the patent application eventually failed), it was pressured to decline any work on sterilizing seed by genetic engineering.

Antitrust busters took an interest in Monsanto, looking into monopolizing practices in the seed market. Customers were rattled by reports that the promised economic benefits of CPPs had failed to materialize. The rapid penetration of the US market slowed down. In Autumn 1999, things were closing in on Monsanto from all sides ...

## Where did Monsanto fail? An interpretation

Monsanto's failure might not signal the end of "Green" genetic engineering, but the standard-bearer failed, if survival as an independent organization is an indicator of success. What went wrong? The following points came out of our investigation: the business model, the mismanagement of stakeholders, communication mismatch and underestimating the adversary.

First, under simple business criteria Monsanto's strategy was risky. To invest more than 50% of the assets and an even larger percentage of cash flow into a new business model with an innovative (that is, untested) technology is more than entrepreneurial and violates the basic rules of risk management ("not putting all one's eggs into one basket"). Competitors developed their genetic engineering business more slowly, although more quickly than originally intended, impressed by Monsanto's forceful advantage. But, despite their huge sizes, their risk exposure was minimal.

What the history of innovations often teaches is that in technology innovations – contrary to product innovations – the potential cannot be reached quickly in one strike; it is more an ongoing "trickle-down" process, which triggers various product innovations, unforeseen at the time of commercial exploitation.

It is unclear what the key driver for Monsanto was to embark on such a strategy: this risky business model became transparent when Monsanto hit public resistance – it was not created by public pressure. Monsanto's strategy was intellectually intriguing, but could it ever have been successful? (One of the biggest mistakes was that Monsanto's board obviously never asked itself this question.)

Perhaps one answer to the question might be the desperation of a mid-sized company, too small to compete globally in any area, let alone the "Land of Promise", using the emergence of GMOs to gain access to the big money.

### Risks of the business model

But the decisive point here is that Monsanto was under tremendous pressure to amortize the huge upfront investments – even if American investors were more patient. The pressure to generate a high cash flow widened the gap between the well-intended corporate declarations on Sustainable Development and the reality of operations management, which is measured through results, not intentions. Monsanto's strategy was not robust – everything had to be going according to optimistic plans. So when Monsanto hit resistance in Europe, it had no time to listen, prepare, adjust or patiently convince.

Although agricultural production is local, trade is global. So Europe could not be divorced from trading in GMO cash crops. Monsanto had to overcome the resistance by all means: by emphasizing the unavoidability of GMOs, by its initial resistance to separate GMOs from non-GMOs, by resisting the labelling of GMOs, and probably by mustering the clout of the US government to push reluctant European governments into GMO acceptance.

### Mismanaged stakeholders

The second and third cluster of mistakes comes from communication and the related stakeholder management dimension. Monsanto never really understood the issues both in the US and Europe. Coming from a science-based, mid-Western culture, it failed to understand the cultural baggage of farming and food in Europe – and how GMOs stirred major concerns regarding food safety, triggered by mad cow disease (BSE), poisoned olive oil, etc. – and the resulting erosion of trust in related government authority and industry research claims.

Offering consumers no additional benefits, but imposing on them the residual risk (however small) has been the recipe for disaster for other "risk technologies" as well (nuclear power being the most prominent, but not the only, case). Why should a consumer undertake risks without benefits? And as every marketing manager knows: you never sell on science.

Monsanto obviously had a specific problem to understand: what they regarded as "unscientific" – that is, the European demand, based on the precaution principle, that *all* potential risks had to be excluded in advance, not allowing emerging problems to be corrected as they emerged (more the US approach). And clearly Monsanto did not have any sensors, no radar or early warning system to detect these issues early on. So their response was always too little, too late, relative to preconceived perceptions.

In addition, the "David" (small farmers) versus "Goliath" (big company) contest was not understood by Monsanto either when it sued its customers. And the PR campaign came too late. People had already made up their minds and did not want a cognitive dissonance – that was the reason they rejected the campaign by Monsanto, not because the campaign in itself appeared wayward.

### Never underestimate your adversary

The last cluster of mistakes lies in the underestimation of the adversary (especially in Europe) and the inability to form a broad supportive alliance (for example, as the chlorine industry had managed to do). Monsanto learned the hard way how influential, skilful, connected and "media-savvy" organizations like Greenpeace and Friends of the Earth actually were.

Monsanto's high moral claims were an additional incentive for their opponents to "unmask the propaganda" and paint a black picture depicting a standardized nature: dependent farmers, producing "Frankenfood" – all driven by sinister profit motives. Further provoked by the supposed "unavoidability" of GMOs, they won early victories (for example, moratoriums) and pushed Monsanto onto the back foot, mostly responding to opinion-shaping actions, slogans and lobbying efforts of their adversaries in the process, which often only served to dilute its own message.

Being a "light-weight" in the European industry, Monsanto appeared "big" due to the support of the US government, and never tried – for reasons nobody could explain – to build broader industry coalitions. Nevertheless, the competitors, unnerved by Monsanto's rapid drive forward, sat on the fence when Monsanto fought its losing battle. Clearly, you don't make new friends in such a crisis.

### To sum it up

Due to a lack of an "early warning system", Monsanto did not realize how controversial genetic engineering technology would become in agriculture, and then did not understand the issues they were confronted with. The result was a "mismatch" in communication (values and emotions versus science), aggravated by underestimation of the adversary and the dynamic of the conflict. Now the to-be-spun-off company is trying to make a new start, from scratch – with a more low-key approach.

Clearly, Monsanto was a dramatic example, but by no means the only one: CFCs in refrigerators, pesticide residue in baby food, the trouble leading Swiss banks were facing in the US about post-Second World War "Swiss Nazi Gold" – to name but a few. Trouble can hit companies any time, anywhere.

So, to review how business has to manage its environment and stakeholders and how to interact with non-market players in a reasonable way, let's look at the empirical evidence first.

## 4.2   DO STAKEHOLDERS MATTER?

The backlash to perceived corporate dominance in the honeymoon of globalization has led to a renewed debate about stakeholder relations.

Often this concept is a simplified counter-position to shareholder value. In the latter, only one stakeholder – the investor – really matters, whereas in the former, firms are seen in a broader network of different stakeholders, and the shareowners are only one of them.

While such a black-and-white picture is appropriate for propaganda reasons, real business life is more complicated. Even the most shareholder value-driven company needs at least two important stakeholders: customers and employees (and probably suppliers). Regulators and media are probably unavoidable, too.

What is really at the heart of the controversy is not that stakeholders, who are defined by market relations (the transactional business environment), do not matter – they do. Although often unsaid, it is the relevance of the non-market-related stakeholders in the contextual business environment that is controversial.

What is the role of governments, local communities, the media, international organizations (for example, the UN, the WTO), or NGOs (or influence groups) for companies? The empirical evidence is in line with what common sense suggests: the importance of the directly business-related stakeholder is far higher than that of the contextual business environment (see Table 4.1). But this does not mean that regulators, NGOs or local communities could not exert pressure on companies, try to influence them or change their behaviour under specific circumstances, but it is often highly contextual and industry-specific – to the point of being arbitrary. But we shall see: there is a pattern.

### Reasons for pressure

But these general results disguise the fact that stakeholder pressure on companies is extremely different by sector and country. Whereas the pressure of the transactional environment – through customers, shareholders, etc. – depends on the industry structure, the capital market depends on the high knowledge intensity of the business (which increases the bargaining position of the employees more than does unionization). As far as the contextual environment is concerned

**Table 4.1** Importance of stakeholder groups. Overall scores for each stakeholder group.

| n = 202 | Current ranking | | Future ranking | |
|---|---|---|---|---|
| | % of overall score | Ranking | % of overall score | Ranking |
| Customers | 23.92 | 1 | 23.70 | 1 |
| Shareholders | 13.90 | 2 | 15.18 | 2 |
| Employees | 13.78 | 3 | 13.34 | 3 |
| Board | 12.25 | 4 | 9.70 | 4 |
| National government | 10.21 | 5 | 8.85 | 5 |
| Suppliers | 5.09 | 6 | 4.89 | 6 |
| Pressure groups | 4.71 | 7 | 5.95 | 7 |
| Media | 3.81 | 8 | 4.06 | 8 |
| Community | 3.65 | 9 | 4.34 | 9 |
| International governments | 2.77 | 10 | 4.77 | 10 |
| Trade associations | 2.11 | 11 | 1.65 | 11 |
| Courts of law | 2.08 | 12 | 1.84 | 12 |
| Creditors | 1.04 | 13 | 0.90 | 13 |
| Political parties | 0.66 | 14 | 0.83 | 14 |

Source: U. Steger, *Mental Map of Managers*, 1998.

(what I call non-market-based relations), an ever-wider variety of reasons came out of our research:

- Rapid social transition in countries (from South Africa or Eastern Europe to the newly industrialized countries in Southeast Asia) exposes companies to specific pressures, from corruption and organized crime to special political relations, which in turn might be criticized in the "home" country.
- The shift from "managerial" capitalism to "investor" capitalism has increased the demand for "good" corporate governance, and the growing sophistication of financial control tools have increased the profit pressure felt by the individual manager who is held accountable.
- The regulatory authorities themselves are responsive to public

opinion because they are looking for political success, but at the same time they are hampered by the necessity to maintain working relations with the regulated industry, needed for information flow and co-operative attitudes. One especially critical issue is to get product approval in rapidly changing market conditions.

- The change in ownership, or the transition from a state or regulated (national) monopoly to a global player in highly competitive markets, creates different expectations in different audiences (for example, investors versus politicians). This often leads to conflicts of interest between different shareholders. Conflicts in the board-room might lead to massive board interventions in operational tasks.

- Maintaining employee commitment and motivation in times of "downsizing" is difficult enough, but it could easily lead to a deterioration of relations with unions and workers' councils. They might turn from being co-operative partners to hostile forces and destabilize pending mergers, acquisitions and restructuring.

- The negative repercussions of the "irresponsible" use of products by customers could ricochet back to the supplier, sometimes even creating severe ethical dilemmas. Such cases range from export control for national security reasons (see Chapter 3) to inappropriate use of chemicals, causing environmental damage, to "unethical" software application (for example, hard Internet pornography).

Given this variety of challenges, companies try to respond in a situation-specific and apparently company-typical way in line with their own political and social environment. This response can be listed as follows:

1  The usual *response* to the identified influence group (hard versus soft stance).
2  The *general attitude* toward its most influential group (confrontation versus empathy).
3  The *posture* when dealing with its influence groups (low profile versus proactive).

**Table 4.2**  Companies' attitudes toward influence groups.

| n = 202 | Response | General attitude | Posture | Relative posture |
|---------|----------|------------------|---------|------------------|
| Average | 3.11[a]  | 3.56             | 3.55    | 3.55             |

[a]Refers to scale (ranging from 1 to 5)
*Source:* U. Steger, *Mental Map of Managers*, 1998.

4  The company's *relative posture* versus other industry players (laggards versus leaders, all on a 1–5 scale).

With very few exceptions, the answers clustered very much around the centre (the 3 in the middle of the scale) leaning slightly toward the positive side, as shown in Table 4.2.

Obviously, a broad majority of managers would neither be regarded as uncaring, confrontational or lagging, nor as a "softy", sacrificing shareholder value or customer needs for the benefits of "outsiders".

## Management as balancing conflicting needs

Balancing needs is a common theme – to weigh the higher economic viability criteria against meeting the public expectation to secure a long-term "licence to operate" by paying the minimal price possible. This is not done in a cynical way; rather, it is regarded as the application of the economic principle and is similar to wage negotiations and so on.

However, this average position does not tell us much in terms of how a company reacts in a specific situation to a specific claim by a specific stakeholder. The research for this book has, however, discovered four "typical" generic strategies in dealing with this issue, because companies develop a specific attitude over time: good citizen, nice guy, lonely fighter and stealth bomber.

## 4.3  GENERIC STRATEGIES FOR DEALING WITH BUSINESS ENVIRONMENT PRESSURE

Companies deal in a specific way with outside pressure. The key variables are the amount of pressure put on them for certain issues through the various "channels" (see Figure 4.1) on the one hand, and the company-specific attitude on the other. This attitude is shaped by the following.

- One dominating stakeholder (for example, the regulatory authority in the health-care industry) or a broader range (as in the case of the automobile industry).
- The corporate culture and the priorities in the corporate mission statements, which might reveal which stakeholders (including shareholders) are regarded as important.
- The political and legal system as well as national culture and history (for example, Japanese companies will shy away from political confrontation, unlike their US counterparts).

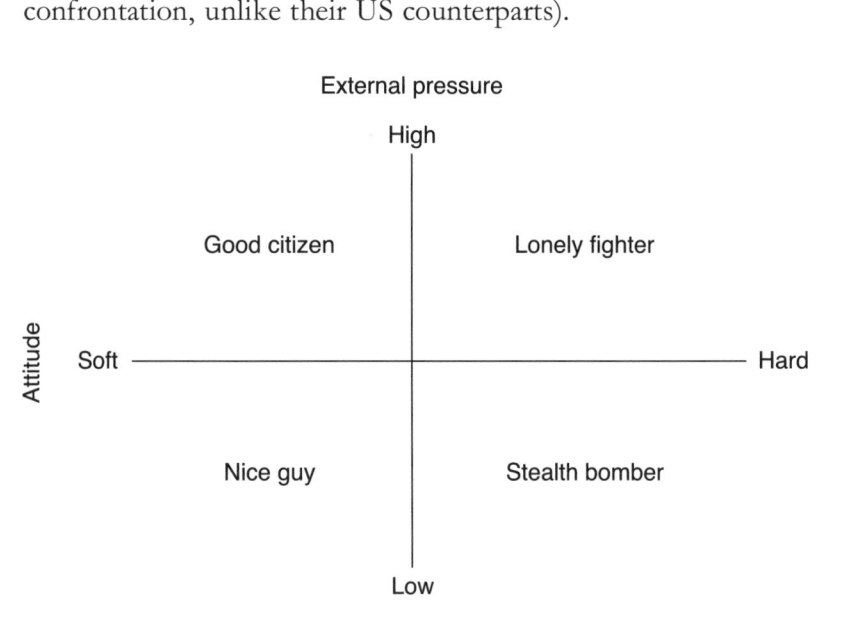

**Figure 4.1**  Generic attitudes to external pressure.

- Past experience and, related to that, the degree of professionalism used in dealing with external pressure.
- The degree of regulation or, more generally, the degree of corporate dependence on the goodwill of other players.
- Size and ownership (large and public companies feel more risk-exposed to external pressure).
- Financial records (in a very ambivalent way: if very good, the company might defend its interests rigorously because it has so much to lose; whereas in the case of a bad record, it might be a matter of survival not to add cost).

The influence of the company-specific attitude explains why companies differ in their reactions, despite the pressure on them being similar. It is therefore not without risk to "pigeonhole" the wide variety of corporate responses into four clusters. This is just a means of simplifying the basic alternatives; however, in real life things are more complex, in particular since every cluster covers a range of its own. The caselet should serve as an illustration, not a judgment. But with this reservation in mind, the four generic strategies are as follows.

### Nice Guy

The "nice guy" approach can be enjoyed by those companies that face only a small degree of public pressure and have chosen a soft stance, either because they can afford it or because they are dependent on a positive image for their market success. Food or consumer goods companies can be found here as, too, can "nice guy" corporations that use sponsoring, extensive consumer surveys, some monitoring of political developments especially if they affect existing regulations, and some "positive tone" public relation efforts. They try to avoid surprises, but sometimes they just "hide and stay happy" (as one manager described his company's attitude).

## Box 4-2   Nice guy: Scottish & Newcastle

If your roots are in northern England and Scotland and you produce beer and spirits, a basic harmony with your business environment is ensured. But Scottish & Newcastle (S&N) wanted to go beyond the obvious. In its annual report for 2001, it identified four stakeholders (the order follows the presentation in the report): "Our Environment", "Our Employees", "Our Community" and "Our Shareholders". S&N committed itself to becoming an active and responsible community citizen in all areas of operation. Special reports are published to highlight activities in the areas of environment, community and shareholders, whereas employee issues are dealt with in the annual report itself. Unusually for a British company, "The full co-operation of the unions concerned" in the restructuring process is highlighted.

The brewery industry has traditionally been a frontrunner in environmental protection, because its business depends crucially on clean water and residue-free agriculture input. Energy cost (and with that $CO_2$ emission) also plays a significant role. S&N's extensive environmental report stresses the performance in this area in addition to packing waste and effluent discharge.

Shareholders not only get a dividend, but also special benefits from the product range (for example, a wine offer from Waverly and a Premier Lodge accommodation offer). This is traditional in an industry where, due to its products, fringe benefits and "payments in kind" are still commonplace today.

But the focus is clearly on community support. In the year 2000/2001, S&N donated £524,000 to charity and community projects – roughly the same amount as its operating profit (on a turnover of £4.25 billion). The money is channelled to charity and community projects through the S&N Foundation (with a focus on Scotland) and the Kronenbourg Foundation (with a focus on France). The areas of funding are broadly described as "alcohol education and awareness, medicine, social and welfare, youth and education, heritage, arts and environment".

Charities excluded from their criteria are, among others, "charity activities in countries outside the group's main area" and "charities linked with children" – as the majority of group earnings come from the sale of alcohol.

In addition, individual brands raise money for specific purposes in tailored marketing campaigns – for example, the Scottish Courage brands for a cancer care charity, and the pubs around London for "Help a London Child".

Strong emphasis is placed on employee and management involvement in the projects and the wider community. Kronenbourg provide the services of a "coach" from the company, who provides professional expertise for foundation projects on social inclusion. The employees are encouraged to take an active part in the fundraising and to complement this with their own initiatives.

On the more contentious issue of "drinking and driving", however, S&N prefers to keep a low profile. Educational programmes to promote responsible behaviour, especially for younger people, are supported by the industry association, which runs national campaigns. S&N regards these issues as general problems, which should be dealt with appropriately at the industry – not the company – level.

## Good citizen

The "good citizen" attitude can be found in companies that are under high external pressure but depend heavily on goodwill from a broader range of stakeholders. Chemical, transportation, automobile and energy companies can be found here.

These "good citizen" companies want to maintain a positive image in the eyes of their customers, and a positive working relationship with regulatory agencies and political opinion leaders. Therefore, they use a wide range of public relations activities, including sponsoring conferences and scientific studies. To build their reputation, they are interested in establishing dialogue, even with their opponents, and try to gain support from third parties who can speak out on issues, particularly to the media or political decision-makers. The companies develop and communicate their achievements based largely on cost–benefit calculations or environmental impact assessments. Often they assume that, to be heard, more lobbying is necessary to create a large network of contacts.

To boost their corporate image, the "good citizen" companies also try to learn from past experience and improve the professional handling of issue management. Instead of being aggressive, they try to neutralize public resistance through a constructive approach: proposing practical solutions (for example, public/private partnership for energy conservation); developing self-regulation through industry standards (for example, the "Responsible Care Programme" by the Chemical Industry); and "voluntary agreements" with authorities to avoid heavy-handed regulation.

They are looking for win–win solutions (for example, in environmental protection) and they "read the future" through early warning systems, the extensive development of which monitor political systems and social trends. "We can no longer afford to be naive," as one executive put it, "especially as our adversaries are no longer well-meaning amateurs in lambswool pullovers and Birkenstock sandals, but highly professional people who know the business."

## Box 4-3    Good citizen: DuPont

By the mid-1970s, the chemical industry was under worldwide pressure as it became evident that its products had not only upside benefits but could also have massive downside risks, their emissions could harm neighbours and their waste was a long-time liability.

The first reaction by the industry was to "circle the wagons". Soon, it was a beleaguered industry, threatened by restrictive regulations and losing public confidence rapidly.

A changed approach was needed, and was systematized in the "Responsible Care Programme", first established in Canada in 1985, moving rapidly to the US and other industrialized countries (today 46). It basically contains a commitment to:

- continuously improve performance in terms of health, safety and environmental issues, by outlining what should be done in seven principles, but leaving flexibility for country- and company-specific implementation; and

- to communicate its activities and achievements openly.

DuPont committed itself to the Responsible Care Programme as early as 1989, jointly with the American Chemistry Council (at that time known as the Chemical Manufacturers Association) to improve environmental perform-ance and to build a public dialogue. As Pierre Trauffler, Director SHE Europe, put it:

"Obviously throughout the 1980s, raising understanding to reverse the nega-tive public perception of the chemical industry required a proactive ap-proach. At the beginning, we were facing two major challenges: the integration of Responsible Care principles into existing practices, and the dialogue with the public. Today most sites have community advisory panels, which allow for proper communication with local communities, business and decision-making processes incorporating EHS issues. For DuPont, it has always been clear that adopting Responsible Care practices is not a ques-tion of 'if' but 'how quickly' the concept can be implemented into our way of thinking. The self-assessment process is considered an excellent tool for driving continuous improvement of our environment, health and safety performance. It is being continued at a global level and on an annual basis."

DuPont's top management was very supportive of the programme, as they are of environmental management practices in general. The company succeeded in implementing the Responsible Care Programme on all its US sites by 1995. From 1997 onward, all the US sites were managed according to the programme. In the current situation, Responsible Care clearly forms the basis for DuPont's best practice.

When Responsible Care was started, DuPont was widely regarded as a secretive, not very caring company, which had for a long time been on the top of the Environmental Protection Agency (EPA) list as a heavy polluter. It had its first environmental success when it found an environmental substitute for CFCs that are destroying the ozone layer. But it was Responsible Care that really changed the company in every aspect of its operations.

However, the "DuPont Way" is going further, as its Chairman and CEO Chad Holliday described in the September 2000 issue of the *Harvard Business Review*: "The company has identified integrated science (e.g. enabling the company to substitute petrochemical-derived materials with renewable ones), knowledge intensity (e.g. licensing corporate engineering guidelines, models and calculations to clients around the world) and productivity im-provement as its three pathways to 'sustainable growth'. Sustainable growth is not a program for stepped-up environmental performance, but a 'comprehensive way of doing business, one that delivers tremendous economic value and opens up a vast array of new opportunities'."

Holliday believes that "applied sustainability will be a common denominator of successful global companies by the end of the 21st century – and most likely much sooner".

## *Lonely fighter*

If pressure increases and threatens the existence of an industry, companies might resort to a "lonely fighter" attitude. It is plausible that such a position is not one of choice, but that companies, as the conflict escalates, are pushed into it (or corner themselves there).

The "lonely fighters" attack their opponents directly, or even sue them. "Strongarm" tactics against regulators and legislators are common. Having no chance to build larger alliances, such companies can afford to be rather blunt in their arguments, even if they try to protect their customers or supporters from invidious feelings through heavy advertising. To safeguard themselves, they have retreated to portraying themselves either as invincible fortresses of loyal and committed customer support, or as an indispensable but necessary evil (the former can be seen in the case of the US tobacco and gun industries, the latter in the case of the nuclear power industry).

Maintaining employee motivation and loyalty is a critical ingredient for their survival, because the damage done by "whistle-blowing" can be considerable.

### Box 4-4   Lonely fighter: BNFL

The nuclear power industry is probably – next to tobacco – the least loved industry. But whereas cigarette manufacturers are at least still enjoying healthy profits today, the nuclear power industry has been shaken economically: worldwide deregulation of the electricity industry has brought the extension of nuclear power capacity to a grinding halt – more effectively than all the political resistance by environmental groups and Green parties.

With capital costs rising above 10%, less capital-intensive and more decentralized technology – especially gas turbines – have proved much more economical. Especially hard-hit is reprocessing: abandonment of huge fast breeder reactor programmes and a long-term glut in uranium markets has made direct storage of spent fuel elements extremely uneconomical.

British Electric, the privatized company that runs the modern UK nuclear power plants, estimates that reprocessing spent fuel would cost £300 million over a 20-year period, whereas its direct storage would only cost around £50 million.

Not an easy situation for British Nuclear Fuel Ltd (BNFL), which is still government-owned and operates the fuel-manufacturing and reprocessing part of the fuel cycle. BNFL is now trying to transform itself into a global nuclear service company. But huge liability from the past remains. BNFL has shareholder funds of £356 million, but clean-up liabilities of £35 billion, which are calculated in a complicated formula. Small changes in the assumption wipe out any positive profit at the operational level (as last year's loss of £411 million easily demonstrates). But BNFL exists. The British government is committed to continuing its operation and even privatizing the part that has transformed itself into a global nuclear service company by acquiring Westingshouse and ABB's nuclear division and offering fuel and maintenance services, next to the reprocessing plant at Sellafield in Cumbria. The liabilities will be taken up by the British government.

In the UK, at both regional and national levels, BNFL faces an entrenched opposition, although not as strong as in northern Europe. Some people literally dedicate their lives to fighting BNFL. The industry trade union, the local Labour MP and – with varying degrees of enthusiasm – ministries, are the company's only few allies. Customer relations are mixed, with falsified documentation causing a crisis with Japan; BNFL's interests in the US suffered from cost overruns incurred in government clean-up projects, and the captive customers in the UK complain about high costs and lack of service. The regulatory agencies have become more critical and demanding over the years.

To break out of the deadlock, in 1997 the CEO of BNFL decided to start a national stakeholder dialogue. Given the tense relations with well-known

NGOs such as Greenpeace and Friends of the Earth, and the company's history of being perceived as secretive and arrogant, this was an ambitious endeavour.

In addition, external communication efforts were stepped up. BNFL's Environmental Report was even prized and rated high in SustainAbility's rating of such reports. As a moderator, "The Environmental Council" was appointed – a non-profit foundation with expertise in stakeholder dialogue – as a go-between for conflict resolution.

At first a four-page "Ground Rules" document had to be negotiated, which established the aims of "non-commitment rules": participation is no endorsement of BNFL activities; outside the dialogue the relationship will be on the basis of "business as usual"; groups will still campaign against BNFL, with no media presence at the meetings.

And then the miracle happened: not only were customers, regulatory and government agencies, unions and local councils represented, but also major national and regional environmental groups attended the dialogue meetings. These included "Cumbrians against a Radioactive Environment" (CARE), Friends of the Earth and Greenpeace, all with a strong record of confronting BNFL and lobbying for the shut-down of the reprocessing plants at Sellafield.

At the first meeting, a certain enthusiasm was perceptible on both sides of the barricades. The "human factor" worked: by discovering that you have nice people with families, hobbies and social values on the other side, too. Working groups were founded – first on nuclear waste and discharging, then on plutonium. A socio-economic study developed scenarios as to how East Cumbria would be affected by a shut-down or growth of Sellafield's operations.

But around autumn 2000, consultation fatigue set in. It was also accelerated by a new top management, called in to sort out the problems with Japan, and a damning report of Sellafield's safety procedures by the Nuclear Inspectorate. The new top management aggressively (no negative connotation – the CEO just felt as a turnaround manager that this was the normal style) communicated the new growth opportunities they saw not only in clean-up, but also in new nuclear plants. A leader from Friends of the Earth described his feelings: "When BNFL talked about new reactors, for me the dialogue was emotionally finished. They just don't get it."

Other environmental NGOs also expressed concerns that they were being inundated with floods of paper (in addition to all the government consultation papers on similar issues), and that no time was left for campaigning. Some even expressed the feeling that BNFL was getting the NGO side to defend BNFL's strategy from criticism, and at the same time not following the NGOs' recommendations. But the NGOs basically told BNFL to get on with the role of cleaning up their existing environmental liabilities and then vanished from the scene – not a very attractive perspective from the corporate view.

However, the NGOs admit that they also gained some useful information (for example, on BNFL's business plan and technical data). But, most importantly, nobody wants to create confrontation and call off the dialogue and then be blamed for the failure. Organizations want to leave more silently – as was the case, for example, with Greenpeace – in the hope that perhaps nobody would notice they had participated in the first round.

So the process goes on – but all have given up on something that was fundamental to change. Back to the trenches ...

### Stealth bomber

The "stealth bomber" attitude is often applied by companies (or industry associations) that are currently not subject to heavy public scrutiny. These companies try to quell public criticism from the beginning, but prefer to work much more behind the scenes than do the "lonely fighter" types.

However, choosing a low profile in public does not mean being soft. "Blackmail sometimes helps," stated one manager quite openly when he described his company's strong-arm attitude toward political critics (of course, this is not meant in a legal sense, but, for example, by threatening to mobilize industry supporters against a legislator in his or her constituency).

Even taking into account that managers from companies in this category are not much inclined to reveal their practices, there is no reason to doubt that "stealth bombers" exist, but they are few in number. The reason might be that such a strategy is very counterproductive once the silence has been broken; a public outcry elevates the company or industry association into the uncomfortable position of a "lonely fighter". Which often happens ...

### Box 4-5   Discovered Stealth Bomber: Interfor

Canada's Minister for Natural Resources was visiting European capitals in late 2000 to discuss the growing pain that global environmental campaigns, supported by celebrities like 007 actor Pierce Brosnan and Robert Kennedy Jr, are imposing – especially on forest companies on the West Coast, operating in temperate old growth rainforest. Most of the companies – with the exception of, for example, Weyersheuser – refuse to live up to the standards of the Forest Stewardship Council (FSC), a WWF joint venture with industry and retailers for sustainable forestry. Customers like IKEA and the Do-It-Yourself chain Home Depot have already made the FSC seal a precondition for their suppliers.

But beyond polite diplomatic exchanges and corporate buying decisions, the real drama was going on in the woods. At the core of the battle was International Forest Products Ltd (Interfor), the company that owns most of the Great Bear Rain Forest, covering the largest part of British Columbia's West Coast, one-and-a-half times the size of the Netherlands. The $600 million company employs 2,800 workers and operates half a dozen sawmills, 90% of its wood supply coming from the Great Bear Rain Forest. But it is this forest that is at the heart of the environmental campaign due to its pristine landscapes, many old growth forests and a rich wilderness of grizzly bears, timber wolves, and natural rivers supporting an unprecedented variety of aquatic life. It is no wonder that US and global media attention is ensured.

For years, Interfor had managed to stay out of the limelight, leaving the debate to the larger companies like Weyersheuser. But, while attempts at negotiation failed to reach a compromise between environmentalists and the British Columbia forest industry, environmental actions and responses became more and more heated and violent.

Just a couple of examples: five Interfor workers face criminal charges for trashing a protestors' camp and threatening to crush one man's head with a rock. Two protestors received an unprecedented one-year jail sentence for defying injunctions Interfor had obtained to stop protestors interfering with their operations. An Interfor employee deliberately rammed a Greenpeace inflatable, when activists tried to hang a banner across a river, wrestling away the banner and slashing it. On the other side, company cars had their windows smashed, bridges and equipment were tampered with. In one case, an employee barely escaped with his life, when someone removed a pin and molly, sending a steel cable slicing through the air as the line grew taut.

While the mayors of forest industry towns support Interfor against "economic terrorism from environmental groups", the company was also fighting on another front: the indigenous Kitasoo/Xaisxais First Nation tribe is claiming huge chunks of the Great Bear Rain Forest for its people. The plan would preserve 40% of the land and allow some logging and commercial activities in the remainder.

Interfor CEO Duncan Davis witnessed a Greenpeace tree-hugging demonstration at his home, condemning him as "the enemy of the Earth". In an interview with the *Globe and Mail* newspaper on 4 November 2000 he condemned violence, but added: "... if somebody threatened me, or spat in my face or threatened my property or my ability to earn my living – and did it over and over and over again – at some point, I would probably reach the breakpoint."

That is exactly where his company is in 2001: in my evaluation he has lost the battle, the morale and trust of his employees, as well as the reputation of the company with many customers. The provincial government, many of its competitors and allies in the media, surrendered when Home Depot, the largest Do-It-Yourself chain in the US, and most printing companies in the US and Europe, went from silent de-listing to public announcement of their boycott of Interfor and other companies that log in the Great Bear Rain Forest. Despite a $100 million (Canadian) subsidy, at least 10% of work places will be lost under an agreement signed by the forest industry, the provincial government and the local "First Nation" tribes and the environmentalists. This establishes a huge protection zone in which no logging will be permitted and a restricted zone in which environmentally sound logging (for example, following the criteria of the FSC) will be possible to a limited extent. As a consequence of the agreement, the boycott against Interfor and others was lifted.

But there is hope. In 1993, another British Columbia forest and paper company, McMillan Bloedel (MB) faced a similar, successful boycott against its intention to log old growth forest. The crisis was the start of a transformation from an insular, hierarchical organization with very traditional logging practices into a progressive, collaborative, value-driven and – maybe not coincidentally – financially more successful company, pioneering sustainable logging practice. Six years after the boycott, MB signed an agreement with its former adversaries for a joint marketing initiative to promote MB's forest and paper products.

As can be seen, there is nothing right or wrong about a specific strategy (although some situations are more comfortable than others). They are quite logical responses to some specific business situations, evolving from the interaction of basic corporate goals, cultures or attitudes with the involved players and their goals and attitudes. More often than not these have developed more intuitively, as a spontaneous reaction to a conflict or crisis, or have evolved in the course of the dynamic (for example, in the protracted and escalating "war" on tobacco).

But companies have to be clear as to where they come from and what kind of strategy they have pursued so far. In particular, with regard to "household names", the public will have a basic understanding of the corporation's strategy reflected, among other things, in its "image". Any sudden shift in the image might cause many problems that may result in numerous difficulties to rebuild the public's perception. And the corporation needs a clear understanding of which "channel" or "transmission belt" pressure is exerted and what are the issues the corporation has to deal with.

## 4.4 THE "TRANSMISSION BELTS" THAT INFLUENCE THE BUSINESS ENVIRONMENT

As described above, the contextual business environment covers all non-market factors and influences on corporations. However, it would be a wrong conclusion to assume that there is no influence from these "external forces" on the markets. As Figure 4.2 indicates, there are several avenues, or transmission belts, through which a "driver" of an

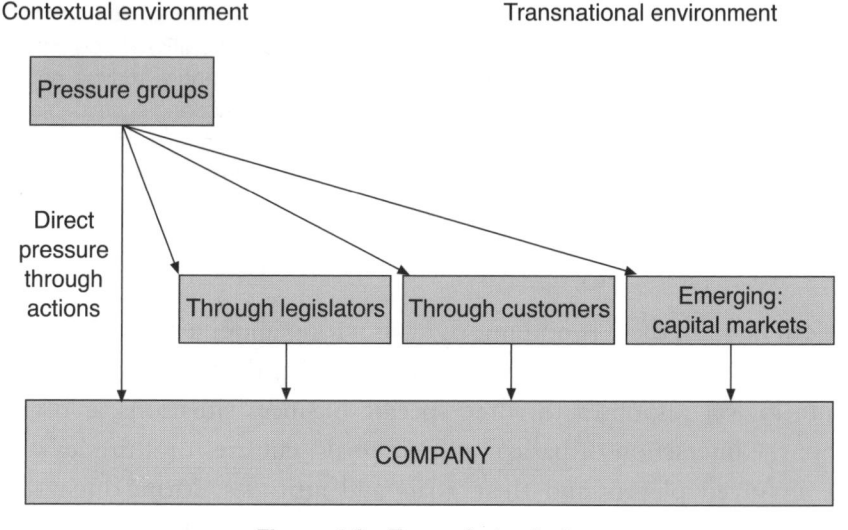

**Figure 4.2**   Transmission belts.

issue can try to influence corporate behaviour. One, if not the oldest, form is through direct action: for example, climbing on polluting chimneys, activists chaining themselves to barriers, interrupting sewage discharge, etc. – or sometimes even resorting to violence (see Box 4-6.)

## Box 4-6   Huntingdon Life Service (HLS): When Activists Resort to Violence and Blackmail

Englishmen are renowned for their common sense, a particular humour and patiently waiting in line at the bus stop or post office, not to mention the National Health Service (NHS). But the UK is also home to the most militant animal rights movement in the world: from the noble Royal Society for the Prevention of Cruelty to Animals (RSPCA), the professional PETA (People for the Ethical Treatment of Animals) to the underground Animal Liberation Frontline (ALF) – the entire spectrum of NGOs for animal rights.

During the 1990s the battle was very much about wearing fur for fashion. The more militant groups sabotaged animal farms and opened cages to release the animals (for example, minks). PETA recruited famous models, advertising them as being "too beautiful to wear fur", and organized demonstrations against fashion designers (for example, Karl Lagerfeld).

However, at the end of the 1990s the pharmaceutical industry became the focus of animal rights groups. The UK alone uses an estimated 2.6 million animals each year, mostly for legally required testing of new drugs. Of these, 70,000 animals are used in the specialized drug-testing company Huntingdon Life Science Group PLC (HLS). This company of 1,200 employees soon became the focus of an especially aggressive and eventually violent campaign.

Brian Cass, the CEO of HLS, was attacked and hurt with baseball clubs, managers have been subjected to death threats and arson attacks. Cars were burnt in front of the company's headquarters, and protestors trampled flower-beds in neighbouring gardens. The corporate web page, the internal email, and database system were attacked and interrupted by an "Animal Liberation Tactical Internet Response Network".

The "Stop Huntingdon Animal Cruelty" (SHAC) group, which had organized mostly peaceful demonstrations, now turned to the financial backers of HLS – and they backed off. HSBC, Citibank, the Royal Bank of Scotland and then Barclays and investment banks and stock-brokers such as Credit Suisse, First Boston, Merrill Lynch, Phillips & Drew or TD Waterhouse – all cut their links with HLS, forcing the company to look desperately for new financial backers and try to secure exemption from the stock market rules that would normally require the disclosure of their identity.

Some banks cited commercial reasons only (for example, the Royal Bank of Scotland, which is assumed to have written off 50% of a US$33 million loan) although their offices, too, had been subject to demonstrations and occupation. But Barclays were more frank: they admitted that their security concerns for their staff and their families was a reason to withdraw from the business.

The new financial backer Stephen Inc. also witnessed demonstrations in front of their London subsidiary branch, as did one of the remaining brokers to trade HLS shares, Winterflood Securities. Stephen also dropped out in late 2001, citing commercial reasons (obviously they lost some equity).

The British government, concerned about the escalation of these actions, vowed to fight militant animal rights groups with more dedication, considered toughening up the law, and allocated approximately US$1.5 million for funding a special police task force. SHAC, obviously unimpressed, announced that they would now be extending their actions to HLS customers.

The wear and tear for the company became clearly visible when HLS chairman Andrew Bake announced a loss of £10.9 million for 2000, admitting that the animal rights groups campaigns had affected orders.

Whereas such – sometimes spectacular – actions have raised public awareness, the overall impact is limited. In addition, after 30 years of environmental policy in OECD countries, the numbers of heavily polluting chimneys have declined considerably. And social issues are often related to developing countries, which makes only headquarter offices a target.

Although some areas for direct action remain (for example, destroying test fields of GM crops), the public increasingly expects to see solutions to a problem once its awareness has been raised. Therefore direct action has to be complemented by lobbying efforts, a cumbersome and slow process in a democracy. And furthermore, every effort by NGOs – for example, with regard to environmental issues – has met a heavy counter-lobby effort mostly by industry associations. To prove the case on scientific grounds, present the solution in a legal framework, promote the proposal through many steps in the decision-building in numerous expert and parliamentary committees, party conventions, etc. and survive "administrative reframing" was often beyond the means of even the best-resourced influencer NGO, or only possible if a focus on one or two absolute priority issues was decided.

Relatively new on the menu are focused company attacks, in an extreme case leading to boycotts (see the next subsection: "Pressure for change").

Previous successful, high-profile consumer pressure campaigns have been organized by activists against: sportswear producers (prominently Nike); Shell in the course of the Brent Spar controversy; fur fashion producers; any producer of GM food, and so on.

### Pressure for change

For brand- and image-conscious companies, the threat of a negative media campaign – and the desire to avoid or stop it – might be enough to change behaviour. Texaco and Coca-Cola, and their Afro-American employees are good examples: both companies not only paid punitive damages, but set up minority enhancement programmes and donated three-digit millions of dollars to foundations promoting minority education and business.

One precondition for any boycott (or credible threat of a boycott) should be noted here: the consumer or customer does not want to make a sacrifice – there must be equal alternatives available to which he or she may switch. This is mostly the case in the consumer goods area, where a "better guy" is readily available – so, it might only be one company that is boycotted.

As became crystal clear in the conflict over the Brent Spar platform, Greenpeace wisely focused on Shell alone in order not to widen the conflict. Three years later in 1998, in the activists' fight with the French government over nuclear testing in the South Pacific, it was clear that it is impossible to organize a boycott against a nation and the range of products it offers on the world market, even if there are alternatives to French champagne or cheese (although there are none for some high-brow gourmets). In short: national governments do not have a "soft underbelly" to attract activist pressure, whereas companies do.

A transmission belt increasingly used by activist groups to influence corporate behaviour is via the capital markets (see also Section 6.5). In this context, proposing shareholder resolutions to be heard at annual general meetings is mostly a tool of public relations, to grab media attention during the meeting. There might be cases where corporate management has to react with a more "reasonable" resolution to rally shareholders behind them, but mostly such actions are about propaganda. As one combattant observed: "The use of a shareholder resolution is the equivalent to dropping a nuclear bomb – the relationship necessarily becomes adversarial."

More sophisticated attempts have been made to alert the financial community to market and regulatory risks: for example, Greenpeace was successful in talking down the market value of DSM, a Dutch-based PVC manufacturer, when it embarked on an Initial Public Offering (IPO). Greenpeace's action alerted analysts and banks to the liabilities and market risks of the chlorine-based product. But often such information is dismissed as biased.

A more indirect, and effective, result might be the neutral-ranking by different bank and rating agencies (for details see Chapter 6). With different approaches, the raters try to assess the social and environmental performance of companies and assess current non-financial risks that might easily turn into such. Or certain normative criteria are applied to exclude specific industries or companies from investing in, notably, tobacco, alcohol and arms production. The amount of such "Green" or "ethical" investment is estimated – in its broadest definition – at approximately 10% of all share investment.

Given this multi-channel reality and the many players involved, how can companies decide early on what is relevant for them? Obviously – as the previous cases and evidence have shown – because players in the non-market environment are not so high on companies' radar screens, one can easily miss "the writing on the wall". But the range of companies and the probability that they are "in the limelight" is increasing because of brands.

## 4.5  WHY COMPANIES ARE BECOMING MORE VULNERABLE: THE ROLE OF BRANDS

### Box 4-7  In the Spotlight: It's Always Coca-Cola

At first glance, it appeared that the series of incidents that hit Coca-Cola during and after spring 1999 were completely unrelated:

- Coca-Cola was under heavy fire from antitrust busters worldwide, over the acquisition of the Cadbury beverage brands in 120 countries. As EU

Competition Commissioner Karl von Miert observed, "Coca-Cola thought we would be too naive or not determined enough to stop them. They were over-confident and a bit arrogant." Since then every acquisition by Coca-Cola is a "way of the Cross": for example, after two-and-a-half years of investigation, France turned down Coca-Cola's acquisition of Orangina from Pernod-Ricard. In Italy, antitrust authorities fined Coca-Cola US$16.1 million, 3% of its annual sales in Italy.

- Also, in spring 1999, US employees filed a class action law suit against Coca-Cola, citing systematic discrimination against Black employees. As one of the plaintiffs explained: "They ignored me, ignored me, ignored me to the point where I felt I had no other recourse." Coca-Cola embarked on a vigorous pre-trial defence and at the same time set up a new diversity council. The co-head, the most senior Black executive, however, was demoted in a management reshuffle half a year later and rehired after Coca-Cola – confronted with mounting boycott threats – settled the race suit for nearly US$200 million in spring 2000 and promised to invest US$1 billion into funds promoting diversity over the next five years.
- In June 1999, a botched contamination scare in Belgium and France reduced Coca-Cola's position from a trusted market leader to having to give away free products in an attempt to restore consumer confidence. Due to heavy-handed management from Atlanta (the *Economist* quotes Coca-Cola CEO Investor as saying "Where the fuck is Belgium?"), Coca-Cola appeared as untrustworthy, secretive and always too late in its responses – but was later forced into apologies to Belgium (which led to an outcry in France demanding the same). Altogether, Coca-Cola had to recall drinks to the value of US$14 in Europe. The overall cost of the crisis was estimated at above US$100 million plus additional marketing costs. Even in Kenya, supermarkets withdrew Coca-Cola products originating in the EU, due to a minor blip in quality control.
- In April 2000, a Greenpeace report embarrassed the Olympic Committee and Coca-Cola in the run-up to the "Green" Olympics in Sydney. Greenpeace stated that Coca-Cola used global warming HFCs throughout the Olympic site, although environmentally friendly alternatives are commercially available. In the much-visited website "cokespotlight.org" Greenpeace featured a mock advertisement: Coca-Cola's polar bear marketing symbol perched on a vanishing iceberg, under the banner "Enjoy Climate Change" in Coca-Cola's trademark banner lettering. After some bickering, the company announced that it was to ban all purchasing of refrigerators containing HFCs by the Athens Summer Olympics in 2004.

But the market pulled these unrelated incidents together: during this time, Coca-Cola's brand value dropped 13% from US$84 billion in 1999 to US$73 billion in mid-2000. The share price development was significantly below the S&P 500 index.

- And once in the spotlight, the story unfolded: for example, unions in the US accused Coca-Cola of allegedly allowing right-wing death squads to terrorize workers and murder union leaders in the bottling plants in Colombia, leading to a union demonstration at Coca-Cola's Annual Assembly in April 2002.

When certain parts of the world think of globalization, they think of a global fast-food franchise, where you (wearing blue jeans) eat a Big Mac, drink Coca-Cola, and pay in US dollars, while watching CNN World News or listening to MTV. To cut a long story short: they do not think of a world going global, but rather of the Americanization of their local, regional or national culture. Be it in Asia, Latin America or Africa: globalization seems to be understood as a synonym for American influence and commercialization.

It is not accidental that many of the companies mentioned in this book are "household names", well-known brands to which many people can relate. Coca-Cola, McDonald's, Mercedes, etc. enjoy a recognition rate of around 80–90% in each of the 100 plus countries in which they operate. Furthermore, nine out of top ten brands are American. But part of this concept is wrong, as the case of MTV indicates. The worldwide music television company tried to establish a global TV station with a global programme structure. The project failed. Nowadays, MTV has adopted local cultural characteristics, and broadcasts via approximately 30 different regional programmes.

### Clichés and brands

If one is to believe the marketing gurus, brands have become commercially more important: it is the only protection against "commoditization", the relentless working of market forces to erode any competitive advantage and related profit margin above the average.

Commodities do not command a premium price – brands do. And marketers pin their hopes on stronger brands as a barrier, to stop the ongoing decline in brand loyalty that can be observed throughout the world over the last two decades. As the number of brands increase in the global village, so does the "noise" that is needed to get attention.

But brands have not only become global – they have moved beyond commitment, and guarantee quality and performance that customers can trust. Today brands indicate a lifestyle, aspirations, a set of ideas or a social cachet. Some consumers even view brands on a par with religion.

Young & Rubicam, one of the largest advertising agencies worldwide, in its "league table of global consumer brands", stated that "Belief in consumer brands has replaced religious faith as the thing that gives purpose to people's lives." Which brand is it that succeeds? The study showed that brands *with strong beliefs and original ideas* were top of the list, as well as the ones with an image of quality and reliability. You can interpret this, however, in a positive way, as did the agency: companies *would therefore come under greater pressure to incorporate social responsibility into their brand value.*

Coca-Cola stands for carefree fun, Nike for a "just-do-it" attitude, and a Mercedes indicates that "you have made it". A brand's becoming a likeable "personality" with which people can identify is the marketing executive's ultimate dream.

Globalization critics such as Naomi Klein take brand personality as an indicator of the manipulative character of corporate marketing, cocooning as in a "brandscape", where no place is untouched. As companies become weightless, focusing on marketing and design only (but reaping with this the bulk of the profit), they are shifting production into sweatshops elsewhere.

The "race-to-the-bottom" – the use of low-paid labour, distraction of the environment and hence violation of human rights – is in her view the ugly side of the "branding coin" with its state dreams of happiness through consumption. And because the dominant brands are American, they neatly serve as the scapegoat for every anti-American sentiment around the world: be it Hindu nationalist authorities closing McDonald's restaurants in India, or pro-Palestine supporters boycotting US goods.

But the dialectic is more complex than the globalization critics assume. Not only are brands less stable than they used to be (for example, Nescafé and Kellogg's – a decade ago at the top, but now lingering somewhere in the middle – not to mention the faded dotcom brands), but through extension into the emotional dimension, "they need to be ethically robust and environmentally sound," as one marketing manger observed. "Enjoy the pleasures of life without remorse" best captures the attitude of the hedonistic consumer.

In today's world, a brand therefore is not only jeopardized by poor product or service quality but also by any whiff of scandal or provoking of public outrage. Arrogance, greed and hypocrisy are proven causes of customers' walking away from a brand – the customer expects good behaviour in every walk of life.

Therefore, alignment of the brand's promises with the values by which a company lives means that these promises and values are shared and executed by all employees in all operational tasks – this is vital. Basically, it is the gap between promises or raised expectations and actual behaviour by members of the organization that allow adversaries to run campaigns against the companies.

Nobody has exploited this lever to influence corporate behaviour as skilfully as the new breed of NGO campaigners. And no company has experienced this new reality more than the world's most famous brand, Coca-Cola. It is difficult to quantify the financial fallout of an incident, especially in the long run – but few question today the need to manage outside perception and reputation as carefully as other assets. Otherwise a boycott is looming.

### Boycotts as an anti-corporate weapon

The boycott is clearly the "ultimate" weapon, using customers and – also increasingly – the capital markets. The Internet is full of pages for all kinds of boycott: searches can easily reveal several hundreds: Exxon, prominently for its stance on global warming; Amazon, for patenting its "one-click" software; Microsoft ("say no to monopolies"); the US Music Corporation for destroying Napster; the state of Texas boycotted by tourists due to its human rights record; Nestlé is singled out time and again for baby milk, coffee, chocolate, GMOs, etc.; Mazda/Ford by the anti-abortion movement because they allow abortion in Mazda's corporate hospital. But one does not only find celebrities: neighbours of the FedEx hub call for a boycott because of hub extensions, and the regional US retail chain Neiman Marcus is boycotted because of its sales of fur. And obscure cases abound …

One can even choose between a more aggressive and a "love-based, compassionate" boycott, or learn how to organize a successful boycott (consuming.com). To bring order to this wide range of causes, boycottindex.com offers a neutral overview. You can choose among a variety that might fuel your boycott desire – environmental, human rights, bad business ethics, etc. – and a click guides you to a comprehensive set of hyperlinks.

So, one can easily find out who is boycotting whom and why. There is even a section entitled "boycott the boycotters", featuring among other items a "pro-Disney" movement. A boycott can be directed at nations (South Africa during the apartheid regime, Libya following Lockerbie, Yugoslavia due to several Balkan wars, Iraq following the invasion of Kuwait), as well as against companies (Shell filling stations during the Brent Spar campaign, or Nike due to its association with sweatshops).

In general, "boycott" *is a negative labelling* for something – no matter whether it is a national government or a company. Boycott always has a negative impact in that it belittles something.

The opposite of negative labelling is *positive labelling*, a method that is not used as often as the negative labelling such as boycott, but also an effective (and cheap!) form of protest. For example, in the 1920s, American trade unions put a label on every product that was produced under acceptable social conditions by organized workers. This kind of labelling system enabled everyone – especially trade union members – to distinguish between what they should and what they should not buy. Today, the many eco-labels try to have a similar impact.

An interesting question concerning the method of boycott is: *Who addresses whom?* In the case of British landowner Charles Boycott mentioned earlier, the ill-treated Irish employees, as stakeholders of Boycott's company, protested and addressed the "boycott" against him (and ever since 1875, his name has become the synonym for this kind of action). In the case of apartheid and the boycott against South Africa, matters were somewhat more complex. On the one hand the White-dominated government was subjected to a regime of international sanctions. On the other hand, professionally organized local and national consumer boycotts, often run by Black communities, targeted large South African companies; for example, the popular brand Outspan was called "blood-stained".

The effect of sanctions is sometimes not too visible: the critics of sanctions against the regime of Saddam Hussein in Iraq are prominent and well-known and say that the sanctions will only punish the public, but not the people truly responsible. Also, calls for company boycotts are not always successful, although refusing something does not cost too much; it is a relatively cheap form of political articulation. A consumers' boycott has a touch of grassroots democracy – which could have an important effect on legitimizing the protest by a broader public.

However, for a boycott to be successful, certain *preconditions* have to be met:

- The issue must grab the attention of a wide audience – this is often achieved by bringing about public outrage (for example, regarding child labour, but not the extinction of rats or spiders).
- The boycott must be focused (this explains why it is easier to boycott a product than a state – as NGOs discovered when they tried to boycott French products to protest against nuclear testing in the South Pacific) and have a clear, achievable goal ("recycling" instead of "dumping").

- The boycott must not call for too much sacrifice. A boycott of all gasoline stations in northern Europe would have probably shown no result, whereas it was easy to "punish" Shell for Brent Spar by stopping at the next station.
- The brand (or the institution) has to be strong and well-known ("household names"), which is not good news for marketers – that is, their efforts make the brand more vulnerable to protest.

This also means that the organizers of a protest will often choose to attack companies with a popular brand (what you could call the "inequality of boycott"). The competitors of such popular brands will be spared from the intended sanctions – life is not always fair.

---

### Box 4-8   Nestlé and the Baby Food – Singled out Again

Founded in 1866 by Heinrich Nestlé (a pharmacist from Frankfurt) in Vevey, Switzerland, Nestlé is the largest nutrition company worldwide (with sales of US$46.7 in 1999). It is a truly global company, located in over 80 countries and employing more than 230,000 people and operates over 500 factories.

The main product during Nestlé's early years, back in 1866, was powdered milk. At that time there was a high infant mortality rate and powdered milk helped to fight malnutrition in babies and small children.

Nearly a century later, the distribution of so-called "breast-milk substitutes", especially in African countries, resulted in an accusation of doubtful marketing practices by Nestlé, and led to one of the earliest, fiercest, most prominent and lengthy consumer boycotts of a global company.

It has been claimed (since 1939) that Nestlé yearly kills 1.5 million infants in the Third World with these substitutes, because of unsafe drinking water conditions. There is no evidence to support this, but the statements are still harmful: in 1979, the International Baby Food Action Network (as a main actor in the protest against Nestlé) was founded. In the US, Germany and the UK boycotts were launched against Nestlé.

Nestlé was accused because its critics said that free breast-milk substitutes distributed in Third World countries both hinders women in producing real milk and addicts them to Nestlé products. In 1981, the WHO passed a codex for the marketing of breast-milk substitutes, which was followed by Nestlé's own guidelines in 1982, which were similar to those of the WHO.

Two years later, Nestlé signed the WHO codex and the boycott ended. In 1986, the WHO passed a definitive prohibition of such substitutes – this was partly broken by nutrition companies, resulting in new boycotts.

At the beginning of the 1990s, the Anglican Church also participated in protests against Nestlé (they called a boycott on Nescafé coffee), as did many other groups in many other countries. In 1999, Nestlé let governmental and semi-governmental institutions certify that they follow the WHO guide-lines. The distribution of breast-milk substitutes is only a very small portion of the Nestlé portfolio, but the problem arose from the fact that, over a 20-year period, the case dominated nearly every discussion on Nestlé.

Nestlé and its image in general (also for other products) was labelled and damaged. The "Nestlé = Baby-milk drama in the Third World" equation seems to be continuing on into the future. Nestlé tried to handle the problem of public pressure as rapidly as possible, and yet the case still haunts the company – although it has no major effects on its sales, it appears to be a never-ending story. No small wonder that the company is ranked high on the list of companies targeted by anti-GMO activists.

## 4.6  DON'T LOOK BACK

There are clearly limits for companies in applying the traditional, more academic approach to the stakeholder concept. Different from the stable, local "good old days", in today's fragmented, fast-moving global business environment neither the stakeholders nor their claims can be known for sure – one of the usual preconditions in such recommendations.

As we have seen, Mitsubishi did not know who the "Rainforest Action Network" (RAN) were – until the protest began to hurt the sale of Mitsubishi cars and do-it-yourself products in the US and Europe. Monsanto did not know that Greenpeace had decided to make the fight against GMO its top priority, and had chosen the much-heralded market pioneer as its core "adversary". However, as we shall see in Chapter 5, the issues – old growth forest-logging and "tampering with nature" – had specific characteristics, which positioned them high on the top list of public attention.

In addition, the claims stakeholders make can easily contradict one another. Often employees (and unions) reject changes in the technology, strategy or marketing being proposed by environmentalists. The conflicting claims on the wealth created between investors and employees has today evolved differently than it did in the "class struggle" of a century ago, but the conflict remains (for example, at the top of the share bubble, investment bankers capture up to 90% of the profit from their activities as a bonus, leaving investors wondering about their shares . . .).

Even among regulators, conflicts can arise. The UK water industry has found itself caught over the years in the different priorities of the environmental agency and the industry regulator. Whereas the environmental officials were expecting – and pushing – for above-compliance environmental standards, the industry regulator was pushing for lower prices as the advocate of consumer interest. Even shareholders can have conflicting interests and clash vigorously. (See Box 4-9.)

### Box 4-9 Société du Louvre: Barbarian at the Gate?

When, in the mid- to late 1990s, US investors were starting to reach out to European stock markets, a number of clashes occurred between US shareholder activists and incumbent boards and owners, especially in family-controlled but stock market-listed companies.

One conflict that made the headlines – and not only in the French media – was that between Asher B. Edelmann and the Taittinger family, who controlled the hotel and luxury goods group Société du Louvre, as well as owning the famous Taittinger champagne brand.

The characters in this scenario could not have been cast better by a film producer. On the one hand the "red-blooded" US raider Edelmann who back in the 1980s was referred to in Wall Street as a "monster"; although not many of his raids succeeded, he was skilful enough to make a handsome profit out of the attempts – enabling him to take early retirement in the late 1980s, and to set up a US$150 million modern art museum in Switzerland. When he taught business courses such as "The Art of War" at Columbia University, New York, he offered every student US$100,000 for an identified takeover target. (Columbia, however, banned that offer.) Returning to business in the mid-1990s, he amassed a 12.2% stake in Société du Louvre, the group that were 36.6% owned by the Taittinger family, who had 54.5% of the voting rights.

The Taittinger family, on the other hand, could not be more French elite than you can be French and elite. No other family lists so many names in *Who's Who*, including the minister of justice, a vice-president of the senate and the director general of the holding, Anne-Clair Taittinger, who was – as were many other family members – educated at an elitist *grande ecole*.

All important units of the holding were run by family members: the Concorde Group of Luxury Hotels (including the famous Crillion Hotel in Paris); Envergure, the second largest economy hotel chain in Europe; as well as the champagne unit and the Baccarat company, producers of crystal glassware and jewellery.

Edelmann's lawyer claimed that more than 50 members of the family were sitting on the various boards of the diversified company. Family members were often also employed – for example, in the decoration of hotels, or for PR activities.

Soon the Taittingers and Edelmann were embroiled in a dog-fight. Edelmann's assessment was that the company traded for approximately 50% of the value of its individual parts, so it would unlock considerable shareholder value to sell everything except the Luxury Hotels group.

Anne-Claire Taittinger refused Edelmann's proposal saying that bringing the economy hotel chain Envergure to the stock market would mean that Société du Louvre would have shouldered the development costs, leaving future profits to others. Selling real estate would mostly benefit the French government in terms of capital gains taxes.

The arguments escalated when the Taittingers refused to disclose information required by Edelmann on answers to 58 questions he put at the Annual General Meeting in 2000. In the next round, not surprisingly, this led to a barrage of lawsuits and Edelmann's lawyer sent several complaints to the regulatory authorities. Among other things, Edelmann accused the Taittingers of:

- manipulating the share price to save wealth tax;
- selling shares below market value to the Peugeot family and Credit Lyonais to ensure further control;
- violating French antitrust and corporate laws through the web of cross-shareholdings;
- offering family members jobs above, and renting company real estate below, the market price.

The Taittingers denied any wrongdoing.

The US media featured this conflict under the headline "Shareholder value vs. family values", asserting that European companies still had a long way to go before reaching the (superior) modern Anglo-Saxon-style capitalism.

But putting tradition, style and pride aside (difficult to do, for sure), a closer look at the management issues revealed that it was more about "how" rather than "if" value is to be created. True, some parts in the group came into it, for example, as a result of a marriage, and for sentimental reasons it was a long time before it was sold. But, even in the most share-holder-driven company, long-serving senior executives have their "pet projects".

At least for the management generation now in charge, value matters (and if not for Mr Edelmann then for the cousins, who would not like to squander their inherited wealth). As for the "how" part, there are important conceptual differences. First, the more risk-averse Europeans do not prefer "pure plays" as US investors do. The latter value transparency rather than com-pensating for the cyclical nature of many businesses (maybe this view is changing, too, in the US due to the stock market development). Second, the Europeans have a stronger tendency to own the property on which they conduct their business, due to high transaction costs and the risk of price increases.

Which, from the empirical evidence, is the "better" business model is far from clear, and up to management judgment under specific contextual factors. However, what emerges as a result of such conflicts is more trans-parency regarding minority family members and family-related affairs (for example, employing family members for "social reasons").

But Edelmann did not want to wait for that development: he sold his share-holding to Albert Frérer, a French-speaking Belgian investor – betting that he could pressure the family more subtly and effectively?

In such (typical) situations, it does not help much to look at the power, urgency and legitimacy of stakeholder claims. This can only work if you know all your stakeholders and their power, can rank the urgency according to an agreed list of priorities and discriminate between more or less legitimate claims along a set of agreed values. But this is nearly impossible in today's global world, because you have high uncertainty, many information asymmetries and most of the claims are legitimate, but come from different values and priorities (this is the heart of a pluralistic democracy!).

Also, the power of a stakeholder often evolves in the course of the conflict when, for example, the influence group can attract political support, mobilize an alliance or their network, raise additional resources, or bet its budget on a victorious outcome. For example, the protracted Brent Spar campaign cost Greenpeace a fortune, far above the originally planned budget, because the conflict escalated in an unpredicted way. But Greenpeace was able to draw on reserves. And eventually it paid off – more in an indirect way than in contributions directly related to the campaign.

Nor does it help to "pigeonhole" stakeholders into categories of, for example, "accommodating" versus "antagonistic". Important campaign organizations – form Amnesty International to the WWF – both co-operate with industry on certain issues while at the same time campaigning against them for others.

The balance between conflict and co-operation might evolve in the course of the debate. Influence groups may start with an offer for dialogue and co-operation, but escalate to an "all and now" position when rejected. Even established routines of co-operation might sometimes get out of hand: normally, workers' representatives co-operate when restructuring and lay-offs, etc. are carried out, trying to get the best deal for those affected. However, when Renault closed its only Belgian plant in Vilvordein, a major social and political conflict emerged, leading to boycotts of Renault in Belgium (for a while . . .).

Nor does it help that industry mostly observes stakeholders from an institutional power base, mainly regulators enforcing (national) laws. As important as they are, they only represent established, not emerging, social expectations, issues or trends – exactly those dynamic factors that create and shape the markets of the future.

Readers may well be feeling depressed at this stage, asking themselves whether it is possible to bring some order and predictability into the chaos that surrounds them. As argued in the next chapter, it takes a different perspective: look at the issues, not the stakeholders (the owner or driver of an issue is one of the characteristics), judge them through the lens of your strategy and understand how you are currently perceived by the external world.

This perspective requires an early warning system, second only to an understanding about the "transmission belts" of external pressure from influence groups on corporations and the criteria set for the characteristics of an issue, on which a company can decide the importance and relevance of specific issues and how this affects its strategy. After all, companies are not organizations designed to uphold the common good, but are set up with a specific purpose: to earn a profit by satisfying the demand that exists (even latently) in the market, and for which the customers are willing to pay. As business organizations, companies therefore have a specific – and legitimate – perspective to look at those (external, non-direct or only indirect) market factors.

# Detecting and Preventing Trouble Ahead    5

To identify issues, a company first needs an "Early Awareness System" (EAS). This does not involve having huge resources or systems, but requires a curious attitude or open-mindedness, and can be exercised by some simple tools. In this chapter, the tools are introduced and, second, two (tested) checklists are explained. These checklists assess the relevance of an issue for a company: one looks from the corporate perspective, the other from the adversary point of view (because NGOs do not choose their campaigns at random). In addition, the transmission belts for pressure on corporations are described, especially when they are exposed by having a strong brand, explaining why companies have to look at issues, not stakeholders (the strength of the stakeholder is one of the issue characteristics).

## 5.1   THE NEED FOR AN EARLY AWARENESS SYSTEM (EAS)

---

### Box 5-1   Swiss Re: From Early Risk Identification to "Top Topics"

The most sophisticated and comprehensive EAS can probably be found in the insurance industry – no small wonder. In the late 1980s, the industry learned the hard way about the cost of risks not being detected early: several billion euros were paid in the US and Europe for the clean-up of contaminated real estate by accumulated diffuse emissions of hydrocarbons.

Reinsurance companies in particular have to look decades into the future to calculate, for example, the impacts of global warming on property and the casualty risks that they cover.

Swiss Re has developed a recognized best practice system called SONAR (Systematic Observations of Nations Associated with Risk). All persons involved in a specific underwriting process are required to contribute their observations to a data bank, where additional information is fed in from public sources. One – typical – issue is the increased propensity to allergic reaction caused, for example, by anti-bacterial additives in food or cleaning agents.

The findings are processed in two ways: first, the technical risk assessment department looks in more detail at identified risks, using a sophisticated but industry-specific risk assessment methodology (for example, one is called Safety Management Audits in the Process Industry, covering industries from oil to chemicals). The quality of the risk is always defined by three factors: "hardware", technical factors covering, for example, process control or the factors involved in fire and explosion production; "software", comprehending organizational factors and management systems; and "liveware", for example, the attitude and awareness of management and employees with regard to safety.

Using this system, Swiss Re recently saved an amount of over 100 million euros because they were the only reinsurer who declined to cover a newly launched pharmaceutical. Only Swiss Re had detected potentially negative side-effects, which then materialized leading to huge liability compensation.

Second, the findings are aggregated currently to six "Top Topics", more than 50% related to sustainable development (for example, climate change, water). The issues are selected by their relevance for Swiss Re, using criteria such as brand reputation, stock market capitalization or business volume.

Top management serve as sponsors, and a senior manager is named "Topic Manager", supported by a "Communication Officer". This indicates that the management of the issue has an internal and external dimension. Internally, the impact on the reinsurance business is managed and a common position throughout the divisions implemented. Externally, Swiss Re is striving for an opinion leadership, based on expertise, trying to educate customers and lawmakers or demonstrate its commitment to corporate social responsibility.

Everybody agrees that preventing a crisis is better than managing a crisis (but, from the manager's individual career perspective, there is a drawback: if you manage a crisis successfully, you become a hero, preventing crises will not be noticed – or rewarded – by anyone).

But time and again it can be observed that companies react to new developments in their business environment when it is too late. What is needed is an EAS, and, as argued in this chapter, it is as much about attitude as it is about (IT-based) tools.

EASs are not uncommon. You can find them in many places: in the military, the Airborne Warning and Control System (AWAC); in the "leading indicators" for detecting the next phase in the business cycle; or an EAS run by the Food and Agriculture Organization (FAO) of the United Nations, on food supply and demand. Companies have their EASs, too: consumer research, aimed at detecting new desires or shifts in attitudes, trading incoming orders, and so on.

All these systems have two characteristics in common: first, they do not require an unassailable chain of scientific evidence before a recommendation is made. What counts in scanning is not established causality, but the plausibility of the findings. Waiting until the danger is confirmed beyond the shadow of a doubt means that in all likelihood disaster already will have struck. The second characteristic is that all these information systems require a capacity for large databases in order to produce meaningful information. Therefore, they can most effectively be run with the support of computers.

All awareness systems (computerized or not) can be classified as aiming for either operational or strategic awareness, depending on the object and the time dimension. The difference between the two is that, in the case of operational early awareness, the potential identified through strategic awareness already has turned into reality. In the military, for example, strategic early awareness wants to know the number and types of enemy weapons before they are even in the arsenal. Operational early awareness systems, on the other hand, evaluate risks that are known already in principle, but where details are still missing (for example, precise enemy troop movements).

## What might an EAS for the business environment look like?

Most EASs seen in researching this book were proprietary and confidential to the companies that owned them. (For a best practice example, see Chapter 8 on DaimlerChrysler.) In general, they can be described as a special application of existing information systems that, by providing early indicators, draw attention to approaching opportunities and risks, the significance of which has not yet been commonly recognized. Such EAS can help a company to stay on track operationally and strategically by taking timely and appropriate action.

They support managers in scanning and monitoring their general business environment. Since, for example, activist groups belong to the contextual environment of an organization and can influence the company's future without being involved in direct business relations or transactions, monitoring of these relevant groups clearly should be part of the scanning process. But basically it is issue management.

Strategic early awareness scanning requires computer support just as much as operational early awareness systems that trace stock or incoming orders. A corporate headquarters can only with difficulty stay on top of all possible developments in all its different business units and all different markets at any one time. So, in the world of business, there is a growing need for IT support in strategic early awareness.

Computerized EASs need to help managers to collect and aggregate data in a systematic way. Even if data collection sources are decentralized, sensors must distribute the processed data to any managers who might need it. The tasks of such a system can therefore be divided into data collection and transfer, information-processing and information distribution.

## Data collection and transfer

Data collection for early awareness of developments in a company's business environment normally use five different information sources. First, employees may enter data "by hand". In this case, people at the peripheral elements scan the information environment in their special area of expertise, which might be customer groups or scientific fields, for example. Observations of interest to the company are, in the former case, entered into the system; for example, sales managers enter information referring to customer attitudes.

Second, data can be collected through the monitoring of press agencies and information services (for example, Reuters) by using key words to sort out topics of interest.

A third source may be specialized databases, that is, scientific databases for the newest research findings or legal databases for court decisions. Similarly, by using search engines (AltaVista, MSN, Yahoo, etc.), managers can scan the Internet for keywords on topics that might be important for the company. Internet chat or newsgroups on certain themes can also help to discern public attitudes.

Finally, company internal information sources provide valuable information. Customer information systems of consumer goods companies, based on free-phone 800 numbers, where companies like Coca-Cola monitor consumer attitudes, provide feedback on issues ranging from product quality to the noise of automatic vending machines. Such systems often do reveal important signals at a very early stage. Complaints and questions from consumers may contain valuable information about developments in the company's business environment.

Once data are entered, they have to be communicated in order to be combined usefully with other data. This communication can take place at the corporation's headquarters, through the company's own network (for example, an intranet) or using public networks like the Internet. The basic design philosophy of data collection transfer is represented in Figure 5.1.

### Information-processing

Once the data have been communicated to the organization, they have to be checked, aggregated and stored. This check includes a review of the logical consistency, a sorting procedure by which the data are

Computerized Early Awareness System

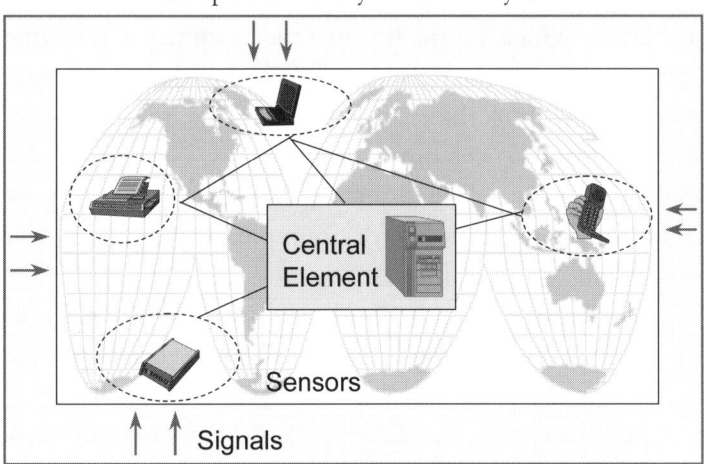

**Figure 5.1**   Data collection transfer.

assigned to certain issues and storage in databases. Groupware programmes may help managers to structure the incoming data.

Any central database should facilitate flexible queries such as a full-
text search (to find everything related to one issue), queries on attributes
(key activist groups, time distribution, media, etc.) and trend reports.
To provide managers with trend reports, the system should be able to
calculate, for example, distribution functions for factors like media
coverage of various controversies.

### Information distribution

Information distribution can take place in a pull or a push form. In a
pull system managers have to access the information system themselves
and pull data of interest out of the system. Examples of these kinds of
systems are intranets or groupware programs. In a push system,
managers get the information that is relevant to them in an automatic
form. They might, for example, get a daily update on an issue in
which they are involved through email. To build such a system, the

central processing unit has to possess user profiles that identify user interests.

However, the best EASs will have no impact if a company is culturally blind to its business environment. This can take different forms: scientific arrogance, that the layman is ignorant and better "shut up"; high identification with its product, where every criticism appears to be malicious; or, in highly political corporations, where attention is inward-directed. But even the most outward-looking managers need some tools to cut through all the "noise" in the system and try to figure out what is relevant for the company.

Two simple tools in the context of EASs are explained here. They will help to figure out what are emerging issues (cross-impact analysis) and how the dynamic of public opinion might evolve (diffusion curve), before turning to the specific characteristics of an issue, which could generate a specific impact on the company.

## Cross-impact analysis

Many companies use Scenario Analysis to alert themselves to the range of potential developments. An environmental analysis is certainly an efficient information instrument, but takes a great deal of time to prepare if it is to meet the purpose. A simpler instrument for the identification and "sifting" of weak signals is so-called "cross-impact analysis", which can be generated, for example, in the course of a brainstorming session. Brainstorming makes it possible to activate know-how which employees in different areas (for example, R&D, marketing, environmental protection) already possess, but which they have not necessarily articulated in an environmental context nor synthesized.

By placing potential environmental developments in relation to corporate objectives (see Table 5.1), an image of a network of interrelationships is produced that gives a transparent structure to various and mutually interacting variables. This method can be used in situations in which, for example, environmental issues cause consumers to direct criticism at a corporation because of its products, and begin migrating

**Table 5.1** Cross-impact analysis

| | Potential environmental product-related developments | | | |
| --- | --- | --- | --- | --- |
| | Potential for public criticism | Ability of consumers to switch to environmentally-friendly substitutes | Stricter environmental regulations | Ability to innovate |
| *Corporate issues* | | | | |
| Safeguarding of competitiveness | − | − | − | + |
| Profit | 0 | − | − | ? |
| Qualified and motivated employees | − | − | ? | + |
| Quality level of products– user-friendly image | 0 | 0 | ?! | |
| Diversification | + | + | + | ? |
| Globalization | 0 | 0 | − | ± |
| Distribution channels | ? | ?! | ? | 0 |

+ = Positive influence
? = Ambiguous/Uncertain influence
− = Negative influence
?! = Unknown if it will have an influence or not and, if so, in which direction
0 = Neutral

to more environmentally friendly products, or those situations in which a corporation finds itself confronted with stricter regulations that could make innovations viable.

Potential developments in the environmental context are systematically mapped out in terms of their effects on corporate objectives and strategies. In this way, it might become clear that the ability of consumers to switch to environmentally friendly substitutes is high −

potentially reducing the competitiveness of the corporation and spurring on diversification – or that one's ability to generate positive innovations is higher than realized. However, the most interesting areas are those in which no clear estimates can be made. Unclear or contradictory evaluations and unknown interaction relationships can be the tip of an iceberg beneath which are concealed changes to the strategic context of great potential strategic significance. These may indicate that something has "started to move".

Deeper analyses are called for in cases that show high sensitivity to new developments, that exhibit paradoxes, or that indicate that there is an information deficit, because only in this way can weak signals indicating possible trend-breaks or displacements of the regulatory framework be recognized. A precondition for the use of this method is that no predominating opinion (even if only informal) be allowed to prevail when preparing the cross-impact analysis, since this would hinder the early preconception-free identification of new developments. Similarly, no attempt should be made in the information acquisition phase to harmonize different opinions by compromises; instead, the causes for these differences of opinion should be investigated.

The latter process will be simplified when advocates of minority opinions are brought into the brainstorming sessions as well as outsiders with a wide background of experience. Only in this way can corporate "tunnel vision" be prevented, which can lead to information being overlooked or ignored because it does not fit into the pattern of experience gained in the organization's history (for example, the "not invented here" syndrome and its environmental cousin, the "not emitted here" syndrome). Minority opinions should be assiduously considered in an unprejudiced manner, because the business environment is characterized by convictions about its own motive force, which in turn can rapidly change both minority and majority opinions – whether based on "objective" findings or sentiment. Such opinion dynamics are naturally painful for a corporation when they produce direct, rapid changes in consumer behaviour.

*Forecasting the dynamic course of public opinion:*
*the diffusion curve*

On social, political or environmental issues, a corporation is faced with the difficulty of filtering out for itself from the daily flood of reports in the media the information that is relevant to its operations. It can frequently be observed that certain problems can rapidly "climb to the top of the ladder" of priorities while others remain relatively unnoticed and dormant.

However, diffusion research shows us that there are some very typical patterns for the dissemination of ideas, the way problems are perceived, and political decision-making processes, and that these can be represented using non-linear trend-lines in the approximate form of an S-shaped curve. Such a path is typical of environmental problems, which characteristically have long gestation periods, a steep rise to the threshold of general awareness, a period of stability at a high level of awareness and finally a slackening of interest after, for example, measures have been taken to solve a problem.

Figure 5.2 shows the plausible dynamic course of a typical issue, for example on environmental concerns. It is thoroughly characteristic that phases of intensive reporting and quieter periods follow one another in alternation. Particular occurrences – such as a crisis or a highly noteworthy research report – can precipitate a whole chain of actions and statements ("the snowball effect").

It is important to note that at the "take-off" point, it is really vital that the company act – and now. Sometimes it has less than 24 hours, but anyhow the initial reaction very much shapes the future path of escalation – or descent. The heightened level of sensitivity leads to a more intensive level of perception, which in turn leads to a higher priority being attached to the particular problem. Reports spawn additional reports and stories in the mass media as well. Each corporation must set for itself a threshold above which it will start to react. The point that is set should depend on the corporate strategy being followed.

A system's ability-oriented market leader is likely to behave in a

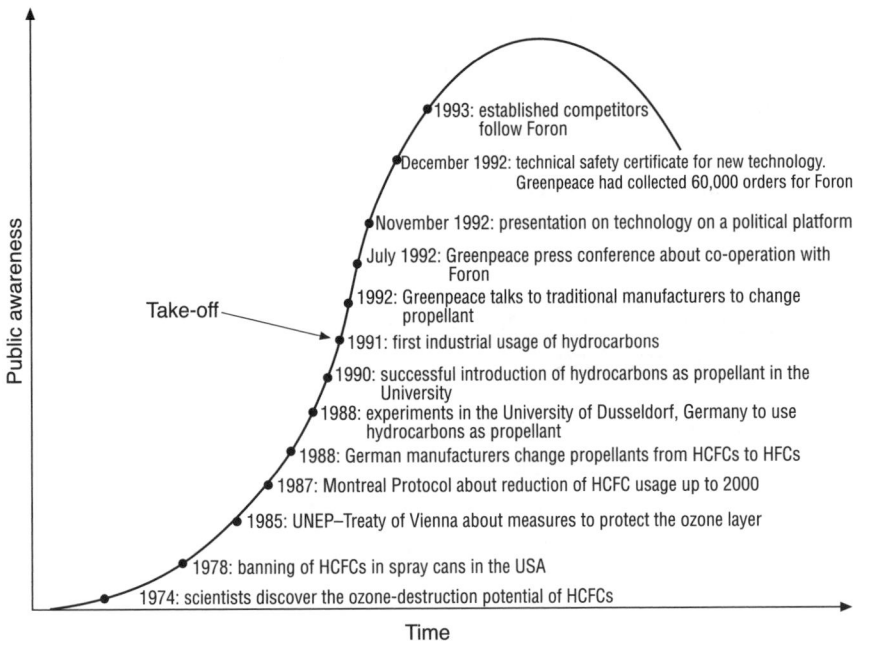

**Figure 5.2** Diffusion curve for CFCs.

manner very different from a corporation with a defensive strategy. Whereas the latter will tend to react primarily to measures taken by authorities, the former will react at an earlier stage. Reacting at an early stage helps, as a rule, to prevent further escalation of the public discussion. This is, however, only possible when the potential to solve the problem is available at the critical moment.

The applicability of the crisis diffusion curve concept has been tested several times and with good results in environmental management research projects (in connection with, among others, foods, textiles and the issues surrounding greenhouse gas). The classic example of the CFC issue is presented here in Figure 5.2. Following initial worries about damage to the stratospheric ozone layer by CFCs, new findings in the first half of the 1980s led first to "false-alarm" pronouncements by sceptics, which then nevertheless had to be revised as a result of new confirmation of the existence of the "ozone hole" over the

Antarctic. Finally, the theme escalated very rapidly and led to an internationally co-ordinated and phased elimination of the use of these chemicals (the Montreal Protocol of 1987).

The diffusion curve concept is discussed here because one of the typical mistakes made by companies is underestimation of the dynamic of public opinion – they did not understand the take-off point.

## 5.2  PREVENTING TROUBLE – THE ISSUE CHECKLIST FOR COMPANIES

As argued above, issues matter more for companies than an in-depth analysis of the range of stakeholders. The question is how to identify the issues that could lead to trouble. Whereas the EAS serves as a reconnaissance for emerging issues and their broader context, in this section "issues on the rise" are tested for their impact on a company, a specific investment, a product launch or a process (for example, insurance for equal opportunities). Basically, this is a screening test for changes, new projects or an assessment of existing conflicts, simmering over a small flame, where a test might reveal the probability if it flaring up.

The assumption – based on empirical research – is that most issues do not come like a flash out of the blue, but could have been detected because they fit a pattern or set of criteria. Matthias Winter and I tested the following checklist – among others – in our book on "managing outside pressure" and put ourselves on the line: we predicted the further development and outcome of nine emerging conflicts (at that time – for example, Swiss Nazi gold or ABB's Bakun Dam). In eight cases, our predictions were reasonably aligned with the real development; however, we underestimated the power of the opposition against genetically modified food (but two companies involved advised us that they had gained a great deal of insight from our research, which is prompting them to revise their strategy).

As with every checklist, it is not a replacement for managerial judgment and common sense. It should not be "mechanically" applied, but should be used as a tool to support systematic thinking and the systematic ability to look comprehensively – that is, from different angles! – at the issues. It is for this purpose that we have also developed the checklist from the point of view of the corporate adversary: you can gain far greater understanding of a "battle" if you can put yourself "into the shoes" of the other side.

---

### Box 5-2   Company Checklist

**1**   Are the arguments against the issue plausible?
**2**   Does the issue evoke emotion? Is it understandable – visual, touching – by the public?
**3**   Is the issue media-friendly?
**4**   Are there connections to other issues involving the company or other companies?
**5**   How strong is the key activist group?
**6**   How isolated is the company?
**7**   How far have the dynamics of the crisis already evolved?
**8**   How easy is the solution?

---

### Are the arguments against the issue plausible?

Two factors determine whether activists' claims are plausible:

**1**   if they are connected to some understandable concerns; and
**2**   if they are communicated through a reliable and credible source.

People can have very strong opinions that are not based on superior logic, but rather on values and beliefs. Therefore, companies should not evaluate activist claims only on the basis of whether they are scientifically or technically justified, but should consider instead whether there is a certain degree of plausibility in the eyes of the public.

Even if public opinion sometimes seems capricious, unpredictable or irrational, managers should try nevertheless to look further than their own scientific data and internal issues. They should, as a rule, listen carefully – and especially to their harshest critics. Falling into the trap of labelling activist demands as "irrational" from the beginning limits a company's ability to gain additional insight and to understand the concerns of the public.

Managers should also take into account the fact that the reference system for evaluating the plausibility of an issue through all activist groups may be very different from the company's own reference system. For example, in the European debate over the use of gene-manipulated maize, industry assumes that the existing, intensive, mono-cultural farming systems will be the norm in the future, and evaluates the benefits of biotechnology with this in mind. Conversely, most environmental activist groups that are against the use of biotechnology see it as binding agriculture to mono-cultural farming systems, and view it as a major disadvantage to the multi-cultural farming system that they favour.

Furthermore, managers should realize that, rather than the activist groups having to prove companies guilty of harmful practices, society is increasingly demanding that companies first give proof of their products' safety.

The second factor determining the plausibility of claims is that of people's trust in the information source. In general, if the source is trustworthy in the eyes of the public, then the information is less likely to be challenged. In the Western world, trust in large corporations is generally quite low. Before US legislation forced companies to report the emission levels of 300 hazardous chemicals in the so-called Toxic Release Inventory (TRI), firms were constantly pushed by activist groups to publish their emissions. Even when they did this, however, nobody believed the data. Since the information has been published through this (relatively) trusted government agency, pressure to disclose the data has subsided.

Many accusations could never be considered plausible and therefore lead only to minor disruptions. A classic example is that of the gossip and chain letters about Procter & Gamble's (P&G) connection with

Satanism, which began in the early 1980s, when certain groups claimed that the president of P&G spoke in support of Satanism on a television talk show. As proof of their arguments, these groups mentioned the company's old moon-and-stars trademark, which has 13 stars and could therefore be seen as a Satanic symbol connected with devil worship. However, the background behind this symbol is in fact that, in 1850, P&G marketed Star Candles, utilizing a man-in-the-moon trademark consisting of a popular figure of the 1800s. The 13 stars represented the original 13 colonies of the US. (They can also be found on the US dollar bill.)

Despite the fact that this rumour came up again and again over the years, the issue never seriously affected P&G's business – it was simply not plausible. To avoid mushrooming negative publicity, P&G sued rumormongers, and sent letters to 10 churches and to the news media, denying any connection with devil worship. (The company has now also discarded its traditional trademark.)

In summary, managers should consider both whether an issue is connected to plausible concerns and whether the public views the company or the activist group as the more trustworthy information source.

### *Does the issue evoke emotion? Is it understandable – visual, touching – for the public?*

This question is probably the most important one on the checklist. Emotions can be the most powerful motivators for action. Emotions are not necessarily negative – they are simply a fact of life, helping people to reduce the complexity that they have to face in their decisions. Only a small number of issues are able to arouse the interest of large numbers of people at a time, but, when they do, the momentum is difficult to counter. Issues that evoke emotion have several characteristics in common and include: easily understood by the public, visual and touching.

People become excited about things that they can see, understand, love or hate. Environmental- or health-related disasters are guaranteed international media coverage when pictures or films of suffering animals or ugly piles of waste are available to create good visuals and touch people's emotions. Social issues become strong when they show a great visual injustice. Everyone can understand the message, and possibilities for public reaction under these conditions are high.

A classic example of a very emotional issue has been the US debate on "dolphin-safe" tuna-fishing. After research revealed that at least one million dolphins died in fishermen's nets between 1972 and 1990, dramatic advertisements with headlines like "Kill a Dolphin Today – All You Need Is a Tuna Can and a Can Opener" were used by animal rights groups to encourage consumers to boycott tuna-canners who trapped dolphins in their nets. Although there are healthy numbers of dolphins on the planet, and the animal is clearly not on the endangered species list, this dolphin-by-catch quickly became a hot issue for the public and resulted in a tremendous outcry.

First, teenagers became active spokespersons against dolphin-killing; then their parents caught on and started boycotting tuna as well. The major contributing factor to this was the fact that most human beings like dolphins – highly intelligent and sociable creatures typified by the friendly character in the *Flipper* television series. The issue of dolphins dying in fishermen's nets is an emotionally distressing one, with all the necessary characteristics – it is understandable, visual and deeply touching.

Attempts at other fishing techniques are fraught with problems, because they result in a larger number of young tuna or tuna in reproductive stages being caught. Arguments based on hard data that the tuna themselves are much more likely than dolphins to be added to the endangered species list do not have the same emotional value with the public, and therefore pressure on companies for a solution for dolphins will always be heavier than that for tuna.

Public outcry in the US and the threat of legislation forced the major tuna marketers to switch to "dolphin-free" fishing methods. The whole issue finally resulted in a labelling programme for tuna cans that became one of the most popular labelling programmes ever.

This case also shows that emotionally charged issues not only attract the public but often lead to legislative action. In April 1991 the US placed an embargo on the import of Mexican tuna because of its non-compliance with dolphin-safe fishing methods. As of 1998, the Mexican tuna industry suffered a 55% shrinkage and 30,000 direct and indirect jobs have been lost, while tuna exports have dropped by 70%. The WTO later ruled this legislation illegal.

However, one should not conclude from this example that animal rights in general are high on the consumer's agenda and are always able to evoke emotion. If many people really felt strongly about animals being driven around the country for long periods, some super-markets might gain market share quickly by announcing that they buy only local meat. But this issue is not as emotional, probably because of missing aesthetics (mistreatment of pigs leads to far fewer and less excit-ing protests than does mistreatment of horses or dogs).

It should be noted that national differences exist concerning such issues. For example, nuclear power finds a much broader acceptance in France, Japan, Korea and Taiwan and stirs up far less emotion than in the US or in Germany. But even in Asiatic countries, which up until recently experienced few activist group demands and where public emotional reactions are generally frowned on, the trend for public pressure on companies seems to be gaining a foothold.

### Is the issue media-friendly?

Highly emotional issues are those most likely to be media-friendly. The importance of the media in raising issues cannot be overemphasized, because media involvement is the way to bring an issue to prominence. Only the mass media are able to disseminate a topic of discussion instan-taneously throughout society (see Chapter 3).

The British media, for example, had quite a decisive influence on bringing the GMO issue to the public's attention, but they did not "invent" it. Following the BSE ("mad cow") scare, food was at the top of people's agendas. To identify this, focus was placed on the impact on personal health (instead of many other aspects such as the impact on farmers) and the issue was simplified to the extreme so that literally no-one could avoid confronting the issue ("Frankenstein Food" was the "creative" labelling by one tabloid newspaper). Strong opinions were expressed: these opinions, however, were not manipulated by the press, but served to rekindle existing concerns, prejudices and perceptions.

However, there are many issues that fulfil all the emotional requirements and still do not gain media attention. This is because it is also very important that an issue be new, extraordinary and accessible to media reporters.

When the media began reporting on environmental and health disasters about 20 years ago, interest mounted quickly because the issues were new. Blazing rainforests, slaughtered elephants, oil-slicked otters, and forced child labour made good stories. This rising interest led to the fact that in the 1980s virtually every consumer magazine was running cover stories on the environment, on health and social injustice.

However, in the 1990s, these stories became commonplace and interest declined. Today, the campaigns still exist but they are mingled with the many "also-rans", buried in the millions of Internet pages. Issues have to be different or extraordinary in some way if they are to grab media attention. If a particular issue, or even a similar one, has already been reported extensively, people tend to skip the story and look for something more interesting – unless they are looking for a story to confirm their opinion (for which, in fact, one only needs to read the headlines).

A "new" story is not always enough: in order to be media-friendly, an issue has to be accessible to the reporters as well. If something happens in an out-of-the-way place that is difficult for even reporters to reach, they are not likely to expend their energy and resources to get there. In the 1990s, to choose a simple example, Hoechst (which split up and is now part of Aventis) was said to be under much heavier scrutiny than, for example, BASF. The reason: the ageing Hoechst core plant lay within "smelling distance" of approximately 120 news agencies, radio and TV editors, national and regional newspapers – not to mention the many political "Greens" in the surrounding suburbs. BASF, on the other hand, located in a more remote area enjoyed the coverage of just a couple of local newspapers and a regional TV and radio station, with a small number of "Greens" living nearby.

Today, however, the accessibility problem has decreased as activist groups learn how to work with the media. Greenpeace produces and provides "video news releases" free of charge to the media. Other activist groups provide material for the press through their Internet servers. So the media can use the material provided by the activist groups rather than sending their own reporters to the scene. Many stations broadcast this material without even changing the accompanying voice-overs.

The media today includes the national and international press, technical journals, television, local radio programmes and popular new forms like the Internet. Activists' concerns may first appear in local or highly specialized media, then may – or may not – succeed in moving into more general publications (see Figure 5.2).

The growing popularity of the Internet is truly helping to make the world into a "global village". Crises, engendered or highlighted, exposed on the Internet will be an increasing problem for companies, because media coverage can be generated by a single person with a complaint.

Boycotts and protests generally spread much faster through the Internet. It took more than a decade for boycotts against South Africa to take hold, but organized protests against oil companies in Burma that continue to do business there have gained support rapidly in only two years, mainly through the Free Burma Coalition website which averages 36,000 visitors a month. Activists use the Internet to monitor

Burma on a daily basis and report to the world what streets the demonstrators are on, where they are arrested and how the government
reacts, thus drawing international attention to one of the world's most
brutal and repressive military regimes – the Burma State Law and
Order Restoration Council (SLORC). This Council has received severe
condemnations from the US Congress and State Department, the European Parliament, the United Nations Human Rights Commission, the
International Labor Organization, and Amnesty International. No
company dealing with Burma has gone so far unnoticed – and
unpunished.

The Internet activists are also taking on corporations directly, with
pages combining text, graphics, video and audio, to spread information
on a company's questionable practices. These groups can use the Internet to challenge claims of companies point-for-point – as RAN did
with Mitsubishi. RAN's website linked its rebuttals back to Mitsubishi's
site, so that readers could check RAN's rebuttals directly against the
statements they refute.

Allan Hunt-Badiner, RAN's chairman, argues: "Despite these new
forms of communication, however, companies themselves can still influence the media through their advertising expenditures, and in most
countries the media depend on their advertisers. Therefore, heavy
advertising can sometimes improve a company's position in a conflict,
or at least force the media to be more balanced in their reporting."

### Are there connections to other issues involving the company or other companies?

Managers must be aware of the connections between controversial
issues, since these may give some issues prominence out of all propor-
tion to their limited, direct, environmental, health or social impact.
Activists' accusations may take on huge proportions, perhaps beyond
all rationality from a company's point of view, if, in the eyes of the
public, they are connected to other events. The list of possible intercon-
nections can be very long. The connections may lie within the

company, with other companies within the same industry or with related effects or results.

One example of connections within the company is provided by the Swiss food giant Nestlé. Since the infant milk formula scare, every new issue that comes up for Nestlé is linked back to that one. Most recently it came back to haunt Nestlé in the controversy over the planned use of genetically engineered soybeans in many of its products, where Nestlé was under heavy scrutiny (see Box 4-8).

Connections can be especially troublesome for managers in the event of accidents. It may be nearly impossible for the company to communicate its point of view to the public, because the public is outraged by linkages over which the company has no control.

One curious example, to highlight this point, is the reporting on Hoechst (now Aventis). After a series of (mostly minor, but widely-covered) spills following an explosion, a fire broke out in a chemical factory in Cologne. The first news to break was: "Fire in a Hoechst factory" – which was in fact located nearby, but not affected. The journalist had assumed: "If there is something, it must be Hoechst …"

### How strong is the key activist group?

As one characteristic of an issue, in this book the key activist group or advocate who takes ownership of an issue away from the company is defined. At this point in the checklist, managers should evaluate the strength of this group (and eventually all groups) involved in this issue. On a case-by-case basis, power is relative – the same group can be very powerful on one topic, but weak on another.

The importance of an issue in the eyes of the public is determined by its own particular characteristics – only one of them being the power of the key activist group. However, even if a certain issue has all the ingredients to become a strong one, if there is no activist group powerful enough to push it to public attention, then the company involved may escape extreme negative effects. Despite the fact that the number of these groups has risen dramatically in recent years, only a few have the power to make a strong impact. Among these are the larger environmental groups such as the Sierra Club, the National Resources Defense Council (NRDC) the Environment Defense Fund (EDF), Greenpeace and Friends of the Earth, some very powerful social issue groups such as Amnesty International, PETA, certain unions, and Public Citizen, a powerful group that focuses on health and consumer issues.

These groups share a few common characteristics: they are large, international, highly professional, and staffed by expert lawyers and scientists. Other groups are staffed by only a handful of people and rely largely on volunteer efforts. So a company that finds itself on Greenpeace's hit list would understandably take the threat much more seriously than if it were attacked by a smaller, lesser known group. However, even small groups can join forces and leverage their power (as in the case of RAN).

But what makes an activist group able to affect companies through media access and customer and legislator influence? In general, their strengths are twofold:

1  A broad base of support.
2  Their internal structure.

### Bases of support

Activist groups provide their sponsors, members and supporters with the opportunity to support certain ideals or goals. As one NGO executive stated: "We deliver 'feel-good'." Supporters can give the activist group financial or other donations, thereby "voicing" their concerns without necessarily becoming active themselves. The more supporters, the stronger the voice. Companies should therefore assess whether the activist group represents the feelings of a large or small part of the population. The Consumer Federation of America brings together over 200 groups that represent some 30 million Americans and defends consumer interests. Amnesty International has over 1.1 million members from more than 150 different countries around the world. Even a very large corporation would have to think twice about fighting with either of these organizations.

In addition to the support of its members, support is also determined by the general attitude toward a group by society at large. While some activism concerns issues that affect the general population (humanitarian issues, ethnic discrimination, environmental destruction, torture, etc.), other issues affect individuals at a very personal level, such as when they fear for their jobs or feel they are being treated unfairly. Public support for those groups is often inconsistent. For example, in many societies, unions may be seen as solely concerned with their own interests, disregarding the good of society as a whole. But when it comes to "sweatshops" in factories of multinationals in Southeast Asia, they are an accepted source of information.

The power of all activist groups, however, is related to their financial power. The more spectacular campaigns, like the Brent Spar campaign, are often extremely expensive and very few activist groups can afford them. This gives unions, who regularly collect dues from their members, power related to their own financial resources (as well as to the number of members) despite the ambivalent public attitudes described above.

But a purely quantitative evaluation of the support for an activist group does not reveal everything. Some groups have learned very well how to bring issues to public awareness and are considered very influential; others are still in the learning process.

### Internal structure

One should also look at the activist groups' internal structures. Contrary to companies, non-profit organizations do not measure their market share in monetary units, but in degrees of change. To change people normally requires a more democratic structure in an activist organization, as opposed to a commercial organization.

The key criterion for evaluating the power of an activist group as a function of its internal structure is the degree of centralization in decision-making. In most businesses, when management takes a decision it is carried out (more or less ...). This is not necessarily so with non-profit organizations: in many organizations of this type, the managing director is required to have every decision reviewed either by committees or a board. And while boards of corporations tend to be small and efficient, they are usually larger and less efficient in non-profit organizations.

Often, in activist groups the board is very strong and tends to over-control. Managers in activist groups often do not have a clear command authority, which creates many inefficiencies and takes away the possible surprise effect. So being able to catch a campaign target by surprise depends largely on the existence of central power structures, not least because of the financial flexibility of a centralized activist group. Greenpeace International, for example, always keeps part of its budget available for contingencies such as the Brent Spar campaign in order to be able to strike quickly.

While some activist groups like Greenpeace have recognized the advantages of central decision-making and have a powerful steering committee that can take decisions on campaigns quickly with little backtracking, other organizations are strongly membership-driven. In these cases, local groups have influence on all key decisions: obviously, discussion takes longer and the probability of compromise is higher. Examples of these kinds of structures are the national chapters of Friends of the Earth.

Naturally, membership groups can only have a limited surprise effect and need much more consensus-building before stepping into action than a highly centralized group. Sometimes groups even require unanimity, which makes the process of consensus-building long and tedious. But once they start to move, they usually build up a strong momentum.

To centralize their decision-making process and move faster on upcoming issues, some groups, like companies, decentralize themselves into "business units" that can act with flexibility in their "market".

For example, Ralph Nader's group Public Citizen consists of six units, focusing on issues such as health and energy.

Another way of centralizing decision-making power is to give national organizations a high degree of independence from the international headquarters. Greenpeace, for example, has worked to achieve this balancing act between central and decentralized power: most of the organization's decisions are taken locally through national offices, rather than at Greenpeace International's headquarters in Amsterdam. These national offices run campaigns on local pollution issues, and are responsible for building contacts with national politicians and journalists. However, when it needs to, Greenpeace can act like a centralized organization: its offices are wired up to an international computer network and, although national offices are given relative freedom from Amsterdam, they are never allowed to change Greenpeace's worldwide policy to suit local tastes. Greenpeace Norway, for example, is obliged to oppose whaling although this goes against a deeply ingrained public mood.

### How isolated is the company?

Activist groups prefer not to attack entire industries. Especially in long-drawn-out debates, industries usually take a common position, making it hard to single out "sinners" and to move them into the public spotlight. If activist groups can target a single, isolated company as a scapegoat, they can frame a case as a symbolic fight.

Many companies try, therefore, to accomplish a "common front" by joining industry associations. This protects them to a certain extent through common lobbying and communication initiatives, but in today's world only helps to a limited extent. When one company is attacked, competitors love to stay on the sidelines – as Shell, Monsanto, Hoechst and many others have discovered.

Front-runner companies are obvious targets for pressure. Opponents find it easy to concentrate on one company, to give the media a clear symbolic fight that can be relatively easily covered. Any company pursuing a project that could be interpreted as being a bad precedent for the whole industry should therefore be aware of the high danger of drawing activist attacks.

This is exactly what happened to Shell in the Brent Spar case. Although the owner of Brent Spar was, in reality, Shell Exploration and Development (Shell Expro), a joint venture between Shell and Exxon, Greenpeace levelled its criticism solely at Shell. This made the message easier for the public to understand and the environmentalists had one isolated opponent on which to focus. When the Greenpeace campaign began, the entire industry left Shell to defend itself alone. Even Exxon, their 50% partner in the venture, would not make any public statement in favour of Shell, and tried to maintain a low profile throughout Greenpeace's campaign, despite the fact that the Brent Spar incident was going to be used as a precedent for bans and moratoriums on decommissioning a growing inventory of offshore facilities around the world.

Another good example of isolation was the reduction in sick payments in 1996 in Germany where the industrial giant Daimler–Benz (now DaimlerChrysler), the largest company in Germany, suddenly found itself in the role of the scapegoat for German industry in general. In this case, the German government tried to cut sick pay by reducing the statutory entitlement of workers to 80% of normal wages for sick days from the previous 100%. The new law became effective in October and Daimler–Benz was the first German company to attempt to apply it. This front-runner activity was, of course, an ideal battlefield for the unions. An immediate wave of protest was unleashed among employees, with workers staging brief strikes at various company sites across the country.

The discussion on German television began to focus increasingly on Daimler–Benz as an isolated opponent of unions' and workers' rights. Other big industrial companies shied away from the issue and told the media they would wait before taking any decision to apply the law – waiting to see whether Daimler–Benz would survive or be ripped to shreds. In December, after weeks of hefty criticism, Daimler–Benz announced that it would hold off implementing the new law until it had reached a "contractual clarification" on the issue with the union.

### How far have the dynamics of the crisis already evolved?

As with the diffusion curve, mentioned earlier in this chapter, issues go through different stages from their first identification to the point where the problem is eventually resolved or disappears.

Once an issue is identified, the next task for managers is to analyse how far it has already developed and what might be its future dynamics. Doing so may help them to predict what may trigger the next stage. Admittedly, this is easier said than done. But two points are crucial: first, to asertain the "take-off" point. As mentioned earlier, companies cannot afford to invest in in-depth analyses of the thousands of issues that are flying around that might potentially affect them. But when one issue is taking off, the (re)action at this point could shape the further dynamic. There is no rocket science available to predict exactly when one issue might flare up. The checklist can only assess the potential, and then managers have to be sensitive to the development and the specific "trigger".

There are some typical indicators of the "take-off". If people are affected directly (for example, in terms of their health), important issues are threatened (for example, baby food), and a scandal is discovered, then issues tend to flare up within days, sometimes hours. If there are more general, longer term threats like global warming, endocrine disruptors, child labour, then the build-up of pressure for take-off tends to be longer, but it will also be more enduring.

Second, once the take-off has happened, the development is not linear (as most executives tend to think), but mostly escalates, leading to a climax, where a solution to the problem is proposed – or interest fades because the limited amount of attention shifts to other issues.

But a new event might easily trigger a new cycle. The diffusion curve can avoid the earlier-described "too little, too late" mistake, which is so typical, by understanding when concessions might be helpful to avoid further escalation and seeing when one has to fight one's way through. This tends mostly to occur toward the end of the cycle, but the end is sometimes unknown or unpleasant – for example, when government steps in and slaps a regulation on an industry that is just hanging on, but has lost the battle for hearts and minds.

### How easy is the solution?

Experience shows that both the public and legislators prefer solutions that do not put the company's existence at stake. But if a "perfect solution" does not exist in most cases, what are the possible solutions?

Solutions to activist issues can refer to changes in production processes (mostly environmental and social issues), in products (environmental and health issues) and in the company's behaviour in general (especially with reference to societal and political issues).

A change in production processes could be, for example, taking measures to reduce the amount and toxicity of emissions resulting from a certain process. A typical example is that of the paper industry, which has been forced by environmental activists to switch to chlorine-free bleaching methods. In such cases, the entire industry is generally affected and competitive disadvantage occurs only on an international basis (if at all). Any first-mover advantage is short-lived.

Whenever a product is attacked by consumers, the easy (although not necessarily cost-efficient) solution is often to take the product off the market and substitute it with another product, or to change the product formula. The classic example occurred in 1984: P&G Germany launched a laundry booster sheet "Top Job" to enhance washing power. The product reached sales of about US$30 million some months after its introduction, until the German government told P&G that "Top Job" was unnecessary and harmful to the environment.

While the German Federal Environmental Office had no power to remove the product from the shelves, it decided to persuade and educate consumers through press releases. As a first response to these releases, P&G bought space in regional newspapers that said: "Many homeowners use Top Job in order to save money and of course it is compatible with the environment." But after calls for a boycott, P&G decided to take the product off the market and cancelled the planned European rollout. The solution was easy to find, since P&G wanted most of all to avoid damage to its public image.

Solutions to social issues refer in most cases to changes in general attitudes and behaviours. An example can be found in the 1997 racial discrimination case against Texaco. In this case, six Black Texaco employees complained that they were discriminated against in promotions, and this could be proven clearly by a secret tape that caught Texaco executives belittling Blacks. As a consequence, the company fired the managers and started a programme to improve the career opportunities of all minorities working in the company.

## What level of change is required?

As discussed earlier, legislators do not normally demand economically impossible actions from companies, because this would go against some of their own interests. They generally know what is feasible and are aware of the fact that they cannot improve companies by imposing crippling demands on them. In the current environment of global competition for jobs and wealth, politicians' success also depends increasingly on the health and success of businesses in the regions they represent. So, for example, legislation for tighter pollution control or social standards is often passed only if the concerned companies are not suddenly put at a great disadvantage when compared with foreign competitors.

Companies are heard in the legislative process and are given the opportunity to communicate their opinions on a piece of legislation. Today's politicians also rely less on the command-and-control rationale, and prefer to work out "voluntary agreements" where industry can exercise some choice in how it will change its practices to comply with legal and political requirements. So, normally, legislators do not make demands on companies where there is no solution in sight.

This trend for consideration of business interests has been growing, especially in recent years, as governments around the world attempt to develop more intelligent legislation.

The situation with respect to the general public is a bit more complicated: even though the public evaluates issues more on an emotional basis, they can usually tell the difference between a feasible solution and an impossible one. Often, the public compares the perceived behaviour of one company with the behaviour of another and evaluates possible solutions on this basis. For example, animal-testing is still publicly accepted as an unpleasant necessity for products that fight disease or save lives. People understand the need for guinea pigs in this context. But animal-testing for cosmetics or other products is perceived as unnecessary: protests are more powerful because many people believe that other solutions are possible. For example, the Boston-based Gillette Company learned this lesson in 1995 when concerned schoolchildren, who wanted the company to stop animal-based safety tests of their products, started a campaign that called a boycott on all Gillette products and the products of its subsidiaries (for example, Oral B).

Gillette argued that the best available safety tests – and the ones most likely to hold up in court in cases of liability claims – will sometimes involve animals. Still, while Gillette were reluctant to forego animal-testing, other companies – such as Avon, Benetton, Chanel and L'Oreal – have given up the practice and therefore become peers against which Gillette has to measure itself.

As can be seen from this example, solutions that are pushed by public opinion should be benchmarked against practices in other companies in the industry. Companies should identify significant differences between their own products/processes/behaviour and that of their benchmarking partners. In most cases, it is in any case difficult for companies to get away with the argument that a malpractice is "impossible" to change.

*Conclusion*

The eight points in our checklist are the characteristics that are central to issue analysis. Together they determine whether a certain issue might become "strong" enough to be a threat to the company.

When corporations have analysed these eight points, they may make a qualitative summary and evaluate an issue from an overall perspective. This is done by evaluating the results of the different checklist items and then assessing the overall danger resulting from the issue. In such an overall evaluation, corporations also rely on their industry expertise and background knowledge to judge the issue in its particular context.

In general, a quantitative measuring of issues should be possible: for example, by assigning percentage values to the different questions and then aggregating the value of each checklist item into an overall value. However, I believe that in most cases managers tend to rely more on their judgment and not on fixed percentage points. Additionally, as already seen, there is some overlap in the different checklist items that would produce inconsistencies in an overall aggregation of all the questions (for example, the ease of solution can be different from an overall or corporate view versus the assessment of the affected business unit).

The following is an illustrative example for the application of the checklist.

*An example: Monsanto's GMO*

As an illustration (of course in hindsight!) to explain the practical application of the company checklist, we have selected Monsanto and the opposition against GMOs, especially in Europe (see Section 4.1). We have selected the year 1998 as a reference point for the assessment: the year of the big battles.

*Is the issue plausible?*

From its scientific findings, the issue is implausible. There are no reviewed, validated studies that show that foods that contain GMOs pose any health threat to consumers. Of course, there is always a residual risk that new GMOs in new plants might change the picture, or that diseases with an extremely long incubation period might show up much later.

However, in Europe, the context of the issue – on the intuitive level – made the issue appear more plausible. Governments and scientists, especially in the UK, had long claimed and insisted that BSE ("mad cow" disease) did not affect human beings – at least until there was evidence that "Creutzfeldt–Jakob" brain disease, related to BSE, suddenly seemed to be getting out of hand. Why could this not happen again in the case of GMOs?

The plausibility of the risk perception was strengthened by the allocation of risk. Whereas all the benefits (mainly cost savings) occurred in the agribusiness supply chain, the consumer gained nothing (industry and agencies claimed that the products were identical), but shouldered the residual risk (such a structure was a recipe for disaster in many cases, not least in the nuclear power industry).

### Does the issue evoke emotion? Is it understandable, visual, touching?

Food issues are always emotional, because they always affect people in a very personal and fundamental way, whereas the environmental issues of GMOs are of a more general nature. However, it will be difficult to get the message across because emotions might be diluted by the potentially lengthy time frame of the impacts of GMOs. Also, the potential for visuals and the opportunities for human touch are limited.

### Is the issue media-friendly?

The sight of limited, destroyed test fields probably does not trigger much support – there might be some action against docking ships laden with GMOs, but otherwise the issue is "abstract".

### Are there connections with other issues inside the company or industry?

The BSE crisis and other food scandals (for example, poisoned olive oil) have made consumers and the media acutely aware of the food safety issue. The handling of the violation of food safety rules (for example, lax enforcement) has weakened authorities' credibility. The EU's Common Agricultural Policy, which favours an industrial agribusiness, is watched with increasing concern as a result of economic inefficiency, lower food quality and environmental impact.

In 1995, the EU placed a moratorium on Monsanto's bovine somatotropin product (used to boost milk yield in cows) due to health concerns.

### How strong is the outside pressure group as an adversary?

Nearly all environmental NGOs, consumer associations, etc. have lined up against GMOs. Some, such as Greenpeace, Friends of the Earth and the Consumer Association, command a large support basis, resources and good media connections. However, not all of them oppose GMOs as a top priority.

### How isolated is the company?

In Europe Monsanto is a "lightweight" and in the US a second-tier player, except in GMOs. It is difficult to form alliances, because for most other competitors GMOs still represent a niche market – but not for Monsanto. Competitors might also be put off due to Monsanto's aggressive and accelerated strategy for pursuing GMOs.

### How far has the issue evolved?

In summer 1996, Greenpeace started its campaign to raise awareness, and the end of 1996 saw the first regulatory action. Uncertainty about the regulatory situation (a de facto moratorium) is increasing, and labelling is now obligatory.

## How easy might it be for the company to contain and solve the issue?

Whereas competitors strategize for a more gradual development of GMOs, Monsanto has based its testing on the rapid communication of new technology. That is, upfront investment in research and development and the high cost of acquisition of seed companies (as the new distribution channels to farmers), which must be paid off as soon as possible, has resulted in relatively high debt.

The markets for soybean, maize and so on (the main application of GMOs) are global, so Europe could not be "left out" in the supply of GMOs. Separating conventional and GMO products seems to be too expensive in a commodity market. As can be seen from the checklist in Box 5-3, it was not necessarily a lost battle from the beginning – but clearly Monsanto underestimated the difficulties it was confronted with in Europe.

---

### Box 5-3  Company Checklist – Monsanto/GMOs

| Assessment criteria | Ratings ++   +   0   –   – – | Comments |
|---|---|---|
| Plausibility | + | In context of "food scare" |
| Potential for emotion | + | Emotions: Yes; Visualization: No |
| Media-friendliness | – | Only in up-market media |
| Interconnection with other issues | ++ | Limited to "food safety" |
| Strength of the potential adversary | ++ | Broad coalition, with Greenpeace in a certain lead function |

| Degree of company isolation | ++ | Competitors kept low-profile |
|---|---|---|
| Ease of solution (general) | + | Food surplus through EU policy |
| Ease of solution for Monsanto | + | Monsanto's "pure play" in the agribusiness arena made for a more difficult solution |
| Overall | + | |

## 5.3 HOW DOES IT LOOK FROM THE NGO POINT OF VIEW? THE ACTIVIST CHECKLIST

Companies should try to understand activists' thought processes in addition to their own, in order to get a feel for their "world view" and anticipate which issues they are likely to pursue.

To analyse the likelihood of coming under attack for a project or decision, the following procedure is recommended: first, analyse the issue against the company's own checklist. One of the characteristics in this analysis is the "strength of the key activist group". To determine whether the identified key activist group might pick up on a potentially "hot" issue (according to the other seven criteria), the company must next analyse the issue against the key activist group's own priorities. If the issue characteristics are high on this list as well, then the company is facing a situation that demands immediate attention.

### Box 5-4  Activist Checklist

1  The campaign has a clear aim or goal.
2  The issue is easily understood by the general public.
3  The issue has a high symbolic value.
4  The issue has the potential to damage the image of the company.
5  The opponent is strong enough (no "underdog" effect).

> **6** The issue can be "packaged" in a campaign in which the public can get involved.
> **7** There are solutions that are confrontational, not gradual (political concepts, management concepts, product or process concepts that are competitive in price and quality).
> **8** There is perhaps a dramatic element in the campaign that will engage media interest.

The checklist can exist either explicitly or implicitly within the activist group and represents factors determining when it will take action. To get an idea of these rules, managers can read the mission statements of the groups, look at their recent campaigns and conduct media analysis of their recent projects. What the checklist might look like also depends on the type of group, which can be loosely categorized as follows:

**1** Large groups with massive membership bases and emphasis on active membership involvement: for example, church organizations like Caritas, the National Wildlife Federation, or the Brazilian social movement "Movimento Sem Terra". These groups tend to emphasize social justice.

**2** Large groups with strong action-orientation and little direct participation by supporters: for example, Greenpeace, PETA, and the National Urban League. These groups focus on issues that have strong pictures and clear symbols, hence inducing a "wake-up" effect on the public.

**3** Quasi-scientific groups: for example, the Foundation for Development and Peace, Ocean Voice, Environmental Defense Fund, etc. These groups generally do not run campaigns, but focus more on communicating their scientific findings and influencing opinion leaders.

**4** Project-specific organizations, often with a regional or single issue focus ("Say No to Microsoft" or INFACT, founded to organize consumer boycotts and campaigns). Sometimes several groups join forces (for example, RAN) for specific campaigns.

The research for this book looked at a large number of issues; it found that many activist groups use a set of guidelines to ascertain when they should involve themselves in an issue. Some patterns were also found in these guidelines that outline the requirements for a successful campaign, which were clearly used to formulate the Activist Checklist.

### The campaign should have a clear aim or goal

In most cases, activist groups prefer issues where they can identify a clear and specific goal. People are more realistic today about what they can expect from companies, and the general tendency is not to target individual companies for general problems such as world hunger or loss of biodiversity (although this might come up in the context of a campaign).

One determining factor for the goal of an activist group is of course the time frame. In the case of an environmental accident, for example, activist groups can fight for fair compensation of financial and other losses, or they may just try to punish the company for its imprudent behaviour (as in the case of the boycott against Exxon following the *Exxon Valdez* accident).

On the other hand, in the case of a possible present or future incident, the goal is often to prevent the company from undertaking the project in question, or to damage a company's image. So, to a certain degree, goals are predetermined by the context, but mostly they are achievable.

With health issues, the goal for activist groups is obvious – they can campaign for a product to be taken off the market or to be changed. Environmental and social issues are generally more difficult to link to a specific goal. In these two areas, single projects that are perceived to threaten the environment, or are socially unjust, can be targeted, but for a debate on general industry behaviour it is indeed difficult for activist groups to target companies. This is also the reason that such groups often go for single-issue campaigns in environmental and social areas, thus attracting critics who blame such "one-sided" approaches.

In some cases, the main goal of environmental and social activists is to create awareness; the goal of solving a specific problem is then only secondary. Still, there are some examples of campaigns with clear goals that go beyond creating awareness in the environmental and social areas. In the issue of animal rights, for example, the "Coalition for Consumer Information on Cosmetics", formed by nine animal rights groups, launched in 1996 what it calls "The Corporate Standard for Compassion for Animals", to standardize industry's claims regarding animal-testing (mainly by pressuring suppliers to pledge that they will abandon animal-testing of their ingredients). And in the environmental field, a good example is the success of Greenpeace in pushing the industry to produce CFC-free refrigerator coolants.

Nevertheless, goals such as "protect animal rights" and "save the ozone layer" are by nature less specific and more difficult to control than product-specific goals. But today's activist groups know how to "disaggregate" them into a specific campaign.

In summary, activist groups know that they stand a higher chance of winning single-issue campaigns with clear goals. Such clear goals are in scarce supply for activist groups. But if a company has somehow created a target and a goal for activist groups, it should be alert.

### The issue is easily understood by the general public

Most people are confronted daily by a vast number of messages, only a few of which will cut through the confusion and make an impression. These few messages are usually the ones that are plain and easy to understand. Therefore, many activists prefer issues where they can point the finger clearly at the "good guys" – and ever more so at the "bad guys". It should be neither too technical nor abstract, and relatively free of complex details.

Very technical issues, even when they do get attention, tend to be misunderstood, and, in addition, people often react to them in irrational ways.

From a technical perspective, risk is defined as the likelihood of a hazard occurring, multiplied by the impact of the event. The impact of the hazard can be measured in terms of money, health impact or lives lost. While this formula is theoretically correct for calculating risk, it has little to do with the way the public perceives risk, and is by no means an indicator of how the public will react to a certain issue. Some companies have nevertheless tried to predict issues by assessing risks involved with environmental and health issues. This has turned out to be rather unhelpful, because what they calculated had little to do with what the public understood as risk.

Risk calculation in itself is a tricky and confusing business, even for the experts, and there are weaknesses and unsolved methodological problems in risk measurement methods. Just choosing the parameters by which to calculate the risk can lead to great frustration, as seemingly small differences cause large variances in the result. The examples below illustrate the extent of the problem.

In the case of breast implants, the probability of an implant going awry was estimated at between 0.2% to 35%. Reasons for these differences may be differing assumptions (different models of analysis), errors of omission (short-term versus long-term effects), unknown latent effects, subjective bias and the difference between animal studies versus human effects. But for the public it was a clear issue of corporate irresponsibility, and the US courts placed huge punitive damage liabilities on corporations such as Dow Corning and BMS.

Given all these technical variables, activists obviously prefer to focus on easy-to-understand issues. The causes of a problem do not necessarily have to be easy to understand, but the effects should be clear for the average person.

Because the "man in the street" does not examine all the scientific data surrounding an issue, activist groups can influence the public's risk perception through modifying, magnifying and channelling public knowledge about possible effects. This is why they are sometimes accused of communicating their points of view selectively, through misuse of scientific data, or by ignoring scientific arguments altogether. (However, companies and industry associations are likewise not always prim and proper in choosing their arguments.)

When an issue is difficult to understand, some groups make use of the "customer segmentation" technique. They target their campaigns to a specific audience who will both understand the issue and be instrumental in the campaign's success. For example, the issue of genetically engineered wheat may be too technical for the general public; therefore, some activist groups began their campaign with paediatricians who would then advise parents against feeding baby cereals containing genetically engineered wheat to their children.

One way for corporations to weigh how understandable the issue might be to the public is to write an imaginary news headline about the issue from the activist group's point of view. If the headline is easy to phrase, the issue might impose a real danger. If the managers in some of our examples had done this, they might have had a better idea of what they were getting into: "Shell Dumps Its Rubbish in the Sea" or "BMS Kills AIDS Patients" (in the controversy over generic AIDS therapy in South Africa). A headline like "Dow Chemical Contributes to Biodiversity Loss" simply does not have the same impact. As a result, the Dow issue stands less of a chance of becoming "hot".

### The issue has high symbolic value

The power of symbols in management was recognized for the first time in the debate over corporate culture in the early 1980s. At that time researchers and practitioners found that symbols can represent many of the hidden agendas in an organization and show the culture in a visible form. The research for this book has shown that symbols have the same kind of importance for activists as well, being the visible parts of the much wider concerns that they represent.

An issue is symbolic if it represents a "picture" to the public that facilitates media communication and public involvement. For example, the Brent Spar platform was a symbol in itself that seemed to epitomize oil companies' lack of respect for the environment, tossing their junk into the sea.

Most activist groups make vigorous use of symbols in their campaigns because they can be used to change society's overall value system. Finding and using symbols can induce a "wake-up" effect to problems that have so far not been recognized. Symbols that are used in campaigns can generally represent "mistakes" made by entire industries or single companies. Some industries that have created very bad images for themselves can easily be used as symbolic opponents, while other industries are perceived in a more positive light.

An example of the power of symbols in a strongly exposed industry could be seen repeatedly in Germany in 2000 when the nuclear industry wanted to transport spent nuclear fuel to the Gorleben nuclear waste storage facility in special yellow containers called "castors". The fear-provoking containers and the fact that the nuclear waste was "escaping" from its maximum security prison became powerful symbols for the German public's anti-nuclear feelings in general. The issue resulted in severe protests against the transport, which were mostly peaceful but which also included sawing through railway lines, setting fire to signal boxes, toppling a power line and making bomb threats. Finally, the transport required a mobilization of 30,000 policemen, the largest post-war operation in Germany, which in addition heightened the perceived danger ...

In the absence of inherent symbols in the issues, activist groups may be able to "invent" symbols themselves. Greenpeace activists always wear their famous protection suits and goggles whenever they protest against toxic waste. Other groups like to get children involved in their protests because they are seen as both highly sympathetic and as symbols of hope for the future.

### The issue has the potential to damage the image of the company

Corporate image, especially for large and well-known companies, is one of the most important assets to safeguard. Therefore, it is an ideal target for an activist group wishing to make such corporations into villains. How this can happen is demonstrated by the commissioning of Asea Brown Boveri (ABB) by the Malaysian Government in 1996 to help with the construction of a dam in Malaysia (see Chapter 8).

ABB was supposed to be the major outside contractor, responsible for the overall project management and supply of electrical equipment. However, the dam project had been condemned by many international activist groups as being socially destructive, environmentally disastrous and economically misconceived (due to the economic crisis, it was eventually delayed indefinitely in September 1997). While some activist groups were trying to persuade the Malaysian Government to scrap the project, it was ABB as the big, rich corporation that bore the brunt of the criticism. This was, of course, because ABB's image is much more vulnerable than that of the Malaysian government.

Even though many firms that have been targeted by activist groups publicly report that their sales were not adversely affected, executives will often complain off the record of the damage the company has suffered to its image. Once a company's image has been tarnished by one issue, the public will be even more distrustful of them the next time around. Multi-brand companies facing negative issues surrounding one product often experience negative consumer attitudes toward their other products as well.

While companies fear negative images among the public, there is also a less evident, but also powerful, effect – employee motivation and a company's ability to attract good employees. Employees who have a good image of their company take pride in working there, trust their future to it and assume that they will be treated fairly.

Hiring highly qualified people is therefore easier: suppliers and subcontractors prefer to do business with a company that has a renowned reputation and, of course, customers prefer to deal with it as a supplier. The opposite is true when a company's image has been destroyed. Employees may even be confronted socially: "You work for THAT company?"

A company's image can be damaged in two ways: first, as a result of its behaviour before the pressure campaign starts (the issue itself); and, second, by its reactions and behaviour during the campaign.

Even in less dramatic instances, simple court actions against pro-testers can backfire severely for the company through adverse publicity. Many activist groups therefore welcome lawsuits by companies, because it shows that they are being taken seriously and it creates public sympathy. Activists naturally prefer to attack companies that have high-profile images. Therefore, consumer companies that are well-known to the general public are preferred targets for campaigns.

Brand names like BMW, McDonald's or Nike automatically attract a high level of attention, and activist groups know they stand a chance of gaining consumer allies in their campaign. Once the negative spotlight lights up a popular brand, years of painstaking image-building can be de-stroyed. Companies that have popular brands are living in glass houses, and should be well aware of the danger that comes with the territory.

Sometimes, activists use one strong brand as a target for an issue that has nothing to do with the company. This happened in 1997 to Burger King in New Zealand. The country's anti-smoking lobbyists en-couraged consumers to boycott the restaurant chain, which had put up large posters depicting James Dean smoking a cigarette, arguing that the practice encouraged smoking, especially in teenagers. Obviously Burger King's objective was not to promote cigarettes. It declared that the boycott was ludicrous and merely a publicity stunt by the lobby group, desperate for any popular brand to target as a symbolic opponent. New Zealand Burger King's director of marketing com-plained: "We have Marilyn who died of a drug overdose, James Dean smoking and Elvis who died of whatever. Where does all this stop?"

### The opponent is strong enough (no "underdog" effect)

Activist groups like to engage with strong opponents so that they can position themselves as "righteous Davids" against "corporate Goliaths". The group may spur on the public with an underlying envy argument: "Look at this company – not only are they taking all our money, but now they are harming the environment/health/social rights."

RAN spearheaded a broad international coalition of organizations to boycott Mitsubishi (the top blue-chip company of Japan) and its subsidiaries until the company stopped logging operations or purchasing timber or timber products from sources that harmed the environment or native communities (see Box 3-4). Exxon is another case where nobody had to be concerned about the underdog effect (see Section 8.4).

Activist groups usually refrain from attacking "weak" companies, because this could cause the "underdog" effect. In such a case, the public may change sides and argue in favour of the company, which they see as having enough problems to deal with already, without being hassled by activists in addition.

Most groups especially try to avoid attacking companies where a high number of jobs are at stake. In many European countries, the problem of job security is uppermost in the public mind, and public opinion could turn against the activists if job losses are threatened.

So, while serious financial problems may be uncomfortable, at least managers can console themselves that there will probably be no major environmental groups knocking down their doors for the foreseeable future: "For everyone has to work – compassion, one can get for free."

### The issue can be "packaged" in a campaign in which the public can get involved

Activist groups have become highly sophisticated in their ability to package stories. Interesting campaigns contain a combination of several characteristics – the possibility of physical action rather than scientific discussion, symbolic fights and a visual and attackable adversary. Such campaigns are more likely to inspire public involvement. Groups prefer issues in which their contact with the public is not restricted to simply informing the world of the presence of the issue, but where they are able to enlist public involvement in stopping or solving the issue. The easiest and most obvious is through the customer transmission belt with a consumer boycott. Large numbers of people can easily and almost passively participate simply by not buying the product of the company in question or substituting a product category in general. It has become the most widely used form of getting the public involved in an issue.

However, as activists have to compete like everyone else for public attention, they need somehow to differentiate themselves from the other activist groups, and try where possible to initiate creative or more active ways for the public to get involved in a campaign: protesting on the street, being invited to a forum, or even writing a letter to the chairman of a company or an important politician can be stimulating life experiences, and activists attract this kind of commitment from people on the issue in question.

Some campaigns are too difficult or complex for general public participation. An example is the debate on endocrine-mimicking, which focuses on the question of how far chemicals such as those found in a variety of products like plastic packaging, fertilizers, etc. are threatening mankind through massively disturbing reproductive cycles. In this case, it is difficult to pinpoint blame on a single chemical, and there are just too many products and companies involved to organize any sort of consumer or other public action.

The level of public involvement an activist group is able to galvanize also depends largely on its talent for motivating people. Some of them purposefully drive an almost overly aggressive campaign to attract attention and gain popular involvement. For example, PETA spokesman Michael McGraw argues in favour of the organization's aggressive, "sensationalizing" approach to public relations, saying that we live today in a tabloid age where things have to be sensationalized and flamboyant to get people involved.

*There are solutions that are confrontational, not gradual (political concepts, management concepts, product or process concepts that are competitive in price and quality)*

Activists try to provide attractive, publicly acceptable solutions for the problems that they are attacking. They are increasingly realizing that they have to become part of the solution instead of just pointing the finger at the problem, knowing, however, that a perfect solution does not always exist.

Most groups, however, are not looking for gradual solutions that involve changing habits, processes or products incrementally over time, but prefer confrontational solutions instead. Means for reaching these solutions could be political concepts such as energy taxes, management concepts such as the introduction of a committee who reviews a company's equal opportunities employment policy or even alternative product and process concepts.

One example of this search for solutions is the case of the SmILE car designed by Greenpeace. Arguments in favour of more environmentally friendly public transport do not have much effect because this alternative is seen by many as a gross inconvenience. Citizens are still not ready to give up their cars. Greenpeace set out to prove that, while they cannot convince people to give up their cars, automobile manufacturers could at least make cars that pollute less. To prove that automobile companies have failed to take even the first steps toward the production of more environmentally sound vehicles, Greenpeace designed and built an eco-efficient car themselves. The SmILE is a modified Renault Twingo that is almost 50% more energy-efficient than its conventional counterpart and other cars of similar size. SmILE stands for "Small, Intelligent, Light, Efficient" and describes the car of the future according to Greenpeace: light, compact, efficient and intelligently built. The modifications were carried out by a Swiss engineering company and financed by Greenpeace. According to Greenpeace, the SmILE confronts the automobile industry's denials that halving petrol consumption is feasible.

Many groups are unconcerned with finding solutions for their adversaries because their level of critique is fundamental. Internally, Greenpeace had problems with its more fundamentalist activists when it was trying to come up with the SmILE solution; the fundamentalist argument was that the SmILE is still not totally clean, healthy and environmentally benign. So the official view of Greenpeace is that the SmILE is not a solution in itself, but serves merely to prove that automobile petrol consumption can be cut in half with contemporary technology.

Companies should ask themselves whether their adversaries might be able to offer solutions that are acceptable to the general public. In such a case, the chances of coming under strong pressure to adopt these suggestions will be high. Likewise, some groups may drop an issue, because they cannot come up with a better solution themselves. However, managers should not rely on the lack of a viable alternative as an argument to force a group to back down, because activists reply, "Coming up with a solution is your problem, not ours."

## There is perhaps a dramatic element in the campaign that will engage media interest

Media coverage is essential to a successful activist campaign, but the media already receive more information than they can use. Unless groups can bring dramatic elements into their campaign, they will not have a chance of making the headlines.

Using the attention-getting "striptease method", groups sometimes present the situation in small doses and with each dose the media have something new to report. They do not give away everything they know all at once. Like theatre, public interest builds slowly until a climax is reached. Therefore, if possible, many activists employ "escalation steps" in their campaigns for dramatic effect. For example, they may start a campaign with scientific discussion, which then builds in intensity and plays more and more on emotions, with a few action elements thrown in for effect.

Take again the example of RAN and its nearly 10-year battle against Mitsubishi that shows a typical pattern of escalation (see Box 3-4). In May 1993 RAN launched a dramatic advertising campaign in the US with a full-page advertisement in the *New York Times*. As the next step in the escalation, they encouraged supporters to send telegrams and letters to the prime minister of Japan, the president of Mitsubishi Corporation and the premier of Alberta. Then, to increase the drama, RAN produced a 20-minute video showing Mitsubishi slashing away at rainforest growth and hauling off precious rainforest wood, leading to many demonstrations at Mitsubishi outlets throughout the world. This always took the local dealers or distributors by surprise, but multiplied the media coverage when huge, inflated "chain saws" bedecked their roofs. To gain allies and keep media interest high, RAN then launched an intensive campaign to get other environmental groups to join forces with them against Mitsubishi. Finally, the group distributed powerful brochures denouncing Mitsubishi's rainforest activity to high school and college students in the US and Japan, who joined the campaign.

Activist groups are well aware that dramatic elements cannot always be planned in advance, and they hope that they do not have to contribute all the drama themselves. They count on provoking their opponents to "bite back" in order to add to the drama. As Thilo Bode, the then director of Greenpeace International reflected after the Brent Spar campaign, "Every time we were stuck and didn't know what to do next to keep interest high, Shell helped us."

No matter how the drama is created, when there is potential for it the probability that an activist group will get involved is higher.

### Conclusion

An activist issue that fulfils the majority of the checklist points will almost certainly attract the attention of at least one group, and this group will try somehow to build a campaign around the issue. As a result, if an issue can be identified with the company's checklist as potentially "hot" and a majority of the above-mentioned checklist items are true as well, then the company is potentially facing severe problems and should immediately develop an action plan.

It is not implied here that companies should only behave responsibly when they fear confrontation. If a company is convinced that it has given social, environmental and health concerns every possible consideration, believes it has come up with an acceptable decision, analysis shows that there is still a high risk of running into strong opposition, then contingency planning for responsive action is justified.

### An example: Brent Spar

When the North Sea Minister Conference met in 1995 to officially assess the state of the environment in all bordering countries, Greenpeace was looking for a symbol of industrial pollution to argue against the expected official "back-patting" for success. High on their list was, for example, short-chained chlorinated paraffins, which are toxic, bioaccumulative and persistent – in short, an environmental nightmare. However, as our checklist reveals, Brent Spar was a much better case to run the campaign:

1 **Does the campaign have a clear and understandable goal?**
   The clear goal of the campaign was to prevent Shell's proposal to use deep-sea disposal of the Brent Spar platform. Even if Greenpeace was unsure whether they would accomplish their goal, they were quite positive that they could at least ignite serious debate on the practice of deep-sea platform disposal.
2 **Is the issue easily understood by the general public?**
   The public was able to understand that dumping 14,000 tons of steel into the sea (an equivalent of 6,000 cars) is not necessarily environmentally friendly. The Greenpeace message that Shell was in effect

"littering" was easy to get across to the public, which is basically in favour of recycling.

**3  Does the issue have a high symbolic value?**

The huge platform was a strong symbol, as were the water cannons and the physical struggles for control of the platform.

**4  Can the way the issue is handled damage the image of the opponent?**

Shell is a well-known, successful consumer brand with a high-profile image. It is vulnerable to boycotts. The public perception that Shell "brutalized" Greenpeace during the campaign and that it was insensitive to the environment took its toll on Shell's image.

**5  The opponent is strong enough.**

There is no underdog effect, no severe economic woes, nor any other trouble. Shell is therefore an ideal opponent.

**6  The issue can be packaged in a campaign in which the public can get involved.**

Greenpeace was able to package the campaign for the media in a way that would encourage public involvement: occupying and freeing the platform, vessels following the Spar, helicopter attacks, etc., inspired the public to boycott Shell stations, organize protests, write letters, etc.

**7  There are solutions that are confrontational**

From Greenpeace's point of view, the "solution" was a simple one; namely, not to dump the platform. They also suggested alternatives to deep-sea disposal, with Shell retorting that these were not satisfactory alternatives.

## Box 5-5   Activist Checklist – Shell's Brent Spar

| Assessment criteria | Rating | Comments |
| --- | --- | --- |
| Clear aim or goal | X | Stop sea disposal |
| Understandable by public | X | Platform is equivalent of 6,000 cars |
| Symbolic | X | Platform, water cannons, physical struggles |
| Image can be damaged | X | Shell acted with force, Shell is a consumer brand |
| Strong opponent | X | Shell is the most profitable company in the world |

# Making Corporate Diplomacy Happen

# 6

In order to implement a Corporate Diplomacy strategy, companies need to design and build a robust business case to see the potential benefits and the potential impediments. Then they have to look for alliances with industry association or pro-sustainability organizations and assess what they can (and cannot) deliver in supporting a comprehensive strategy. Finally, we discuss what the new buzz is about – that capital markets push companies via social responsible investment to "good corporate citizenship".

## 6.1  BUILDING A ROBUST BUSINESS CASE

The economic imperative for companies is not denied, but it is argued that within these boundaries there is a lot that can be done to meet and to shape this expectation by what has earlier been called "Corporate Diplomacy".

But the reverse argument also holds true: if a company does not meet the economic imperative, when its survival is in question it will probably focus on the economic imperative, putting everything else on the back burner. This can be observed in companies that run into deep trouble, such as Metallgesellschaft, once an environmental, very proactive company, or Levi Strauss, once known for its social engagement.

Unfortunately, the academic and popular literature is of little help on how a business case can be built. The academic research focuses very often on the macro level, trying to correlate some plausible variables, but is altogether very inconclusive. Such research, too, can never answer the "chicken-and-egg" question: are companies successful because they behave "socially responsibly" (or whatever buzzword is used)? Or, are they a "good corporate citizen" because they are financially successful?

Nor are the smooth PR stories disseminated by companies, politicians and NGOs convincing in their efforts to push other companies to follow their lead. Every manager knows that there is never a "free lunch", but always hard work needed to achieve any result.

But building a robust business case for "Corporate Diplomacy", with a proactive approach in considering social and environmental criteria as well, is highly company-specific and contextual, as argued throughout this book. A limited set of tools could be used for a more methodological, systematic consideration by senior management about a reasonable strategy to manage the broader business environment and stakeholders (for example, the Issue Checklists in previous chapters). And it is possible to identify the main components of a robust business case:

- After the honeymoon of globalization (and the stock market boom) is over, global companies will again come under heavier scrutiny. Their freedom of action will be more limited if power is not exerted wisely. And with some serious thought, many positive actions can result in "win-win solutions" – the room for manoeuvre in integrating social and environmental considerations into the corporate strategy is obviously not exhausted yet.
- In today's global "goldfish bowl transparency" and the orientation of the media and hundreds of thousands of NGOs to scrutinize companies for bad news, the probability of getting away with "bad behaviour" is clearly declining.
- Mutual trust, respect, integrity and a positive attitude by stakeholders clearly pacifies the unavoidable friction in fragmented, pluralistic societies throughout the world – and leads to a more rational resolution rather than escalation of conflicts.
- In particular, companies with strong brands – and many companies are striving to build strong brands – are highly exposed to any

kind of tarnishing of their image in not living up to their brands' values and promises. The "lifestyle brands" in particular need ethical robustness and environmental cleanliness.

- Early awareness systems do not only indicate trouble ahead but also new business opportunities, which result from shifting values, behaviours and needs. This can be both new products and services as well as process innovations and potential options.
- Last but not least: better employee motivation as well as hiring and retaining talented people. "Knowledge workers" in particular can choose among companies and tend to apply for employment where they think companies fit best with their own values. And an outstanding company reputation through environmental and social performance is clearly a priority with high potential. Particularly when wages and working conditions in an industry are similar across companies, these might be the differentiating factor.

As can easily be seen, the main components above cover both better risk management and creating or influencing new elements in the business portfolio. It would be helpful if at least some factors could be quantified (for example, option value or cost saving due to lower employee turnover).

However, the research for this book revealed that there are also many "bumps in the road":

- The mindset and values of top management that may be concerned with finance alone and too risk-averse to chart uncharted waters.
- A corporate culture and organization that is very science-driven and inward-looking, which – as we have seen – can only be maintained as long as it does not clash with the outside world.
- Difficulties in co-ordinating social and environmental issues along the supply chain, with customers and suppliers reluctant to buy in because of mistrust or not seeing enough benefits on their part.
- Regulatory barriers that prevent social and technological innovations (from antitrust rules preventing new, progressive industry

standards to environmental innovations forbidden by firefighting rules).

- Lack of knowledge, tools and processes that puts first-movers at a disadvantage, because they have to deliver more upfront investments to develop such knowledge and tools (from which followers might profit).

Nevertheless, it is strongly recommended that executives in charge develop such a robust business case and communicate it widely internally. They have to identify change-resistors and see how they can get around them, build alliances by communicating the benefits of a "Corporate Diplomacy" strategy to the individual business units, functions and key decision-makers. Basically, this does not differ much from any other change initiative. But evidence abounds on how many of these initiatives have failed. So, additionally, a power-promoter – in the best case the CEO – is needed to support the "Sustainability Champion" in implementing the strategy that is derived from the business case.

But once a robust business case has been built and communicated, the real litmus test is the implementation of the strategy, which is deduced from the business case. In every aspect of strategy, the design is easier than "getting it done" – this is where most companies fail. Typical questions with which executives are confronted are discussed below.

We have phrased the most common obstacles of strategy implementation that we observed in our research in the form of questions, and we endeavour not only to give a description of the problem but also some hints for solutions.

## 6.2 THE HARDER PART: IMPLEMENTING A STRATEGY

Regardless of what strategy a company has chosen (or has been pushed into) or with whom it is confronted, it faces a series of common obstacles for implementing the strategy. This comes as no surprise – designing a strategy is always easier than implementing it – but it is mostly in the implementation and the consistency of implementation that companies "make" or "break".

### How to get top management's attention?

This is *the* question. In today's world, financial performance is the Number One priority for top to middle managers and it has focused the attention of top management on immediate issues in the market environment. Some share price dynamics – as irrational as they often are in their short-term fluctuations – guide more strategic decisions than they used to. So, longer term issues or latent problems regarding "soft" facts easily slip out of sight. This is why a robust business case is so important.

There is no institutional or organizational solution to this problem of top management support; support, because it depends first and foremost on the core values of the corporate culture. If a company hopes to remain a "stealth bomber", believes that nothing is at risk and that nothing could be gained through greater openness to the broader business environment, then there will be no organizational solution to correct this. Either the company is "learning the hard way" through a crisis, which will change its corporate priorities, or it will get away with it.

For companies that are sufficiently open about their culture, or are risk-exposed and aware of the risk – today this probably includes all energy, resource, extracting, chemical, pharmaceutical, transport, packaging and auto companies – the "function" of scanning and dealing with the business environment needs to be "professionalized".

There needs to be a specific assignment at the level of either a management board, or a board committee (the times when, for example, BMW had a special board member for societal and foreign affairs are probably over). Alternatively, someone reporting directly to the CEO takes over the task: this could either be the head of strategy or a "corporate sustainability officer". In most cases, it should be a manager with operational credentials and an in-depth knowledge of the company, not a "typical PR guy".

His or her main task is to build a business case as the principal means to get top management attention and support.

Issues can arise in every function and at every step in the value chain of a company (and beyond), so the professional must have a "helicopter" competence – to be able to take a broad view, but dig into details quickly – *and* must have the ear of the CEO, who listens to the findings – not only the warnings – of this function.

In all other arrangements, the results get drowned in the general "noise" of the system and fall victim to the flood of over-information under which senior managers struggle today. But the clear, personal reporting line to the CEO should be complemented by an "overlay", such as a board of directors or a senior executive committee, in which the main issues are discussed, coordinated and progress reported.

### Do you need a comprehensive strategy or is a "case-by-case" approach sufficient?

Here is the classic answer of an economist to this question: it depends, first, on the risk exposure or importance of the business environment for a specific company. The above-mentioned risk-exposed industries definitely need a comprehensive strategy, as do those who want to be "sustainability leaders" through their core values (for example, companies like the Body Shop or Ben and Jerry).

The case-by-case approach definitely lacks any forward-looking element so that, normally, companies are taken by surprise when something emerges – and react too late, therefore being forced mostly to make defensive moves. The conclusion of this is that some kind of early awareness system is an absolute must, because without some lead time there is rarely any intelligent action.

And, to repeat the observation: a successful strategy does not mean thick corporate manuals, but a clear set of guiding principles and goals, supported by consistent actions. This can be achieved easily in any mid-sized company or business unit.

### How can you ensure you are heard in the "information flood"?

As a rough estimate, the media process approximately 10% of the news with which they are confronted, and their audience is exposed to approximately 10% again of the media news, leading to a 1% "exploitation rate". How can one ensure one is heard in such a situation?

There are three approaches: you are especially shrill (which, for companies, is probably only possible in the case of negative news); you consistently repeat your message; or you focus on clearly defined target groups for your communication and reporting (see also Chapter 7).

Many companies believe that they need to constantly develop something new – but the evidence shows the contrary to be more successful: like a woodpecker, you have to pick constantly at the same spot in order to make an impact. So, consistently repeating the message greatly increases the probability of its being heard. The chances in the market for public opinion are increased if neutral, third parties speak favourably (for example, through ratings, awards, media reports) about the company.

### How can you ensure that the company speaks with one voice?

In global, multi-product companies, this appears to be an unsolvable dilemma: every region or product division has its specific interests and claims to be the exception to the rule. Examples abound: although Novartis is one of the leading GMO companies, its baby food division Gerber was in the forefront for touting its GMO-free products. Tetra Pak is very much committed to recycling, but the Asian region claims that there is no chance to live up to that commitment due to a lack of infrastructure (for example, recycling facilities) and collecting systems.

There is no "silver bullet" to shoot at this problem (dilemmas cannot be solved, only resolved) – there is only a rule of thumb: on issues for which companies have internal control, global consistency is needed. When a company claims, for example, that all its facilities are certified by ISO 14000, then there is no excuse for not delivering on this commitment everywhere. However, when different cultures, market conditions or laws prevent a company from adopting a unified approach, it should be explained (let us give an extreme example: even the most committed feminist would not push a company to set up an equal opportunity programme in its Saudi Arabian operations, because the employment of women is generally not permitted there). However, this can easily become a touchy issue when other basic rights such as child labour or collective bargaining are at stake, and collaboration with an ugly dictatorship is suspected.

### How can one close the credibility gap to "non-profit" NGOs?

By all accounts, companies are less trusted than non-profit NGOs (and official spokespersons without executive power are even less trusted – the famous "They would say that, wouldn't they?" syndrome). Although NGOs also have their own organizational interests, naturally the list of sinners is much longer on the corporate side (no wonder – few NGOs produce chemicals or energy, or employ indigenous people in the Third World).

And there are plenty of examples around where companies have indeed hidden or suppressed safety-relevant information (for example: Mitsubishi), spoiled the environment due to lax enforcement of rules and standards (*Exxon Valdez* still stands out in the public's memory) or lied or cheated (just think of the many insider scandals on Wall Street). The list could continue indefinitely.

So, everybody has to live up to the fact that, for various reasons, the public (and even the company's own employees) are more mistrustful of the company than most NGOs. However, there are companies that have even earned the respect of their adversaries and have earned trust – just by consistently and transparently "walking the talk".

This is the only means of closing the gap. Real-life experience tells us all that a global company cannot be everybody's darling everywhere, but people expect respect and consideration for balancing conflicting interests.

### How to balance openness with the legitimate corporate interest for confidentiality?

This is only a conflict in rare cases. Normally, the public do not expect to gain access to business secrets that are legitimately protected. However, pollution data or employment conditions in a Third World country are today no longer regarded as legitimate secrets. This is the basic difference between the "trust me" and the "show me" world – and companies have to deal with it.

Obviously, some executives have no idea of the huge amount of information that is available, especially about larger global companies. Switch on any intelligent search engine, find the company, and having digested the corporate dissection by financial analysts, there is not much left that is relevant to the public or might lead to any additional information request. The main problem for companies lies in selecting the relevant criteria and the right level of data collection in their reporting, as discussed later.

### Is a specific organization design needed?

Every manager yearns for a clearly structured, stable, simple and transparent corporation. Unfortunately, however, we have to face the fact that today's organizations are hectic and messy; the more global they are the more complex structures they have – and they are *never* stable.

There are at least six axes of management that are continually shifting in relative importance: functions (still!), business/product lines, geography, processes, customers and projects. Even more buzzwords exist: "Flexible matrix, knowledge and network organizations, boundary-less companies, virtual organizations" ... Consultancies sell the latest design like fashion styles at the Milan clothing fair.

Only "stubborn" people, who struggle to survive the umpteenth reorganization in their career, remain the same, sticking to proven behaviour (even in a boundary-less organization you need to cover your back ...).

But, beyond the hype, one has to recognize that the complexity of today's organizations reflects the complexity of the business models that are applied. If you only sell in one regional market, you do not need this dimension in your organization – this is the limit of your organization's scope. But if you sell – like Tetra Pak – a range of products in 125 different countries, there has to be a dimension in an effective organization that optimizes the way it reaches its strategic goal under set (not a single) criteria.

And with changes in the business environment, organizations have to adjust and the sooner the better. In the pre-European Union economy, where national boundaries mattered, many European companies (or US subsidiaries in Europe) were little more than loose confederations, run by powerful, local chiefs. When the internal market became a reality, the product dimension at the European level became dominant in most cases, although it still needs to be close to the customer and to speak his or her language.

But given today's multidimensional, chaotic and hectic organization of the marketplace, how can concerns for the business environment and the stakeholders possibly be considered in the organizational design? Fortunately, the answer is more straightforward than one might expect:

- First, as pointed out throughout this book, it is more a matter of goals and the strategy implemented ("structure follows strategy"). The corporate attitude/culture and top management attention are more important than additional organizational axes or units.
- Second, everything has to fit in with the existing organization, which

(in most cases) has to fit in with the strategy, in order to avoid an uphill battle for recognition or even turf wars.

- Third, it depends on where you anchor the responsibility (and as pointed out time and again, it *is* the issue that is relevant). If you have a major controversy over production (for example, with chlorine chemistry) it would be better to choose a regional or functional anchor. If public concerns are product-specific, it is better to deal with them within the business units responsible, and in any event with the operational management, rather than headquarter staff.

After these more strategic considerations, there is an especially relevant issue that companies need to consider: Where do you find allies? The obvious choice here is the industry associations or trade bodies, especially if you need to create a "sustainable" industry standard. The reality, however, indicates a mixed picture.

## 6.3 PROGRESSIVE COMPANIES – RETARDED INDUSTRY ASSOCIATIONS?

Companies have traditionally influenced politics – for better or for worse. The "Banana Republic" typifies one extreme, with huge US fruit companies literally running small Central American countries through their influence. The support of Germany's heavy industry for Hitler is a well-known example of how bosses, due to a mixture of naivety, short-sighted self-interest and over-estimation of their political leverage in a dictatorship, can contribute to a catastrophic development.

And the lesson learnt: there is no known example of a global company that openly or directly supports an authoritarian regime or movement, either in their home country or abroad; most struggle to detach themselves as far as possible (so as not to damage essential business relationships with the few dictatorships left in the world). It is simply too dangerous to give such support, given global scrutiny and the inevitable trouble waiting at home . . .

But business is deeply involved in democratic policy, both in their own countries, their host countries or in international negotiations. For example, in Germany alone some 15,000 people work for the different chambers of commerce, industry or employer associations, not to mention those serving in government information offices and PR officers of individual companies. Every country has specific rules as to what is and is not acceptable intervention or lobbying efforts.

In the US there are restrictions on candidate and party contributions, but until recently not on "soft money", which is spent, for example, via "political action committees" in a more indirect, but nevertheless effective, way to promote their cause in the political arena. A federal election in the US easily amounts to a billion dollars in business today, and it remains to be seen what changes the projected campaign reforms really will induce.

In Europe, monetary influence is not as great – simply because political parties, which exert a wide influence via their rank and file, are supported more by taxpayers' money (often introduced after a series of scandals of influence-peddling by business). Japan suffered from a string of political bribery scandals for decades, and it remains to be seen how the latest efforts for a "clean-up" will go.

### Sources of influence

But – legitimate and less legitimate – use of money is not the only leverage industry has for influencing policy decisions. Regulators depend to a large extent on information that only the regulated industry can deliver. This creates an interdependence and a delicate balance of conflict and co-operation between the industry watchdog and the industry. Mostly, the balance is lost if there is collusion, but there are a few cases where regulators are completely at odds with their counterparts. However, in more cases the regulators were so close to the industry that they forgot their public mandate, especially that of protecting the less organized consumer. The BSE crisis in the UK is a telling story in this respect – and explains why there is often more trust in NGOs than in government.

Sponsored research and creating events to set issues on the agenda – in a favourable light, of course – are other options that are often employed. Industry associations and NGOs apply a strikingly similar set of tools to influence policy and public opinion. But NGOs, being generally outnumbered by people and money in comparison with industry, tend to use both much more creatively than the somewhat bureaucratic industry associations, which shape to a large degree how the public perceive "industry". And that is mostly defensive.

The reason industry associations are often the "rearguard" of many issues comes down to two specific characteristics: first, the high degree of consensus they have to create in order to keep their membership together. This makes it much easier – as in any other political organization – to block something or engender a negative attitude than to agree on something new and positive – not to mention innovation (which always comes from outsiders and mavericks).

Second, accompanying this are those who have to lose something (often prior to the benefits of change becoming visible), who tend to be more articulate and more ready to become organized than the potential winners. The result is a bias for preserving the status quo. However, with enlightened leadership, even these obstacles can be overcome, and the industry association can play a supportive – and in some areas of their responsibility even a leading – role in delivering accepted results in the context of sustainable development. (See Box 6-1.)

---

### Box 6-1   How Can Industry Associations Support Corporate Sustainability? The International Zinc Association

Industry associations are easily blamed as the "rearguard", protecting only laggards in an industry. However, there are exceptions to every rule. One involves associations made up of proactive companies (see Section 6.4). However, "normal" industry associations can also support their members on the long road to sustainability as the example of the International Zinc Association (IZA) demonstrates.

The membership of IZA is mainly zinc-refining and smelting companies that are located in the value chain "below" mining, but "above" the applications in, for example, galvanizing or die-casting. These "first-use customers" deliver mainly to the construction and automobile industries – although zinc is found in many other applications, from medicines to batteries.

Although the zinc industry was not under severe direct pressure, Antoon Franckaerts, Chairman IZA Environment Committee and Vice President, Environment Health & Safety at Union Minière, and Dr Edouard Gervais, IZA Executive Director, were disturbed by early warning signals: a lack of good quality data for risk assessment, the poor image of mining and the frustratingly complex discussions about life cycle analysis without any strategic direction. Together with others they convinced IZA's directors to launch a major sustainable development action plan in 2000 and face the budget implications.

A sustainable development working group was formed to develop a strategy proposal. IZA also commissioned a stakeholder analysis by an external researcher. Customers, environmentalists, journalists, regulators, scientists, etc. were interviewed and came up with their view of the zinc industry. Although the image of zinc was, in general, positive and diffuse in some dimensions, two clearly distinct clusters of issues were identified: the "spill-over" from mining's negative image and a cluster of issues related to scientific risk assessment of zinc inputs to the environment through corrosion of steel structures, tyre wear and agricultural feeds containing zinc. Given the wide range of background natural zinc concentrations in the Earth's crust, however, it is close to impossible to find an appropriate benchmark of what is the "right" concentration. But, for business, stakeholder views matter more than mere science, as noted by task force chairman Doug Horswill (Cominco Ltd, Canada): "As a result of the stakeholder analysis it suddenly became pretty clear what should be the priorities for our strategy."

The strategy itself was developed through a string of workshops and discussion events at IZA meetings, bringing together for the first time managers from marketing, research and technology, and environment. "Most important for the process was that proposals were not 'watered down', but improved in quality and commitment. Of course, we learnt a lot, changed our views in the process and made some compromises in the end," observed Antoon Franckaerts, "but we maintained the spirit that we did not want to end up with something mediocre ..." The strategy focused clearly on what an industry association should do. But, in building a business case for a more sustainable zinc industry, it would be hard for member companies just to stay on the sidelines. Furthermore, a detailed action plan for 2001/2002 operationalized the strategy and included the following:

- A sustainability charter of responsibility principles for the zinc industry with a strong product stewardship component, codes of conduct and a change in IZA's mission statement and a clear description of the benefits of zinc for society.
- Consultation with customers to learn about their needs and their own efforts in sustainable development. Based on this better understanding, a tailored market development approach, including innovations (for example, the zinc–air battery that could be instrumental for a breakthrough in electric cars) to increase zinc's contribution to society, was developed.
- An elaborate "Proactive Environmental Plan", including, for example, generating sophisticated risk assessment information and guidelines for dealing with the outcomes.
- A "Zinc Recycling Initiative: Towards Closing the Loop", emphasizing that metals can be permanently recycled and provide sufficient value to cover the cost of the process.
- Promotion of environmental management systems, by experience-sharing, providing support through training and information and a related code of conduct.
- Encouraging reporting along the guidelines of the Global Reporting Initiative and a related code of conduct.
- A "Voluntary Emission Reduction Initiative Zinc", where national or regional industry associations should negotiate with governments (or the EU Commission) clearly defined and monitored emission reduction targets (as alternatives to regulatory action), especially in areas where the risk assessment indicated the need for action. Any progress would be monitored by the IZA Secretariat. In addition, IZA will co-operate with similar initiatives, for example, the Global Mining Initiative of the World Business Council for Sustainable Development (WBCSD), basically a multi-stakeholder research project, looking at how best practice can be made the average industry standard so that mining becomes more sustainable.

"Clearly the industry has a long way to go but at last they spend their energy in moving forward instead of wasting their time with defence and justifica-tion," a German environmentalist commenting on IZA's strategy reluctantly accepted. "But we will monitor progress, looking for results, not words. For the time being, we keep zinc on our watch list."

But the IZA example shows how little and how much is needed to move an industry before a crisis hits. "An awareness of and sensitivity to 'weak signals', a dedicated team to push the process with determination over many hurdles and some attractive, business-related ideas to generate a positive momentum, which feeds itself with early wins," is the summary of Edouard Gervais.

## The "rearguard" function

However, the "rearguard" position can often cost industry a great deal of credibility. A typical example is the lobbying of the US automobile industry in 2001 and still ongoing – probably the most powerful industry in Washington next to the oil, gun and tobacco industries – against the CAFE Standard, which regulates the "Corporate Average Fuel Efficiency" manufacturers and importers have to meet over their whole fleet.

Since 1985 – with little variance during the Reagan years – the standard was 11.5 km per litre of petrol for four-door sedans (approximately 9 litres per 100 km, nearly two litres more than the European average). However, for "light trucks" – SUVs, pick-ups, mini-vans – which now make up 50% of the US car fleet, the standard was a low 8.4 km per litre (approximately 13 litres per 100 km).

For years, the auto industry lobbied successfully against any increase in the standard, drawing scenarios of multi-thousands of job losses that a higher standard would result in – or even arguing that higher fuel efficiency would hurt passengers' safety. But three events undermined any credibility:

1  When high petrol prices peaked at US stations, the car companies competed in presenting more fuel-efficient "studies", cumulating in Ford's announcement in July 2001 that it would increase the fuel efficiency of its SUVs by approximately 25% in five years.

**2**  The advancement of foreign competition ( particularly Honda) in the light truck segment, which exceeded the current CAFE Standard by up to 100% (in its recently launched models).
**3**  A study by the National Academy of Science, which ridiculed all the official arguments of the auto lobby.

These three events left the auto lobbyists in disarray, frustrating their supporters on Capital Hill.

### Division of labour

As a simple rule, one can assume that the higher the political influence via regulation or subsidies on an industry the higher the efforts to influence the decisions (and the higher the temptations to stretch the limits of accepted rules ...). Subsidies, protection from competition, etc. do not fall from heaven, nor are they invented by politicians and imposed on a reluctant industry. A good deal of today's complicated and extensive regulation is induced by special business interests.

This issue easily deserves a book of its own, but for our purpose two developments should be noted: the first is the tendency by exposed companies to put on a sympathetic face for themselves and leave the rougher work for the industry associations. A well-documented case is that of the Global Climate Coalition (GCC). Despite its title, it consists of US members only. Founded in 1989, it was to represent the fossil fuel and energy-intensive industries at the Rio Summit in 1992. Often allying itself with OPEC countries, GCC's main task was to spread counter-views on the findings of the Intergovernmental Panel on Climate Change (IPCC, a body co-ordinated by the UN) and to paint doomsday scenarios as to what would happen to the economy and living standards when measures were taken to limit $CO_2$ emissions.

GCC gained special prominence before and during the Kyoto negotiations on limiting greenhouse gases when it literally served as the "Rambo" of the opposition to any agreement. Being only partly successful, but highly visible, it drew fire from all the environmental

NGOs. Its influence was becoming more transparent (for example, its participation in international government negotiations), and its members exposed.

The European-based oil companies such as Shell and BP, in order to maintain credibility, withdrew the membership of their US subsidiaries from GCC, as did DaimlerChrysler for the Chrysler Group. And, when "Greener" chairman Bill Ford took up office, Ford's publicly claimed corporate stance on climate change was declared not reconcilable with the GCC propaganda. Probably this decision was taken without any government consultation. And the peers in industry reacted more with indifference than with outrage.

However, an indirect link remained – although much criticized by environmentalists. For example, through the American Petroleum Institute, the industry association for the US oil industry and still a member of GCC, Shell and BP contributed resources indirectly to the work of GCC. But eventually GCC had run its course and was abolished at the end of 2001.

### Expect more transparency

But it is becoming more difficult to hide: for example, SustainAbility, the interesting mix between brainy campaigners and influential consultants, has set up a special programme to create more transparency in this area (including the privileged access to information often enjoyed by the business community in particular), and has developed four other criteria under which corporate public policies are to be assessed:

1  Legitimacy. Is the means of influence a proper use of corporate power?
2  Consistency. Is a system in place to ensure that lobbying activities are aligned to environmental, social and ethical principles, policies and public commitments?
3  Accountability. Do companies take responsibility for the impacts they have on public policy?

**4** Opportunity. Do companies proactively attempt to influence public policy to support the transition toward sustainable development?

Given the instrumental role SustainAbility played in promoting sustainability reporting through its research, rating and conceptual-framing, there is little doubt that corporate-lobbying, too, will come under more intense scrutiny.

## Conflicts within industry

The second trend to be noted is that more often the interests of different industries are pitched against each other. Gone are the times when powerful industry leaders chaired the national federations of industries – and if necessary brought dissenting interests together, like shepherds rounding up sheep into their flocks ... Nowadays, even open conflicts are not uncommon. A typical example occurred in the "Auto Oil Program" sponsored by the European Union since 1993 (see Box 6-2).

---

### Box 6-2   Auto vs. Oil Industry: Flirting with the Enemy

The research outcome of the EU Auto Oil Program in 1993 promised to lead to lower levels of emissions, for example, of sulphur and benzene, and the abolition of lead or lead-based components. The original consensus between the auto and oil industries was met by universal, political rejection from all parties.

The auto industry, which was more ready to accept higher standards for the next generation of motors, did not want another "battlefield" in the political arena, where its image would surely be damaged (without gaining much economically), given the experience with the catalytic converter debacle in the mid-1980s. The oil industry, concerned about much higher investments in their refineries, continued to fight. A political stalemate occurred, in which the auto industry and the oil industry were pitched one against the other.

The auto industry finally "made its move" and joined the "Alliance for Cleaner Fuels", which was composed of several environmental organizations, the German environmental agency and the biggest German automobile club, ADAC. In a joint press conference held on 8 December 1998, the Alliance proclaimed that cleaner fuels were essential to efficient use of low-emission engines and exhaust filter techniques and campaigned for reducing taxes on cleaner fuels. This tipped the balance, but the oil industry continued fighting.

The German government favoured the introduction of higher standards from 2000 on (on the occasion of the second phase of the eco-tax reform). However, when in summer 1999 Veba Oel consequently threatened to close down its refinery in Gelsenkirchen, the Cabinet postponed the tax differentiation. Eventually, low-sulphur fuels were offered at virtually all German petrol stations from 1 November 2001 onward (sulphur-free fuels will follow by 2003). Refineries were rapidly upgraded after the tax differentiation had been decided on, although according to EU legislation high-sulphur fuel can be sold until 2005.

The more fragmented the political system becomes the less the *esprit de corps* of industry (the "old boys' network"/solidarity) will give way to a more individualistic approach and the more such conflicts will appear: export-driven industries vs. protectionist industries, small- and medium-sized companies vs. big multinationals (for example, in taxes), progressive companies vs. conservative companies, beneficiaries of regulation against those who pay ... The list could continue endlessly. Both sides will battle for public support and media attention as a precondition for favourable political treatment or new regulation.

Sometimes such a split can even occur within a company itself. For example, at the time when the energy companies were more diversified, there were instances where the coal division of one company normally lobbied against the Clean Air Act, whereas the same company's gas division was normally more in favour of it.

Today, one can see a more diplomatic version: an analysis of the speeches made at professional events by senior executives from major European oil companies reveals that speakers from the natural gas industry always touch prominently on the issue of global warming, whereas speakers from the traditional oil business tend to ignore such themes. And it is a similar scenario with car companies: whereas members working for the Volkswagen brand relentlessly promote the fuel efficiency theme, one rarely hears statements from Audi executives. Even tough-minded managers do not like to put another conflict on their plates . . .

### Conclusion: split, ignore or push

A more company-specific problem arises when a company has a vested interest in breaking publicly with its peers on a certain issue. As long as it is a minor member, it might get away with it – provided it does not team up with Greenpeace and serve as a witness against industry opinion (as Feron did on the CFC-free refrigerator issue – but at that time Feron was near bankruptcy and the CFC-free refrigerator was its only means of rescue).

Here, a company must weigh difficult trade-offs: that is, the immediate advantage in terms of positive commercial gain, or gain in terms of reputation, against the longer-term impact, when the company needs the industry association or the co-operation of its peers again. This explains why companies normally avoid breaking up openly with their industry associations – the risks are too high compared with the gains. Often, the industry position crumbles in any case before dissidents appear (as in the above-mentioned case of Ford for the CAFE standards).

It is much easier just to ignore the industry position or – more sophisticatedly – to use a general industry standard statement. Such statements appear in their dozens in press releases by companies, to ensure the companies are seen as being in line with general industry trends without losing the clear message that they want to attach to their own brand or corporation.

Sometimes, the importance of a member is sufficient to block any communication by the industry association on a specific issue, so that no difference in opinion can be detected by the public. This happened, for example, in the mid-1990s in the chemical industry, where some of the larger companies from more environmentally sensitive countries opposed resolutions by smaller producers of chemicals to oppose the phase-out of the "dirty dozen" – that is, bio-accumulative, persistent and toxic chemicals (for example, Lindan) and short-chained chlorinated hydrocarbons.

But whatever the tactics, the corporate priorities are clear: "First, we work on our strategy, guided by our goals and customers," explained a board member responsible for strategy. "Then we look around to see if we can put a 'red cherry on top of the ice cream' [some icing on the cake], and enlist the support of industry associations or initiatives like WBCSD." But sometimes life is not like that. In order to purchase from "sustainable sources" (for example, in the food industry) or to ensure compatibility between technical standards (see the MSC case in Section 7.2), it might be necessary to create an industry standard (without running into opposition from antitrust authorities). Here, a two-step approach often works: interested companies form a coalition, agree on the things needed and then push the industry association in the right direction. Unilever, Nestlé and Danone, for example, teamed up to define the technical meaning of "sustainable agriculture", and then moved on to create it as an industry standard. Their strategy stems from their inability to source from niche markets or buy to regional differentiating standards – to do so would jeopardize the quality promised by their brands.

But luckily there is a new kind of industry association or multi-stakeholder platform that could support proactive corporations.

## 6.4  WHERE THE NICE GUYS MEET

In addition to normal industry associations, today there are more organizations for "good citizenship" corporations than this book could ever cover. In every nation there are specific organizations – for example, environmentally proactive companies, with or without stakeholder participation. Sometimes proactive companies team up with public institutions to provide solutions (see Box 6-3 – ChemSite).

---

### Box 6-3   ChemSite: Preventing "Brown Fields" in Industrial Change

Old industrial regions are notorious for their decaying infrastructure: high unemployment leading to social problems, deserted industrial sites that nobody wants to touch due to environmental liabilities – "brown fields".

But countries learn from past mistakes, as do corporations that realize that, instead of leaving a lot of money on the table when they move out, they should leverage the assets still remaining.

There are many examples of this in the Ruhr: once the powerhouse of Germany's industrial might, since the late 1960s it has suffered due to the decline in coal and steel production. In the late 1980s the chemical industry, predominantly basic and petrochemistry, also came under increasing pressure from competitors in Asia and Eastern Europe. The result was a wave of mergers and restructures, followed by unavoidable downsizing in order to remain competitive. This left "empty spots" in the once densely integrated chemical plants; contrary, for example, to the US structure, the Northern European chemical industry was characterized as "compound chemistry", meaning that from basic chemical production – for example, chlorine and propylene – most of the value-added steps in further production of the end-product occurred onsite, leading to a succession of individual plants where one "feeds" the next.

To avoid existing plants becoming burdened with the additional cost of the infrastructure at the site and high unemployment leading to a vicious downward spiral, five regional chemical companies, led by the E.ON subsidiary Degussa-Hüls, formed a partnership called "ChemSite", which operates in liaison with the State government, the local chambers of commerce and the chemical workers' union.

Adhering to "Industrial Ecology", the task force actively seeks companies that fit nicely into the existing infrastructure (including ones using a different energy supply, for example high-pressure steam) or can process existing output components further up the value chain. A typical example is a joint venture between the US company Rühm and Haas and the German chemical company Stockhausen, which built two "world-scale" production facilities in Marl, for acryl acid and butyl acrylate, fed by plants from the area.

Special attention is given to start-ups, of which there are already 17 since the ChemSite initiative began in 1997. If needed, start-ups receive cost-efficient support services from laboratories, from logistics to environmental protection control and audits.

The partnership with authorities is helpful in expediting decisions through Germany's elaborate bureaucracy. The commitment is to obtain each licence requested in less than six months. Also, the union has promised flexibility in the application of existing labour contracts and laws: "No start-up or investment will be impeded either by too high wages or too high taxes" is the commitment of all partners in the initiative. Firms can tap into a pool of highly qualified industrial and technical workers and engineers.

Michael Czytko, head of the ChemSite task force, summarizes his experience: "In the first round we established credibility: the idea works. Now we have to catch some big fish with a 500 million euro investment. This could trigger a snowball effect, giving a whole new industrial perspective to the region."

The same is true for social responsibility issues. Here the most important global organizations are described in brief, beginning with the Global Reporting Initiative (GRI) because it is setting standards in non-financial reporting, even for those companies that do not participate.

### Sustainability Reporting: The Global Reporting Initiative

Founded in late 1997, GRI (www.globalreporting.org) is by its own definition a "multi-stakeholder initiative to develop, promote and disseminate a generally accepted framework for voluntary reporting of the economic, environmental and social performance of any organization". "Sustainability reporting" should become "as routine and credible as financial reporting in terms of comparability, rigour and verifiability." Instrumental for the founding initiative was the "Coalition for Environmentally Responsible Economies" (CERES), which also became known in the US as the initiators of the then "Valdez Principles" for corporate, environmentally responsible behaviour, together with the United Nations Environment Programme (UNEP) and a host of environmental, human rights and labour organizations.

Business companies from various sectors – for example, Baxter (pharmaceutical), Shell and BP (energy), Ford (auto), Electrolux (electric goods), Henkel (light chemicals) and British Airways – were actively involved in GRI, as well as large accounting companies and rating agencies.

A steering committee comprising 17 members represents and organizes the more than 1,000 participants. Working groups cover areas such as measurement (with 10 subgroups), verification and financial services (not only looking into the specific information issues and needs of the finance sector but also acting as a potential pilot for sector-specific guidelines). Funding comes from a variety of (mostly US) foundations and government agencies, and currently GRI is in the process of being transformed into a permanent institution, with its own governance structure (board of directors) and a permanent location.

The GRI has published "guidelines", first with a pilot in 1999, followed by a fuller set in 2000. A broad but systematic feedback process is organized, in order to improve, update and clarify the provisions (for example, the 2000 version is comprehensively on all three dimensions of sustainable development, whereas the original intention was focused predominantly on the environment). The year 2002 will involve another structured feedback process, including verification issues, which are particularly tricky in the social area.

More than 2,000 companies have used the GRI guidelines for their reporting, and rating agencies are starting to use the guidelines for their information requests. In short, a global standard is emerging for sustainability reporting. Organizations such as WBCSD now focus on tools to effectively implement these reporting requirements and integrate the thinking and the system into daily operations (for the full guideline content see Section 7.3).

In the view of Paul Hohnen (at that time a leading figure in Greenpeace), the further "virtuous circle" for GRI will depend on the rigorous implementation of the basic principles:

- Independence from and integrity accepted by all major stakeholders.
- Credibility by evolving the content and high professional standards.
- Participative and transparent processes that allow everybody to become involved.
- A clearly defined product with distinguished and measurable results.

### Global compact

Initiated by the UN Secretary General Kofi Annan in July 2000, the "Global Compact" (www.unglobalcompact.org) has today been signed by several hundred companies. Its aim is to promote sustainable growth and more inclusive globalization through a nine-point corporate commitment to human rights and high environmental and labour standards. These are derived from the UN Charter for Human Rights, the declarations of the International Labor Organization (ILO) and the Rio Declarations.

In addition, the Global Compact offers a platform for dialogue between companies, unions, NGOs and UN agencies (for example, the High Commissioner for Human Rights, UNEP).

Despite a generally positive response, some NGOs and politicians are critical about the lack of an enforcement mechanism and monitoring system for compliance with the principles signed by corporations.

### The World Business Council for Sustainable Development (WBCSD)

Formed following the Rio Summit of 1992 at the Business Council for Sustainable Development (led by Stephan Schmidheiny) and the environmental branch of the International Chamber of Commerce, the WBCSD (www.wbcsd.org) serves as a platform for some 150 multi-national companies with an interest in sustainable development. Based in Geneva, the WBCSD conducts research projects and multi-stakeholder dialogues, facilitates the sharing of experiences among its members and disseminates information on corporate sustainability issues, serving as the "spokesperson" for industry at all international conferences.

As was the case in Rio, it was very active at the Johannesburg Summit, providing input as to what industry can or will do to promote sustainable development. And its research shows that industry can do a lot: as several of the WBCSD's industry branch studies (for example, that on pulp and paper) reveal, most of the progress in polluting industries could be achieved if the laggards move up to the best practice standards in the industry (often implemented by successful companies, so it cannot harm business . . .). Another central theme will be the "Global Divide" between the "haves" and "have-nots" in information technology. An innovative business model is developed, so that now the poor can leapfrog from poverty to wealth creation by a tailored use of IT.

## Orgnization for Economic Cooperation and Development (OECD)

The OECD (www.oecd.org) is not exactly an NGO for "nice" corporations – however, its *Guidelines for Multinational Enterprises* (2000) set standards for corporate behaviour in developing countries.

First designed in 1976 and revised in June 2000 (updated to the Sustainable Development framework), all OECD member states and threshold countries such as Brazil and Argentina have committed themselves to supervise the implementation of OECD guidelines. Their content is similar to the Global Compact and often serve as a reference point when NGOs accuse companies of violating human rights or environmental protection standards.

*Global Responsibility Founding Forum*

The Global Responsibility Founding Forum was initiated in November 2000 by very progressive companies (for example, the Body Shop or cooperatives), NGOs, academia and the media. Its basic philosophy is the "Natural Step" concept, which formulates certain rules for sustainability (for example, "do not use non-renewable resources faster than renewable substitutes are developed for them").

In addition to organizations, companies can sign up to "Principles" (for example, the CERES Principle or the Global Sullivan Principles), or specific codes of conduct (for example, from Responsible Care to the Ethical Trading Initiative Base Code), committing themselves to a specific behaviour or application of rules (for example, not to buy from suppliers who use child or slave labour, see also www. codesofconduct.org)

Signing up to these and other initiatives can be a mixed blessing for companies. On the one hand, they demonstrate good intentions and even commitment, if they join; they meet peers in interesting networks, which can accelerate the internal learning process. In the case of a conflict, however, they are easily accused of not living up to what they have promised (which is mainly an interpretation of the case in question relative to some general, but sometimes high-flying principles).

But, generally speaking, companies must get something in return, otherwise these kinds of organizations, codes of conduct, etc. would not flourish. Another approach to promote "corporate social responsibility" can be seen in the influence of the capital market, by including an extended set of criteria in the stock market evaluation of companies.

## 6.5 CAN FINANCIAL MARKETS DRIVE "CORPORATE CITIZENSHIP"?

There is a lot of discussion currently about Socially Responsible Investment (SRI). The idea is simple: risks in the non-business environment – for example, due to a lack of good corporate citizenship – are still business risks and should be looked at more closely than "conventional" financial analysis practices. Generally, these risks are not captured in investment banks' analytical frameworks.

### Market developments

SRI activities clearly show a global scope. Markets have grown considerably and development in Japan has been particularly drastic. Currently, at least €2.1 billion (US$1.8 billion) assets are under management worldwide accounting for a market share of roughly 10%. Many of these exclude certain types of investment (for example, tobacco).

However, for the first time in many years, some of the largest and best known SRI funds performed worse than the S&P 500, as a US benchmark. This is largely attributed to their overexposure to technology stocks that were hit hard in 2000. Nevertheless, smaller and more aggressive funds holding large shares in alternative energy companies and biotechnology outperformed the market.

The Dow Jones Sustainability Group Index (DJSGI), launched in 1999, is one of the best known rating agencies. It developed a sophisticated, proprietary system of assessing the sustainability of a company, relative to its peers in a defined industry. The system covers both performance criteria (for example, the amount of toxics released) and behaviour, attitudes or reporting practices. Being part of the Dow Jones Indexes gives DJSGI high visibility.

European companies currently account for 53% as opposed to a 37% share of US companies in the DJSGI. The European bias of the index is also reflected by the fact that not one US financial institution has signed up to use the index. However, the DJSGI intends to break even in 2002. It has recently outperformed its mainstream "relatives". Researchers currently argue about how much this can be attributed to better sustainable performance of the selected enterprises. In July 2001 the DJSGI got a new prominent competitor, the FTSE4Good that placed itself alongside several other rivals such as Sweden's Etik-analytikerna and The Netherlands' "hard-line" Triodos.

Two of the largest US money-managers, the Teachers' Insurance and Annuity Association–College Retirement Equity Fund (TIAA–CREF) and the Vanguard Group, established new SRI funds in 2000. Both funds primarily focus on the "screening" component of SRI, and put less emphasis on shareholder activism and community development investing. Apart from an increase in visibility of SRI investments, this trend – as it is argued by sceptics in the sector – could also lead to the development of "light" versions of social investment.

In July 2000, the UK's Pensions Act 1995 was amended requiring pension funds to reveal their SRI policies. According to the UK Social Investment Forum, only one year later, 60% of the funds had incorporated SRI principles into their investment processes. Similarly, SRI disclosure rules were included in Germany's new capital-based pension scheme, according to which private schemes must disclose SRI policies in order to be certified and thus qualify for tax deductions.

From the *auditing and reporting* point of view, the complexity of measuring soft social issues such as community involvement or labour relations is the major challenge. One way of meeting it could be third-party certification, which features an accreditation body performing audits on certification bodies on a regular basis. In addition to the reduction of the number of audits, this would set national and international quality standards. As an example, Social Accountability International (SAI), a non-governmental and non-profit organization started up its SA (Social Accountability) 8000 workplace standard and verification system in 1997. Since the International Organization for Standardization (ISO) relies on a consensual and voluntary approach to establishing international standards, the process takes more time. There are currently no active projects to prepare screening standards. However, the ISO committee on consumer policy is assessing the feasibility of ISO standards in the area of social accountability and will submit recommendations on possible future steps.

### Challenges of ratings

The awareness of *consumers* regarding environmental and health issues is traditionally strong compared with their knowledge of SRI funds. Low awareness and penetration rates reveal large, unused potential for marketing and distribution. As pointed out earlier, the SRI market will grow with more and different types of mainstream as well as pioneer products. Japan and Germany, in particular, are "sleeping giants". Unfortunately, however, they are not natural pilot markets for innovative finance investment projects.

From the viewpoint of the *rated companies*, there is a clear need for more efficiency. Leaner interfaces require more transparency and consolidation. This holds especially true regarding the immense number and diversity of questionnaires submitted by financial institutions, let alone the different measurement systems, methodologies and criteria currently being used in assessments. Rating agencies should first look for available public and, in particular, online information before sending out their own questionnaires. This would naturally be an incentive for companies to place as much information as possible on their websites. Those withholding relevant CSR data are punished by additional inquiries from rating agencies wishing to clarify issues.

More cohesive standards will also increase the effectiveness (that is, credibility) of the measurement. Of course, *rating agencies* have to manage the trade-offs between completeness and applicability. Here, one major challenge will be cross-company and sector comparison of "soft", complex social issues. Equally important will be differentiating between analysing performance as opposed to judging values and thereby excluding certain industry branches (for example, GMOs, weapons). Here, NGOs usually voice conceptual criticism. The DJSGI, for example, measures *how* companies produce, not *what* they produce. NGOs argue that some sectors such as the nuclear power industry can never be sustainable. Furthermore, continuous monitoring encourages companies to persistently self-assess their business practices. For example, Credit Suisse, the Number One company in the DJSGI banking sector, was downgraded, after questionable financial dealings with former Nigerian officials came to light.

Further *research*, especially in the linkage between environmental and financial performance, is also necessary. Furthermore, there is a strong need for developing adequate performance indicators, integrating different standards and conducting cross-country studies in order to further increase the transparency of the methodologies used by rating agencies.

## Conclusion

Despite recent promising trends, one can conclude that the financial potential of SRI still remains largely unexploited. However, new marketing expertise and distinct regulative and market developments for driving consumer (that is, the private investor) and company behaviour will engage more private and institutional investors in socially responsible investments. At this stage, it may be inappropriate to speak of a paradigm shift. Recent trends, such as the increase in short-term investments and day-trading, need to be reassessed. It remains to be seen what the prolonged downtown in the stockmarkets will do to this SRI initiative. As pointed out earlier, the mainstream of rated companies, rating agencies and investors is beginning to realize that success requires sustainability in the long run.

But sophistication and applicability of financial reporting needed centuries to develop. Given the complexity of the issues to be measured, progress made in developing SRI is significant. Although it is not the main driver, it clearly supports, even today, corporate diplomacy efforts.

But as Sulzer (the Swiss engineering company) has experienced, you can easily be kicked out of an index once you run into any kind of controversy (in this case a product liability in the US). Claiming that Sulzer did not communicate this issue openly, the former "best practice" company was shamed (which we doubt – obviously nobody in the rating consultancy had ever had to confront a US court lawyer . . .) So communication is key – but how?

# Corporate Communication 7

The key element to all constructive interaction is communication. The main factors that shape today's communication of global companies – different from a decade ago – need to be considered by companies, and the target groups and the content standards identified (for example, by the Global Reporting Initiative) for a Corporate Diplomacy strategy to be successful.

## 7.1 WHAT IS THE DIFFERENCE?

Companies have always communicated with their business environments by means of multi-channels: some under the control of a company (for example, PR and marketing activities) and some free from any control (for example, from what others say about "you" to what your own employees say about their company in a pub or at a golf course).

Unfortunately for any director of communication, employee comments are often more effective at shaping perceptions about a company than is the official "gloss". People tend to be sceptical if the originator of the message has something to gain.

So what is different today in the global goldfish bowl transparency? The answer is the already mentioned power of information technology and the impact of the revolution in "instant 24-hour news", as well as the availability and accessibility of data to a degree never seen before.

In addition, there are five other factors that shape the different communications landscapes: the erosion of local roots; the decrease in the importance of politics; the increase in the perceived power of the corporation rules and regulations; and the "agenda of nations". These five factors are examined in detail below in terms of their implications for global corporate communication.

### Erosion of local roots

In the "good old days" of industrial feudalism, the influence of large employers on local or regional politics was natural and important – for better for worse – because it often led to a structural conservatism and monoculture, closing the door to new developments and change. Employees tended to live near the factory and managers started, and often ended, their careers in the same location. The web of social and communicative relations was stable and dense. Company employees were a large chunk of the city council, senior managers played a leading role in sports clubs, cultural and special interest associations, where they met members of parliament, administrators and other influential VIPs.

Today's world is different: individual mobility has scattered employees across a wider local area; no longer are large factories the dominant workplace. Managers are staying only two to three years in the same location, which is not enough to put down roots and become acquainted with the "locals" outside the business context. Important channels to present one's case or interest are lost, because at the end of the day all business is local – even in the Internet age – and so is politics. And what was once communicated automatically now involves making a deliberate effort.

### Erosion of political importance

As was argued in Chapter 2, although the decreased importance of politics and the role of the nation state is often exaggerated, it must be admitted that perception is reality. Global companies are regarded as more powerful than governments and, accordingly, media attention has shifted. Today, one can read, see and hear much more about business and companies (including stock prices) than was the case a decade ago. And the image of powerful leaders, created and communicated by spin doctors, does not differ much – be it a prime minister or a CEO, only that the latter is often more successful . . .

Add to this communication the "convenience promise" with which companies promise to solve all problems immediately – from headaches to investing money – and you will once again see the image of an omnipotent power. But there is a side-effect: if the almighty business communicates that it "cannot be done", it is always read as "we do not want to do this". Why can a CEO shake up whole industries, make billion dollar deals, but not be able to save an indigenous tribe from a corrupt government?

So, this "power image" also nurtures the growing expectation for corporate responsibility and sets the stage for companies to build their case when they try to influence public opinion.

### Expectations for corporate behaviour

Whereas the first two trends are universal (at least in OECD countries), expectations about corporate behaviour differ widely. In the US it is more widely accepted that companies clash aggressively with their governments, sue them and lobby with big money against government regulation. The same behaviour in Japan would be a definite recipe for disaster. In Europe one sees a division of labour with companies trying to be the "nice guy", communicating their good deals and leaving opposition to government regulations or defence of criticized products (for example, PVC) to industry associations.

On the other hand, the transparency legally required in the US – from payments to corporate offices to emission data – is much higher than in Europe or Japan. But the trend toward more openness and reporting requirements is again universal – just the "starting points" are different.

It is very important when planning communication strategy to acknowledge these differences in expectations, because one has to build on them, not violate them. The "mismatch" between the self-assessment of corporations and the expectation of the public is the root cause for many communication disasters. (See Box 7-1.)

---

### Box 7-1   Ford and Tyres – You Might Be in the Right, but Never a Know-it-all

When Ford CEO Jacques Nasser left the company in 2001 in disagreement with his chairman of the Board, the grandson of the founder, a long list of "sins" was circulated: being the best-wired executive (with 12 screens in his office), with up-to-the-second information, had induced more hectic confusion than leadership – the quality cars were deteriorating as the drive toward the car-related service business stalled. And in addition, Ford is said to have lost hundreds of millions of dollars in e-commerce, alienating its dealers along the way.

But as the *Economist* observed (on 3 November 2001): "All might have been forgiven or tolerated a little longer were it not for the Firestone Fiasco . . . Ford was forced to recall millions of Firestone tyres. It blames the tyre manufacturer for a series of accidents that have now claimed more than 300 lives. Firestone insisted that the problem lay with design defects in Ford's Explorer SUV. Hauled before Congress and pilloried in the press, Ford faced a year of excoriation. The campaign greatly damaged the firm's reputation as being customer-friendly."

One has to go back to 1982, with the recall of the popular analgesic Tylenol, to find a product recall of a similar dimension in the US. But whereas the Tylenol case can be found as a best practice example in many textbooks, few disagree that Ford messed it up. Why? In the framework of my analysis, three attitudes led to Ford's disaster:

- The self-opinionated statement that only the tyre was to blame, although it was common sense that SUVs tend to roll over due to their higher centre of gravity. Being built on a smaller (existing) platform and the fact that the problem only occurred with Ford's most profitable SUV were further blows to the credibility of Ford's argumentation. Still, today, experts disagree about the "real" reasons – but Ford's case was not compelling enough for them to take such a strong position.
- The claim that Ford was not aware of the problem before ("We virtually prised the claims data from Firestone's hand and analysed it," said

Jacques Nasser before Congress) was undermined by the fact that personal injury lawyers detected a "pattern" as early as 1996, but decided not "to tip your hands to the defendants out of concerns that private law suits would be compromised." In addition, product recall had already occurred outside the US a year earlier. And the media soon pointed out that Ford's "not knowing" was company-specific: different from that of General Motors. Ford's warranty did not cover tyres, so warranty claims go directly to the tyre manufacturer. But the customer simply asks: Why is Ford's warranty more limited than others? For a company claimng to build "life-long relations with its customers on all car mobility services", this was a damaging blow.

- The decision of Nasser at first not to appear before Congress, and then to back-pedal as the public outcry forced him to do so, was a misjudgment of the "consumer-versus-big business issue", which Congress was more than happy to jump on during this pre-election period. Nobody believed that the tough-talking Australian wanted to duck a fight, so arrogance and not caring for the customer were the dominant explanations remaining.

Observing how Jacques Nasser was "shredded" and remembering other cases – for example, *Exxon Valdez* – you can now see that "sorry CEOs" abound. Whether it is flight delays, payment errors on telephone bills or spoiled food, more companies than ever before are ready to appear apologetic and ask to be forgiven. But the suspicion remains as to whether or not they really mean it.

In any case, it is a clear indication that companies do not want to be caught violating the basic values of society by insisting on their own value system and internal assessment of a conflict. So it is a good starting point – but in the end, it is only action that really counts . . .

And these expectations change slowly – just because shareholder value has become (for the time being) the mantra of CEOs, this does not mean that the public will buy-in easily and quickly, and accept this as a benchmark for corporate behaviour and communication.

## The new role of regulation

Laws and regulations are the "set-in-stone" expectations of society about the "dos and don'ts" of behaviour, not only for corporations.

They differ through tradition and legal systems (more "case law" in the Anglo-Saxon world vs. a more detailed legalistic framework in Continental Europe).

Despite the clichés however, regulations are important for corporate behaviour in every part of the world – and in no country is a corporation capable of communicating convincingly why it was good to violate the law. But compliance with the law, on the other hand, is not something for which one gets a reward – it is the expected norm.

Increasingly, however, companies or industries are expected to regulate themselves through a code of conduct, self-obligations or commitment in order to avoid more "clumsy", inflexible and therefore costly legislation. This is an indicator of the changing expectations of companies as "problem-solvers" in areas that were previously the domain of governments, and has to be taken into consideration in global corporate communication.

### The "agenda" of nations

Last but not least, global communications become more complex through nations' different "agendas". There are specific issues that will be more important to one nation than to others, and they are shaped by cultural traditions, actual experiences and the interconnectedness of issues (see Chapter 5.2), which are often not seen by companies.

So, while the British are not perceived as strong on environment issues, they are the most sensitive and concerned people regarding food safety, haunted by BSE, foot-and-mouth disease, etc. In the US you can pump calves full of growth hormones, but you had better not dare to sell tuna that has not been caught in "dolphin-safe" nets. Japan and Norway, on the other hand, chose to be the international community outlaws before finally bowing to the anti-whaling pressure. And let us not forget national symbols: the German forest is more than just a cluster of trees, and – contrary to the UK monarchy – the Japanese Emperor is still today sacrosanct.

But it is not only the Japanese Emperor who is surrounded by taboos – the US has an entire catalogue about "political correctness", which describes how to address whom, which jokes are acceptable and which are better not referred to at all, what is regarded as discriminating behaviour – in short it is a bonanza for lawyers, a nightmare for human resource and marketing executives, and a dangerous trap for naive and ignorant foreigners . . .

Issues are often seen by the public in a context that companies do not see due to their "blinkered vision" for their particular market segment. Coca-Cola did not understand why the spoiled cans in Belgium created such an uproar. The public were generally concerned about risks in food, but obviously Coca-Cola did not see the interconnection between the meat and the beverage industry. And the company still grapples with the fact that the biggest impact was in Italy, a country where people do not trust authorities to guarantee food safety, but where Coca-Cola was the incarnation of a "clean drink" – a confidence that was shaken by the Belgian scandal.

## Implications

The five factors analysed above shape the communicative environment for corporations and are preconditions to whether a message is going to be heard, understood and accepted, or is going to create an outrage. We give them again in brief:

- Erosion of local roots that had "natural" communication channels.
- Decline of politics and raised expectations due to corporate power.
- Conforming behaviour and conduct of companies as envisaged by the public according to the public's own values.
- Laws and regulations as "set-in-stone" expectations of these norms.
- Country- or cultural-specific issues.

Some readers might question whether it is possible to communicate anything globally that is not going to offend somebody, somewhere, in the world. The answer is clearly "No" – but does it matter? The porn industry probably could not care less that most religious people hold their products in contempt – the industry is targeting a different crowd. Arms manufacturers have learned to live with a pacifist movement that disdains their products. The question of the relevance and strength of your opponent was dealt with in Section 5.3 and need not be repeated here.

A second fact is that often it is not so important *what* a company says, but *how* they say it. A message delivered in a manner that is perceived as arrogant or uncaring can destroy even the very best content.

And thirdly, the question is to whom you communicate. Despite global transparency, the information explosion has made it impossible to follow everything. Everybody is "fishing" for the information that is relevant to him or her and that fits into his or her world view. This is why a clear target group for communication is so essential. "One size fits all" just creates noise, no impact. This is the result of individualism, described by widely varying, fluid and fragmented life situations, lifestyles, values and interests.

## 7.2  TARGET GROUPS FOR CORPORATE COMMUNICATION

### *Customers*

For companies, customers constitute the most important group of stakeholders. This is not only because they are subject to (product-related) marketing efforts. Since products of a given nature are becoming increasingly alike, the customers' perception of the company and its business practices gains importance. The strength of this influence is debatable; however, its existence has been empirically detected.

Consumer behaviour is not homogeneous. Presumably, there is a wide range of behavioural patterns whose effects differ from sector to sector: for example, the market for emotional consumer goods is likely to be more sensitive toward company image than the market for technical intermediate goods. Nowadays, companies are battling for every bit of market share. This competition makes corporate "appearance" an important issue, not necessarily to win something, but to avoid putting yourself in the position of the sector's "baddie". This can also be understood by just looking at the criteria that determine the "image": credibility, clearness, reliability of statements, transparency, tolerance and understanding (as opposed to arrogance). They substantiate trust as a basis for doing business – not as a means of positive differentiation.

### Analysts

The second significant target group consists of financial analysts. Over the years, they have been promoted from mere "number-crunchers" to high priests who were more drivers and protagonists than rational analysts, as all the Wall Street scandals indicate. This is quite understandable from the viewpoint of the analysts: their reputation and payment depend on whether their forecasts eventually occur. Different from the media, good news that is generally associated with rising stock prices sells better than disappointing bulletins. That's why analysts search for "stories" that quicken market prices and follow certain fashionable trends: the "new economy" is currently somewhat "out", whereas its "old" counterpart is seen as a bit more favourable again.

As long as investors keep buying and selling, thus generating revenue for stock exchanges and investment banks, everything is fine. Nothing is more ancient than yesterday's news. According to the theory of efficient markets, this information is already reflected in the current price. Analysts are most interested in information that provokes aspiration, for example, rumours about mergers or acquisitions, because they drive the markets (nevertheless the "bubble" often bursts soon afterwards). Consequently, markets do not react to assessed results, but to divergence from original expectations, meaning the consensus of the analysts.

Reacting to these market "needs", companies have established specialized divisions that communicate with investors and their customers ("investor relations"). CEOs and executive boards spend a lot of time with "roadshows" thereby sometimes neglecting other management duties.

In general, the global network of stock exchanges hardly reacts to events that have no financial implications. Stock prices rarely suffer just because a company is under public pressure – as can be seen from the example of BMW after the planned disposal of Rover (the British public are upset, the share price rises). Hence, it might actually be appropriate to conclude that unpopular measures such as lay-offs and closing of factories tend to be assessed positively by financial markets.

### Administrative–political environment

High-level employees in government and "official" authorities constitute another important group. Although considerable efforts of deregulation are being made, the number of laws and ordinances continues to increase worldwide. Hence, companies and their individual constituents and facilities are more often confronted with enforcement agencies than with the legislators at the political top (MPs or ministers).

On the one hand, authorities are legally bound to treat everyone the same – at least in democratic, constitutional states. On the other hand, they naturally perceive political developments as well as public opinions and act accordingly. Every piece of legislation leaves room for discretionary decisions; for example, the frequency and duration of inspections. The use of such areas of discretion is not only difficult to challenge legally but also humanly quite understandable. A worse company image usually results from more frequent violations, scandals and incidents; it is only natural that such companies are more thoroughly scrutinized. Authorities are "stricter" with unruly companies to avoid becoming subject to scrutiny and criticism themselves. More and more of them are becoming part of a global network that facilitates exchange of information and experience. This collaboration was also a major reason why Coca-Cola was subject to so many antitrust investigations in different countries.

High-level regulators are primarily interested in scientific information in their field. This is due to the fact that, very often, only the companies have the data available, which regulators need to assess the matter of fact (such as environmental effects of a particular substance). Therefore, authorities dispose of various information sources enabling them to relatively quickly identify cases in which companies release sugar-coated information. That's why it is essential for companies to establish good communication relations early on and to persistently cultivate them – before "things go wrong".

### Diversity in the global village

Finally, there are the many groups somewhat embarrassingly called "non-governmental organizations" (NGOs) (see Section 3.4). They comprise traditional groups such as churches or unions, relief organizations, action and campaign groups such as Friends of the Earth, or special-interest groups (for example, those partly organized around gender issues). Their range of subjects is unlimited, so is their regional focus: one can find anything from the "global multi" (for example, WWF or Amnesty International) to the local citizens' initiative (possibly also part of a global network). No other type of organization has grown so quickly over the last two decades; their total number is unknown. The UN estimated that there are around 29,000 international NGOs. In the US, supposedly 2 million exist (accounting for every kind of non-governmental group).

NGOs feature two important "generic" characteristics: first, they make very specific demands of companies; second, they are able to set up political campaigns very quickly. Consequently, they are able to hit companies where it really hurts.

Many of these NGOs dispose of considerable expertise and, hence, are very good at processing and analysing information comprehensively and contemporarily. As far as this scrutiny goes, company information is only one aspect of communication. Discussion and, partly, co-operation is welcomed: one learns and gets the chance to maybe even make an impact.


## 7.3  THE CONTENT OF COMMUNICATION

When it comes to companies' non-market activities, at least in the area of sustainable development issues – and this probably covers most corporate messages, especially in the environmental and social domains – a great deal of clarification has been provided by the Global Reporting Initiative (for the organizational context see Section 6.4).

The GRI consolidated the many different approaches used at the time of its inception into one widely accepted standard for sustainability reporting that will probably "blot out" the others. Although tailored to an (annual) report, it develops criteria and standards that are useful when applied to other communications efforts as well. The ingredients and indicators for credibility of such reporting can be summarized as follows:

- The involvement and commitment of top management (as a precondition to move a hierarchical organization forward).
- Vision and strategy: Where is the company heading? What are its incentives, barriers? How is sustainability part of the overall corporate strategy? What are the avenues of integration? What are the goals for the future?
- How is the corporate policy formulated? What is the content, subscription to codes of conduct? What management systems are used to ensure compliance (for example, ISO 14000 or EMAS in the environmental domain)? What are the reporting lines, the resources and the people to make the strategy happen?
- Performance indicators (painstakingly described in the GRI with no less than 69 obligatory guidelines), so that development over time can be assessed and progress measured quantitatively.

As a whole, the GRI certainly serves to create transparency for the "show me" world. To further ensure that the data and reported facts are reliable, more companies are now also providing third-party verification, mainly by one of the major accounting firms or certification agencies (for example, SGS, DNV) – although the methodology of this assurance is still being developed. Pioneers go a step further still: Shell asked a renowned "Green" research institute to write the environmental report for its German facilities.

In order to establish a better balance between the different needs of the stakeholder and limited print space, many companies simply print an executive summary and put the "full Monty" on their web pages. This, too, has the advantage of keeping information up-to-date.

But the three features that currently differentiate a brilliant report from a merely good one are as listed below:

1  Building a business case: nobody believes that companies are in business "for the common good" – therefore, the more compellingly the business case is built (why and how are non-market activities part of the strategy and how do they contribute to the economic success of the organization) the more credible the communication will be (see also Section 6.1).

2  Going beyond the obvious, politically correct "hot topics" (for example, climate change) and using the early awareness system to highlight emerging trends and sense new opportunities indicates that this is more than "business as usual" and is in fact part of the corporate culture or "genes".

3  Not only covering the industrial world but also activities in developing countries (including joint ventures or reviewing the supply chain).

Having gone through the "heavy lifting" required by such a demanding report, the day-to-day communication of special events (for example, stakeholder dialogues) are much easier to run once a base line is established, to which everybody can return if doubts arise or if more detailed information is required.

But even in the best communicating companies, things can still go wrong (as the previous example of Sulzer showed us). How are they to behave then?

## 7.4   HOW TO SOLVE THE WORST CASE SCENARIO

### Box 7-2   Does It Pay to Tell the Truth?
### BP Amoco Tries to Find out

In the litigious society of the US, the typical advice of corporate lawyers is, on any occasion, just to bear down, deny everything and reveal anything only if you are forced to. The justification is that, otherwise, class action suits with horrendous punitive damages will ruin the company. Without evidence, the reasoning goes, the plaintiffs might not be able to bring their case to court.

Many of the largest PR disasters – *Exxon Valdez*, Coca-Cola, McDonald's, Ford, to name but a few – can be traced back to this kind of legal consideration. And the impact for the credibility of the companies is obvious.

BP Amoco is now trying a new avenue: full public disclosure. The case refers to six scientists, all of whom worked for a long time in Amoco's chemical research lab, and who now suffer from a rare form of brain cancer during retirement.

Amoco brought in top scientists and built up a medical history of nearly 1,700 people who had worked in the "cancer wing" of the lab, to uncover any on-the-job links between those with the rare, but fatal, cancer, and all the other people who worked there.

The report failed to identify a specific chemical or combination of chemicals as being responsible for the cancer, but the occurrence of the cancer in the group was 12 times higher than would be normally expected, suggesting that it was something related to the workplace.

BP Amoco settled with the families of the victims out of court and released the full report of the medical findings. Some were concerned that this could be a bonanza for lawyers to sue the company, because it might provide evidence. Two dozen plaintiffs are currently suing BP Amoco for a variety of seemingly unrelated tumours. However, without the report, the plaintiffs would be in a better position to take the moral high ground.

The first would-be class action was thrown out by a court. The judges obviously believed that the fully disclosed, comprehensive research only established a workplace link to the already-settled, specific brain tumour. Other cases are still pending.

But if you run through my issue checklist (Chapter 5), there in little doubt that the brain cancer cases had the potential of making a strong issue. By providing transparency through full disclosure, any attempt to exploit the issues was firmly defused.

Even emergencies have their up-sides – the advantage of late intervention is that the company does not "waste" its efforts on issues that may not justify the attention. But few will argue with Norman R. Augustine, President of LockheedMartin: "When preparing for crises, it is instructive to recall that Noah started building the ark before it began to rain." Prevention is better: that is, more cost-efficient than intervention. You should monitor your business environment and develop a reasonable response based on a clear understanding of what the issues are, what your previous positioning/strategy has been and how you can communicate your case. (In brief, what this book is all about.)

## Box 7-3   Reputation Assurance

If there is a clear indication that companies are grappling with specific issues, consultancies will develop a tool for "fixing the problem". Pricewaterhouse Coopers (PWC), the largest of the "Big Five" accounting firms and consultancies, recently presented its "Reputation Assurance", a mixture of a diagnostic tool, strategy design and implementation/monitoring set-up. It is based on the experience and basic principles of Total Quality Management.

The first "package" is an audit to evaluate the outside monitoring of stake-holder demands – the established policies that are in place, the resources and people to implement these policies, and whether there is a drive for continuous improvement and innovation.

The second module looks specifically at deploying the principles estab-lished: an effective stakeholder communication programme (a glossy brochure detailing the company's business principles will probably not be sufficient), the way awareness is raised and educating the stakeholders on important issues.

But most of all: Is this all lived up to by the leadership and employees? Does the company serve as a role model and encourage consistency of behaviour through incentives and, if needed, sanctions?

Monitoring the results and giving feedback and input to reputation assurance is the third element. Perceptions of reputation have to be monitored, as they are bound to occur alongside changes in corporate behaviour and the intended results of actions.

This needs structured research, although informal opinion polls during a dinner conversation might be just as helpful (assuming that the executive is able to listen and not sound defensive). As with all management systems, this must then be linked to prioritized goals, measured by some key performance indicators.

However, one has to accept that in every global company things can go wrong, forcing the company to shift gear into crisis management, followed by crisis prevention. So what should you do when the crisis has hit you?

First of all, remember and accept W.I. Thomas's ("perception is reality") theses: what is relevant is what the public feel and believe. It does not matter if a crisis follows scientific guidelines, logical structures or rational thinking, emotions are empirically evident and one will have to deal with them.

Given that circumstances, issues, context and interconnectedness vary widely, it is difficult to give advice in a general format (our diligent MBA task force on crisis management discovered eight different types of crisis). Better managed companies have detailed crisis management plans, even facilities, which fit their needs and the scenarios they have dreamed up – covering eruptive, cyclical and continuous crisis types. But some basic lessons hold true from the trends in every situation.

## Seven golden rules of crisis management

1 Murphy's law is true: "What can go wrong, will go wrong"; this is especially true in companies that are scattered around the globe, with overworked management structures and a corporate rhetoric of risk-taking. So remember: Murphy was an optimist – don't bet the crisis will only affect others.

2 Life is not always fair (and the media even less so), but a mighty company whining about the injustice of the world is the least acceptable response to any criticism or even unfounded accusations. Resist the temptation to fight the media – the crisis issue often blows over quickly, but not through bullying the media. Don't fight your critics: willingness to listen, compassion and responsiveness under the stress of a crisis moves you away from the prisoner's dock, where you always find yourself, pushed by those who claim the moral high ground.

3 Get it over fast: a crisis does not improve with age. "Too little too late" is the sure way for an agonizing prolongation. The fastest way out is to accept responsibility and take some tough decisions pretty soon. Although these decisions may be surrounded in uncertainty, there is only one thing worse: no decision at all. If you are a principled company, then you know on which values you can fall back, to guide your decision.

4 Do not try to find allies after the crisis has hit you. You can only count on those relationships and any trust you have already built up. And after a crisis, you will be much more aware of who your friends are. And don't forget in the media hype who your potential allies are: your employees, customers and suppliers. Their hunger

for information is greater than the interest of the average reader/ viewer.

5 If you don't talk – someone else will. "No comment" is the least acceptable answer in a crisis. State clearly what you do and do not know. Don't speculate. Put one face before the public – opting rather for a senior executive with operational responsibility than a smart PR type.

6 Don't listen to the lawyers, and avoid the language of denial. Your brand reputation is more important than legal-positioning, and avoid making statements like "No comment" or using incomprehensible jargon when explaining your position. As the *Exxon Valdez* case demonstrates so well, it will not help you in court if you have said nothing.

7 Evaluate the crisis in human terms: the outrage is not based on science, but that the company has – mostly unintentionally – violated some values of society. And then appearing (remember: perception is reality) uncaring, arrogant or even disdainful is the surest way to escalate a crisis into a full-blown disaster.

Readers may wonder why I list here some pretty obvious, common-sense rules. I wonder, too – but my own experience and empirical evidence tells me that they are violated time and again ... What is not so evident, however, is when to co-operate and when to fight the activists or NGOs.

# "Suits" and "Sandals": Balancing Conflict and Co-operation

# 8

Despite the official rhetoric, companies are facing options to co-operate *and* to conflict with activist groups at the same time. Here, we analyse the different options and learn how to map the territory using the Marine Stewardship Council and Exxon's more confrontational stand as a template.

## 8.1 HOW NICE WILL NGOs BE TO CORPORATIONS?

In his Millennium Report, the UN Secretary General, Kofi Annan, highlighted the role of civil society organizations and the important contributions they make in advancing the debate and solutions on complex issues. He also predicted that: "The partnership of NGOs, the private sector, international organizations and governments ... is a powerful partnership for the future."

Similar statements could be heard at the G7 or G8 Summits, at the EU conferences, at "Rio + 10" and at the New Earth Summit in Johannesburg in summer 2002, for which sophisticated procedures existed to collect, process and document the inputs of thousands of NGOs (including those that are business-based, some industry associations and others such as the WBCSD).

So, is this a sign of biblical peace between lion and lamb to come? Hold the applause – because the disagreement has already started as to who is the lamb and who is the lion ... While business often feels persecuted by NGOs and their media campaigns and grossly misrepresented in their intentions, NGOs mostly feel bulldozed by the mighty corporations and struggle to make their voice heard.

But business and NGOs have one thing in common: both are "single issue" organizations. This differentiates them from governments (or political parties) who have to "cover the waterfront" on all issues of concern to those who are governed. Therefore, governments struggle to get their priorities right, without alienating too many of their constituency in the process. Business and NGOs are much more focused, but on different areas of life: "Earning money by satisfying market demand" is the predominant priority of companies. "Promoting the chosen issue to satisfy members and donators" is the golden rule for NGOs whose causes generally have nothing to do with market demand. However, NGOs often care passionately when they think markets harm their cause or feel that companies could do more to support their cause – and will do their utmost to change this situation (and remember: perception is reality).

### Box 8-1   Novo Nordisk: Engaging Stakeholders

One of the undisputed leaders in building stakeholder dialogue as a tool to develop and strengthen the business is the Danish Novo Group, which employs 16,000 people around the world in two main businesses: biotechnology-based enzymes for industrial use (Novozymes) and diabetes care and related pharmaceuticals (Novo Nordisk). The Group has received many awards for environmental and social reporting, is praised on many occasions for its social responsibility and its Senior Vice President for Stakeholder Relations Lise Kingo is a much-sought-after speaker around the world. This does not come naturally. After all, the Novo Group is dealing with two hot, controversial issues: genetically modified microorganisms (GMMs) and the use of animals for testing purposes.

Maybe it helped that it all started with a disaster. In 1993, during the initial, somewhat tense stakeholder dialogue on GMMs, an accident happened at Novo's main site, leading to an escape. The participants were openly informed and updated. Contrary to the spontaneous wish of the NGO representatives to leave the discussion, the open attitude of and the frank discussion with Novo's managers convinced them to stay and to continue.

Over the years, Novo Group's sophistication in dealing with stakeholders has been built-up by learning from what has gone before and by creating transparency through extensive reporting and provision of information. Today, its success rests on three pillars:

- Building partnerships, even with adversaries. The Danish Society for the Conservation of Nature and Novo Group are engaged in a common project to develop educational material for older schoolchildren on genetic engineering. Although the partners disagree on these issues, common ground is the belief that knowledge, transparency and debate are the preconditions for the use of – and setting the limits for – genetic engineering. Similarly Novo Group invites dialogue with the many NGOs who oppose GMOs in general, but are ready to co-operate with Novo Group on specific issues such as biodiversity. For a number of years Novo has had a Biodiversity Foundation with WWF to sponsor students who research in biodiversity issues.
- Exploring new business conditions and opportunities. Health care is in every country a tricky political issue, not least because of the many vested interests at stake and the emotional nature of the issue. Recently an accusation jumped to the top of the political agenda that pharmaceutical companies care only for the health of rich people, not the many poor. Novo Nordisk set up a health policy committee, headed by the COO, along the same lines as its committee on bioethics. It is reviewing and re-evaluating Novo's role in helping to bring about better diabetes care globally. It stated: "Globalization is un-discovering the complex issues of poverty, inequity, discrimination, patents of medicine and the allocation of sparse resources in the provision of health care." But Novo Nordisk admitted openly: currently there are more questions than answers. But such a process, especially with the involvement of external experts and NGOs, can sharpen the eye for emerging, new business models or at least it can enlarge or deepen the existing health care offer to Novo customers around the world.
- Explaining to stakeholders the need to use GMMs. Novo Group learnt that it is important to get public perception of bio-safety about antibiotic resistance markers, a field where they now lead research and application. Future business improvement and reduced use of animals are expected from the switch to pharmaceutical testing methods through validated in-vitro analyses. And the Danish Animal Welfare Society helps Novo Group to improve the housing conditions for the test animals and these conditions are now considered the global industry standard. And few people in Novo have doubts that the high standards in

environment, health and safety that it sets for itself plus the far-reaching transparency required by stakeholders are also good for productivity and capacity utilization.

Stakeholder dialogue, however, does not mean that a company has always to be the "nice guy". When certain NGOs argued that Novo Group had to stop using their patent rights, Novo Group was crystal clear that patents are the foundation of its business model. "In the dialogue process we had the opportunity to explain to the NGOs that we do not have patents on our pharmaceutical products in developing countries, but – on the other hand – that we cannot attract investors without patents on new products that are very expensive to develop," observed Lise Kingo, "so not only are we learning, but stakeholders start to understand much better what it means to be competitive in a global marketplace. So the focus is now on innovation to improve the Triple Bottom Line."

As described above, the issues represented by NGOs include every aspect of life – from the protection of birds in rural Wales to slave labour in China.

My central thesis is therefore that – against the official "partnership" rhetoric – it is unavoidable (even if often unintended) that corporations get in the way of one or more NGOs (or vice versa). Nobody is to blame: the free organization of interest is a cornerstone of a democratic society – it is legitimate to have and to set different agendas. But it would be naive to assume that these interests are basically harmonious and can coincide.

As in industrial relations, where companies have developed in northern European welfare states side by side with organized labour, it is more realistic to expect co-operation *and* confrontation. There will be a continuum of full-blown battles at one end of the range (similar to fighting Monsanto or Exxon) and co-operation (similar to MSC) at the other end.

## Range of options

In between, there is a range of interactions and dialogue of different kinds. In an attempt to break down this continuum statistically, I expect in about 25% of cases that NGOs plan, conduct and try to win a campaign that is confrontational against a company or industry, using all channels available (see Section 4.4). In addition, there are a few entrenched wars that are likely to continue unabated for quite some considerable time: the "chlorine industry", GMOs, animal-testing, etc.

About 50% of issues involve confrontational debate, trying to win over the public, pitching the lobbyists from either side against each other (for example, in setting regulatory standards). This is typical when governments, parliaments and regulatory agencies need to be influenced. A further 25% will involve a more constructive, problem-solving type of dialogue, and less than 5% would involve co-operation.

Looking first at co-operation, the decisive question is: why are NGOs ready to co-operate? The first and obvious answer is: to promote their cause. It is often forgotten in the co-operation rhetoric that NGOs – as businesses – have their goals, which they want to see furthered.

So the basic question – from both sides – is: does this co-operation suit my interest? Especially at a time when business is courting well-known NGOs almost to excess, professional NGOs make their choice under criteria such as "what is best to leverage our scarce resources".

They are under a similar efficiency pressure to companies: first, NGOs know that, after decades of awareness-building, they also have to show results and contribute to the solution of problems – but they have only a few levers to pull. And, second, the competition among NGOs for the different issues they promote is immense. This is not only with regard to resources (for example, donations) but also with regard to political and media attention. So co-operation must fit into their strategy and deliver results.

Corporate attempts at what an NGO official called the "3-I" strategy (Inform them extensively, Involve them in many debates, Ignore their recommendations) are short-lived. Even for a less engaging stakeholder dialogue, some rules need to be followed (see Box 8-2: the Ten Dos and Don'ts of Stakeholder Dialogue).

## Box 8-2   The Ten Dos and Don'ts of Stakeholder Dialogue

The following rules appear simplistic and self-evident – a kind of "Forrest Gump of Management". However, as in other areas throughout the book, I have seen that often they are not applied. So further repetition seems to be needed:

1   Be clear what *you* want out of a stakeholder dialogue. Is it a test for your formulated strategy, an input to a problem you are grappling with or do you want to discover a new perspective?

2   Understand why stakeholders participate: it is not money – it is normally the opportunity to better the world by promoting their cause. Are you ready to move in that direction?

3   Honesty sometimes hurts, and the diplomatic style you apply to customers and your direct reports may not be in line with the tone in which the discussion started – especially at the outset or after an experience of confrontation. Do you have the patience and emotional detachment to remain calm?

4   Put marketing last. Stakeholders are normally suspicious that you want to use them as a "Green fig leaf", and tend to withdraw if they perceive that dialogue is being misused for PR purposes. Publicity can therefore only come very late in the process, when results are achieved, and even then only with mutual consent. Are you ready to stay out of the spotlight for so long?

5   To listen is often the hardest part for managers – after all, management is about action. Do you have the patience to listen very carefully, to ask additional questions instead of responding, and not simply to look for confirmation of the prejudice you already have?

6   Appreciate the diversity of perspectives. Business has its logic, but it is not the only "rational" view – with other goals, you have another logic. Are you truly appreciating diversity and different logic as a source of learning? And are you ready to put yourself, for the purpose of understanding, "in the other side's shoes"?

7   Select the participants carefully. Do they bring specific competence to the table? What is their reputation? Do they have experience in dealing with companies? Can you trust them – especially to keep sensitive business information confidential?

8   Negotiate the rules and document them transparently, because nothing is as obvious, self-evident or legally framed as business-to-business

relations. Are you ready to embark on new rules and act according to a different script from the one with which you are familiar?

**9** Agree on a neutral, professional moderator who is looking for results and can serve as an "interpreter" for both sides, calming the waters if needed. But are you ready to relinquish control of the meeting and to obey a referee for implementation of the negotiated rules?

**10** Take your time, because such a dialogue is like arms control negotiations: first, you have to build trust; then each side has to understand the issues from the other side; and only then can you start to work on the solution. Do you have a strict deadline or need a quick-fix or are you in for a longer learning process?

If you cannot answer the questions confidently and meet the criteria – you better abstain from stakeholder dialogue for the time being. Save yourself from the frustration and wasted time you are otherwise going to face. Rather, invest in getting ready and then move on – life is full of second opportunities. And never start a dialogue with the enemy when the battle is already in progress.

(Translated, adapted and extended from Heike Leitschuh-Fecht, *Societal Expectations for Corporate Stakeholder Dialogue*, 2002.)

## Types of co-operation

And companies have to be aware of which type of co-operation they are embarking on (see Figure 8.1), using the degree of commitment from both sides as the dominant selection criteria:

- There are some ad hoc *opportunistic coalitions* possible, which have an affect only on current specific issues. One example is the "clean fuel" controversy that has been raging in the EU over the past years. The automotive industry wanted clean fuel (for example, less sulphur) in order to further reduce emissions, given the better fuel-burning features of their motors. The oil industry was opposed because it meant additional investment in their refineries. In order to push the new regulatory standards through, automotive lobbyists

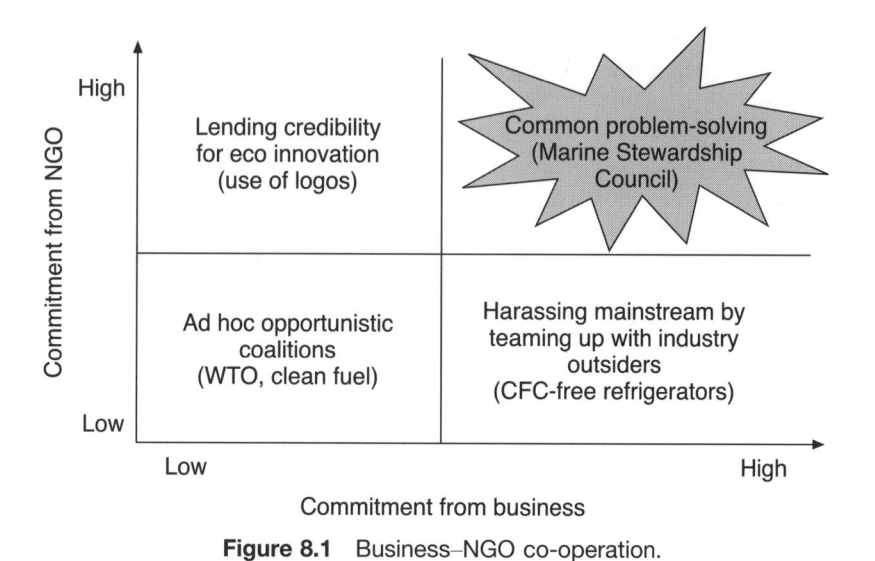

**Figure 8.1**   Business–NGO co-operation.

teamed up with environmentalists, and together they beat the oil industry on this issue. Similarly, sometimes protectionist interests try
to team up with environmental or consumer groups (for example,
to prevent imports of cheap T-shirts from low-wage countries).

- NGOs are *putting their credibility* on the line when they allow companies to use their logo – as is the case, for example, in corporate
communication, in the co-operation between Lafarge and WWF
for the wide range of co-operation they have agreed on to establish
new industry practices in quarry rehabilitation, $CO_2$ reduction,
waste-recycling and environmental audits. The German Chapter of
Friends of the Earth, BUND, helped to select outstanding environmentally friendly products for a German retail chain, and agreed to
use their logo on these products – often as a substitute for the
brand (normally these products come from niche players).

- Sometimes NGOs *team up with industry outsiders* to demonstrate the
feasibility of a solution they promote. This is a preferred Greenpeace
tactic – one which it applied, for example, in the case of CFC-free refrigerators, or the "3-l car" (for US readers: this is not the volume

of the motor, but the equivalent of an 80-mile-per-gallon car). The purpose is to show that these demands could be fulfilled if the dominant players wanted to do so. Despite having limited success in the Greenpeace case with fuel consumption, NGOs clearly managed to set new industry standards in Green freeze, GMO labelling or logging practices (mostly by convincing the customers of the attacked company to join forces with them).

- And last but not least, there is *institutionalized co-operation* on a high-profile project in which a leading corporation and a well-known NGO co-operate in a way that puts both their reputations on the line. This dual commitment of heavyweights is the "height of co-operation", and we should look into one example – the Marine Stewardship Council – in greater detail, because it contains a wealth of general learning points for business–NGO relations.

All this calls for careful mapping of the "territory", not necessarily a mapping of "institutional" and visible stakeholders.


## 8.2 MAPPING THE BATTLEFIELD

In the past, companies have usually been advised to "map" their stake-holders, using different criteria (for example, power or media leverage). Nowadays, as argued earlier, such an approach, coming from a stable world with known (and sometimes proxy) players, cannot be recommended. In today's world, attack (and support!) can come from anywhere (see Section 4.6).

The previous examples in this book – like many others – indicate that the "static" and general mapping of stakeholders does not make much sense. Therefore, the best course is to look at the issues that are high on the corporate radar screen. And one of the characteristics of an issue is (as argued earlier): who is opposed to or supportive of the company's position, how dedicated are they, and what resources and strategies do they have?

Indeed, as Tom Curtin also pointed out (in his book *Green Issues*, Macmillan Press, 2000), it is too simplistic to divide (with different shades of grey) stakeholders involved into a "for" vs. "against" situation. They come from very different angles and these need to be recognized:

- The "dependents" (for example, employees, suppliers) who have a definite interest in the issue or project and are likely to support the company.
- The "unknown", who mostly only become visible in the escalation of a conflict (for example, the local church supporting workers protesting a plant closure). Often the "unknown" have a history that makes certain behaviour probable or even predictable (for example, when the priest has been involved in several community conflicts).
- The "impacted", who might be positively affected, but also negatively, or both (for example, a worker might benefit from the better local labour market conditions if a plant is expanded, but all the additional traffic passes in front of her house). An often-made mistake is that the "impacted" are treated as enemies *per se*, which underestimates the "cross-pressure" people are often under (as the example of the worker above indicates). Often only specific features of a project or issue create opposition and can be settled by mitigation measures (for example, a company voluntarily committing itself to decreasing emissions even if the capacity of the plant is extended). This is the area of the NIMBY ("Not In My Back Yard!") syndrome, whereby people accept the need in general (for example, waste incinerators), but do not want them in their neighbourhood . . .,
- The "intractable" (as per Tom Curtin's classification) – those who oppose an issue in principle or for moral reasons (for example, opponents of GMOs) or they are so negatively offended that they will oppose with great dedication and energy.

However, with the exception of hard-line opposition, there is often the potential that support can be mobilized and people turned into "third-party advocates". Companies are often ambivalent because they cannot "control" these outsiders who might have other reasons to be supportive or do not speak the company language, etc. But the price that companies pay for only relying on internal resources is clear: often the conflict is perceived as the "organization against the rest of the world". Outsiders, who speak for themselves and independently have much more credibility than those who are expected to say certain things (the famous "They would say that, wouldn't they" syndrome).

### Bringing in third parties

In today's pluralistic, flexible world, nothing is certain, and this "third-party advocacy" sometimes brings together strange bedfellows. It is no longer any surprise that unions oppose companies on wage and internal issues, but support them in securing approval for investments, government subsidies, etc. And, as reported earlier, the fact that the car industry and environmentalists co-operate together to beat the oil industry might be surprising, but it has happened at the EU level (see Box 6-2). This is also another example that demonstrates that it is issues that matter – not the study of stakeholder maps.

Another frequent mistake in dealing with stakeholders – next to the inability or unwillingness to form alliances – is the attempt to convince the adversary, as Monsanto tried in its "dialogue phase". Once the battle is running, no dialogue with the adversary is possible – at best there can be truce negotiation if both sides are exhausted. The real target group for the debate is the observers, the bystanders, especially if they are opinion leaders or official decision-makers.

Just one example: a couple of years ago, the then Hoechst Company designed a chemical waste incinerator which, with its energy efficiency, low-emission standards and near invisibility, should have impressed environmentalists. Unfortunately, the management forgot to convince its own workforce, who were for other reasons in a bad mood and started to criticize the project in the (many) pubs around the huge factory. This had a negative influence on non-employee neighbours, who passed on their views to local politicians ... and so on. The project was "dead in the water".

As one manager learned, "Once you lose air supremacy over the 'Stammtisch', you are lost" (a note for the non-German reader: the "Stammtisch" – a table reserved for regular guests – plays an important role in forming public opinion because the people who sit at it check what they have heard or read and form their own opinion by discussion with their peers).

These considerations can be applied to the question about whether and how a company should co-operate with NGOs.

*net neutrality*

## Box 8-3   Cyber Activism and Hacktivism

Not only has the World Wide Web driven the globalization of markets and revolutionized the internal structure of companies – it has also helped to organize corporate opponents.

As Lynee Elvins from SustainAbility has observed: "For businesses, the Web was supposed to be the world's great tool – not a forum for its enemies. The Web was supposed to weld markets into one enormous worldwide trading floor, not organize thousands into picket lines." But indications abound that this is what is happening – at the same time, on the same server.

Since the early 1980s, skilful activists have developed independent computer networks as communication resources for NGOs, eventually merging them into the Association for Progressive Communication (APC), committed to using the Internet as a platform for communication and a strategic tool for the needs of the global civic society. The APC website offers a calendar of events, provides advice on how to build a website and effectively use e-mail.

And scholars have been able to mastermind the organization of mass demonstrations, from Seattle to Geneva. This would have been unthinkable if the Web's potential to communicate quickly to a great number of people had not been applied.

Even anarchists, notoriously hard to organize, use their own website (infoshop. org) to communicate with like-minded people. To guide interested surfers through increasingly crowded cyberspace, a special website (ethical-junction.org) gives advice to activists and consumers.

But alongside "cyber activism", there is "hacking". Since 1998, when the first "virtual sit-in" was organized by the Electronic Disturbance Theater with its Floodnet tool, more than 10,000 hacker attacks of a political nature are reported annually. These can take a wide range of forms – some aggressive, using a kind of electronic civil disobedience by breaking into government databases or corporate computer systems, or flooding them with requests so that their websites deny services.

Not only are companies affected, but also governments – for example, when hackers protested against the Mexican government for the treatment of Zapatistas. Sometimes the act is simply one of self-defence, such as in the case of the US toy retailer, eToys, when it tried to persuade US courts to withdraw the rights of the domain name of a European net-based art collective "e toy", even though the latter had been in existence for longer. A cyber war started, which observers called the Brent Spar of e-commerce. Finally, the mighty eToys dropped the case ("without prejudice", of course) and agreed to pay the small "e toy" court costs of approximately $40,000. However, in comparison with the dramatic drop in its share price, not only caused by the cyber war, this was a small amount!

Business with China attracted the activist group "Yellow Pages", which operates in North America and Europe fighting for human rights in China. The group attacks companies' networks – creating severe damage – in order to deter companies with high involvement in China, such as AT&T and Motorola, from investing further in that country.

This combination of hackers and activists is increasing.

## 8.3  PROBLEM-SOLVING CO-OPERATION: THE LESSONS FROM THE MARINE STEWARDSHIP COUNCIL

The overfishing of our seas is a typical example of what economists call "the Tragedy of the Commons" – a freely available, commercially exploitable natural resource that is soon overexploited and depleted.

Although everyone has seen the writing on the wall for some time, until 1996 when Unilever and the WWF got together nobody had any interest in addressing this problem. The only solution was through government regulation or the allocation of property rights – both of which mean putting a "price tag" on the resource.

National governments, however, used to fail miserably on global commons: they were also, in this case, more interested in getting the highest quotas for their heavily subsidized (national) fishing industries than ensuring sustainable fishing. The result, according to the UN's Food and Agriculture Organization (FAO), was that 70% of the world's commercial marine stock has either been fully fished, over-exploited, depleted or is only slowly recovering.

The inefficiency is huge: one-third of the world's total fish caught is classed as unwanted per catch (for example, sea turtles, marine mammals) and is simply discarded. Also, "fishing-down-the-food-chain" (for example, using sand eels for fish oil, thus diminishing the food base for commercially caught fish), is accelerating the downslide, leading to volatile price increases and the breakdown of century-old fishing communities.

Given this environment, in 1996 two leaders from very different "businesses" decided to tackle this pressing problem together. Unilever, a leading consumer goods manufacturer and the largest seller of frozen fish sticks in the world, and the World Wildlife Fund for Nature (WWF) decided to start the Marine Stewardship Council (MSC). Its goal was to establish a certification scheme for sustainable fishing.

### What Unilever and the WWF brought together

Unilever and the WWF had different goals for starting the MSC. For Unilever, it was a way of protecting market share and ensuring long-term survival. Moreover, the company expected some spill-over in goodwill/corporate citizenship among its consumers. For the WWF, the establishment of the MSC also implied entering new grounds. Michael Sutton, the WWF co-ordinator for the MSC, explained:

"We had to change the rules of the game. People had to come to us because they needed our competence and reputation, if they were looking for new ways of problem-solving and substitutes for reg-ulations. I believed that governments were not able to stop the overfishing. Therefore, we had to develop long-term solutions, which were environmentally necessary. The next step was to create economic incentives in order to make them politically feasible. One thing was certain: where industry and the market led, governments were likely to follow."

The key instruments for "sustainable fishing" should be a worldwide standard, which could be audited by independent certifiers. The logo or label should allow retailers and consumers to discriminate in their fish purchases, based on criteria indicating whether it has come from sustainable or unsustainable fisheries.

In February 1996, Unilever and the WWF set up a "joint working party" to fund the start-up of the MSC. In the summer of the following year, the organization had its own governance structure (under the UK's not-for-profit-foundation law), with an "Advisory Board" as the Democratic Chamber to include all stakeholders, and a standard council for all the technical discussions to define the certification process and the content (for example, the ecological criteria necessary for sustainable fishery) in order to grant – or deny – the logo.

## Managing stakeholders

The massive process of stakeholder consultation started around the world. However, some critics claimed that this came too late, only after the foundation of the MSC. Pilot projects tested the certification of fisheries – a scientific-based process that examined not only the details of data but also the social and political conditions to meet the three sustainability dimensions (or what some mockingly refer to as "the new holy trinity") of environmental, economic and social criteria. A critical bottleneck occurred regarding what auditors could really certify (for example, when a fish factory ship, which can easily catch

1,000 tonnes per day, catches in certificated and non-certificated fisheries during the same trip).

But the MSC not only needed to get it right professionally. Critics were many: on the one hand, there were befriended environmentalist groups of the WWF who refused to accept the MSC standard, because it was too weak under their own criteria or did not restrict the use of very large fishing trawlers. Greenpeace was the most significant opponent in this respect. And not everybody at the WWF was happy to team up with the "enemy" – Unilever – after so many clashes.

While establishing the MSC, the challenge for the WWF was to "keep the sandals" without moving too close to the "suits". After all, the WWF was an environmental NGO and their most important asset – their credibility – was on the line.

On the other hand, heavy opposition also came from the fishery industry associations, especially in the US, the UK and Norway, lambasting Unilever as "sleeping with the Greenies" (and, in the US, using WWF's Panda bear to draw similarities to the former "Soviet/Russian bear").

Attempts to abort the MSC were manifold, including charging the FAO to develop a logo of its own, or self-certification systems where everybody could declare themselves a member of the "Responsible Fishing Society". But in 2000 MSC was up and running and the first certifications were issued.

It was not easy either for the two partners, with different agendas, language and mindsets, to work together. Co-operation at the MSC did not stop campaigning on other issues. Unlike a corporation, the WWF does not (and does not want to) control all the activities of its national affiliates. So WWF USA had just started a campaign against large fishing trawlers, when WWF International was in a dialogue with the US fishing industry, trying to convince them to participate in the MSC effort.

Unilever often had the impression that they were left to "clean up the mess" the WWF left in industry. The WWF, on the other hand, wondered why Unilever moved so slowly on environmental issues (including GMOs). "Just look at the language," observed a key player, "business speaks about emerging markets, environmentalists of developing countries . . ."

### Key success factors

In the end, however, the "rocky path" could not stop the MSC. The factors for its "staying the course" were as follows:

- Shared and important interest between the founders. Unilever and WWF both saw the tragedy of the – global – commons strike in the fishery industry. As the largest producer of processed fish, Unilever would be hit hard by a collapse of fish supply, and the WWF knew that a recovery would take decades. Something needed to be done.
- CEO involvement and entrepreneurial implementers. On both sides, the CEOs were heavily involved and present, when needed. This gave the project a "political invincibility" against internal resistance. But equally important were the entrepreneurial implementers on both sides who understood how to drive the project through many difficult situations.
- "Big splash first", then build consensus. Although partly criticized, Unilever and the WWF did not build a consensus first, but decided to start, then involve other stakeholders and "sell the idea". Given the manifold resistance, both from the fishing industry and more fundamentalist environmental groups, the project would probably never have taken off. Innovation is a contradiction to consensus, because it always starts with minorities. But the effort to get many other interests on board needed to be made (and was done by the project management).
- Isolate the project from other conflicts. There was a mutual understanding – sometimes stretched to the limits – that the common project did not pre-empt or prevent controversy in other areas.
- But NGOs and industry cannot have the same agenda. Positioned in between, MSC has a sophisticated corporate governance structure that allows it to handle emerging conflicts between different interests

(even between different business interests; for example, retail versus fishing industry) and solely focuses on certification, so that other conflicts "don't rock the boat", even if organizations or persons clash who are important supporters of MSC.

- A win–win potential. Approximately 30% of the fish harvest is unwanted per catch (from sea turtles to small fish). Better, but not necessarily more expensive, fishing practices could reduce this number significantly. Adopting such practices would, over time, yield a higher volume than short-term overfishing and slow recovery.

- Instead of second-guessing the perfect methodology, readiness to experiment. To certify a fishery is truly entering into "uncharted water". Abstract discussions cannot lead to a tested and transparent methodology, but thoughtful and systematic experiments with professionals provided the insight, know-how and error corrections that were needed as part of an organized learning process. Now the methodology is largely unchallenged (though of course, not the practical application: so protested New Zealand's Royal Forest and Bird Protection Society against the certification of the New Zealand hoki fishery. The complaint was dealt with under the MSC rules).

- The measure of success – create an industry standard. Co-operation does not make much sense if it is limited to a niche, leaving unsustainable industry standards untouched. The real purpose is to shift the prevailing industry practice to a new level. MSC has focused on this by two means: lining up the demand side – in this case the big retailers – and creating a visible, easy-to-communicate differentiation (in this case a logo that differentiates the "sustainable" caught fish from the "non-sustainable" catch). This is creating a certain dilemma for the commercial innovator (in this case Unilever).

- Normally, you take the risks and make efforts to reap a specific benefit; for an industry standard, you have to invest – but your competitors benefit, too. However, if a higher standard means higher cost, it is vital for the innovator to move the in-dustry, otherwise he or she would suffer from competitive disadvantage.

It is not just in a responsive co-operation that you can be successful, but also – under specific conditions – it can be done in a confrontation. For the time being, the MSC is firmly established. But the jury is still out: in order to be effective it needs to become an industry standard – and four years later it has now just left the pilot phase of testing and training the certifiers. Despite celebrating its first victories, it has not yet won the war. In April 2001 the EU was forced to impose harsh fishing restrictions in its waters – there were no longer many fish to be caught!

## 8.4 EXXONMOBIL: ENJOY THE CONFRONTATION

In contrast to the responsible attitude of oil companies like Shell, or food multinationals like Unilever, is the stand of ExxonMobil, the world's largest oil company, after Exxon bought Mobil in 1999 and absorbed it (which was obviously an easier job than in other mergers, given their common roots in Rockefeller's Standard Oil).

If there is a corporate equivalent of the "axis of evil" for environmentalists, Exxon is part of it. The UK Friends of the Earth called Exxon's CEO Lee Raymond the "Darth Vader of Global Warming". The German environmental conservationist Group NABU declared him the "Dinosaur of the Year 2000". On many NGO web pages you can find long sin-lists of Exxon as "quite possibly the worst oil company in the world" (Friends of the Earth), touching upon nearly every country on the globe – about corruption in Kazakhstan (*Wall Street Journal*), oil spills in rainforests, plans for extracting oil shale on or near the Great Barrier Reef World Heritage area, or the two hundred violations of environmental laws in the USA (*Ends Report*) for which Exxon was fined up to $4.7 million. Not to mention the *Exxon Valdez* oil spill in Alaska, for which the company has already paid approximately $3.5 billion – and for which court cases are still pending.

## Involvement in Indonesia

What could evolve into the equivalent "pressure cooker" of Shell's Nigeria experience, Exxon critics claim (and obviously hope), is its involvement in Indonesia, in the civil war-torn area of situated in the north of Aceh.

The former Mobil gas field in Aceh (Sumatra Island) was once a "crown jewel", providing nearly a quarter of Indonesia's revenues in the early 1990s. Now it is caught at the centre of a secessionist conflict that is increasingly bloody and has cost uncertain numbers of lives of Mobil employees, civilians, guerrillas of the Free Aceh Movement and soldiers – not to mention countless production interruptions. Although ExxonMobil does not release figures on individual fields, Aceh is certainly now more of a liability.

When the *Wall Street Journal* first covered this case in a front page story on 7 September 2001, it became pretty clear that ExxonMobil now had to pay the price for its close relationship with former President Suharto and his family and proxies. Although, since 1971, Mobil had tried to support the local workforce and population with schools and housing, it is obvious that this was perceived as "peanuts" in relation to the huge sums that go directly to Jakarta – and straight into pockets, difficult to track.

Worse for ExxonMobil is the fact that (armed) security is provided by the Indonesian army, known to the broader Western public for its atrocities in East Timor. The facts as to who started what violence when are always fiercely contested. The guerrillas deny, for example, any involvement in the shooting of two (unarmed) Mobil security guards, claiming that the army is only looking for reasons to go after the guerrillas. The civil population suffers most, with reports by human rights groups that rapes, torture, even massacring of civilians are on the rise.

But the military received most of the blame: recently an Acehnese court convicted 24 soldiers of massacring 57 villagers. Although Exxon-Mobil offered shelter for civilians and their property, the *Wall Street*

*Journal* observed: "The refugees expressed an intense hatred not only of the armed forces, but in many cases of Mobil, too."

Since then, the gas field has had to be shut down several times, and Exxon is a permanent object of demonstrations, attacks and a permanent target for additional negative press coverage, especially in the Asian media.

### Fighting against the tide

But what environmentalists are really up in arms about is Exxon's stand on global warming. In addition, many NGOs are suspicious that campaign donations from the Texas-based multi would have played a part in influencing the Bush administration's opposition to the Kyoto Protocol

The UK is currently at the centre of the "Stop Esso" campaign (Esso is the European brand of Exxon), with a campaign coalition being formed by Greenpeace and Friends of the Earth. Greenpeace activists interrupted the operation of the UK distribution centre in July 2001, whereas demonstrators took to the streets on 1 December 2001, distributing leaflets and displaying protest banners at more than 300 petrol stations throughout the UK.

In the US, Pressure Point, a Seattle-based NGO, is coordinating the protest and has demonstrated at Exxon's Annual Shareholder Meeting in 2001, including displaying a banner during Lee Raymond's speech. Resolutions for the General Assembly to stop Arctic drilling and move into renewables received close to 10% of the shareholders' votes, while 13% agreed to an equal employment opportunities resolution. Probably both votes are below the threshold for Exxon's top management to consider major shifts in policy.

And Exxon's response to the outside pressure? In my view, they enjoy the fight, because it sharpens the sense of self-confidence and gives a mission to be fulfilled: the defenders of prudent science versus the "stampede of public opinion", misled by "extreme activist groups who choose to demonize society's use of fossil fuels".

One cannot help it, but this is the impression given, when one analyses Exxon's (public) documents or talks to its executives. Admitting that such a position is not always comfortable, Rene Dahan, Executive Vice President, claims: "Comfort is not on our menu when we determine what we believe in and decide to speak up" (Exxon's web site: www.exxon.com).

### Self-confidence or arrogance?

The drivers of this self-confidence (what opponents call "arrogance" – for example, when Exxon lawyers in court openly label requirements by regulatory agencies as "meddlesome") are manifold. In our analysis, the following factors play a role:

- An optimistic view of science and the answers science can give (of course, only prudent, rigorous science, understandable by those who bring a "basic level of scientific competence" to the table). Contrary to other oil companies, Exxon has, since the early 1980s, an in-house competence on climate that has shaped the internal decision-making process. Confident that they always have the best scientist in their labs, it doesn't matter that the scientific mainstream is moving in the opposite direction.
- The performance track record. Exxon is definitely an extremely successful company financially, with a lot of professional and technological competence. Its highly structured and disciplined management systems are tailored in the environmental, health and safety area (called Operations Integrity Management System) to achieve "consistent, reliable and incident-free results". Indeed, opponents will be hard-pressed to make the case that operational, environmental performance indicators on Exxon's platforms, in refineries or chemical plants are less than in the industry's top 25% range.
- A knack for "shareholder value". This does not allow for long-term investment – for example, in renewables, as long as they are niche markets – plus the confidence of always being cash-rich enough to

buy into these areas once they have picked up, and to have the scientific competence to bring enough technology quickly to the selected markets and keep up with the competition (Exxon's strategy in fuel cells is an example of this attitude).

- Last but not least, a greater, cultured homogeneity in Exxon's top management (as an insider described it, "church-going, button-down, Republican blue-blazer, conservative and mid-Western – probably only Mormons have values to match Exxon's culture today"), combined with a more centralized company. Although BP and Shell put an end to the country–global matrix organization, and centre around global product lines, they are still miles apart from Exxon's headquarter-driven, more centralized organization (although it is said that this has also loosened up a bit as a result of Mobil's integration and the sheer size that comes with that). The Exxon arguments probably are welcomed in the main street in Texas (and especially in Irvine). So, peer pressure – relative to intellectually more fluid capitals like London – is smaller on the top team, not to mention the consensus-building attitude that shapes Dutch behaviour.

How long can Exxon withstand the NGO pressure? The gap between the European oil companies and Exxon in public opinion polls becomes visible, but does it matter who is more likeable? Excluding a major policy shift in the US and a dramatic erosion of its profitability, my hunch is: a long time. Although Shell's Stuart Moody says, "a tobacco industry-like reluctance to admit the possibility of global warming", the analysis tells us that Exxon will continue to "speak up based on our experience and knowledge of science, technology and economics." And it has banned the words "sustainable development" from its corporate language as long as it does not feel a commercial pressure to change its behaviour and fundamental attitude. And this is not on the cards just yet – despite the many actions against the company. However, such a "war of attrition" is not without longer term risk for the brand. Coca-Cola once thought that it too was invincible.

But we have argued throughout this book that there is not a "right" position – it is fair to state that Exxon's anchoring in the US market and policy, its core values and tradition, its attitude and argumentation reflect this condition and are consistently communicated and implemented.

In the final chapter, we will pull the learning from the previous chapters together in three more extended case studies, which are written under specific criteria: development over time, processes needed and issues to be managed.

# Learning from Three Reference Examples

# 9

In this chapter, three in-depth case studies about Corporate Diplomacy are examined: ABB, describing the evolution of its sustainable strategy; DaimlerChrysler, looking mainly at the processes needed; and Shell, reviewing the issues that needed to be covered.

## 9.1  ABB: FROM CLEANING UP TO PIONEERING CORPORATE SOCIAL POLICY

Sometimes personal experience helps. Jörgen Centerman, CEO of ABB up to August 2002, remembers vividly the time when he was at the centre of a public outrage. In Sweden in 1987, he had just been named responsible for ABB's Swedish automation business. Under his supervision was an electronics factory that still cleaned printed circuit boards with a fluid that released CFCs. The emissions contributed to ozone layer depletion and global warming. A task force was set up and presented a new solution: soap and water! "We were challenged and we changed," said Centerman.

Percy Barnevik, who was the legendary architect of the 1987 merger between Swedish ASEA and Swiss BBC and builder of the world-class electrical engineering giant (a success story that is taught as a case study in business schools across the world), had another reason to drive ABB toward environmental excellence: for him it had a compelling business logic.

His successor Göran Lindahl saw the necessity for global companies like ABB, doing business in more than 100 countries and with more than a quarter of its revenues and workforce in developing countries, to "put a human face to globalization", and added the social dimension to the environmental dimension.

Put together three CEOs with different personalities, leadership styles and motivations, yet a shared business case for Sustainable Development, plus a fast-driving company with a thirst for excellence and you get within a decade a dynamic that catapults you into the leading position in your industry (if the Dow Jones Sustainability Group Index is any indicator).

### Getting started

The beginning at ABB was modest. After the merger and the rapid globalization process, consideration to strengthen the Corporate Environmental Function started in the early 1990s, without any visible pressure (for example, a crisis or a business unit in jeopardy). In 1992 ABB signed the environmental Business Charter for Sustainable Development of the International Chamber of Commerce and took the Charter's 16 principles as its environmental policy – the benchmark against which ABB reports progress.

It set up the Corporate Staff for Environmental Affairs, which never had more than three to four full-time employees, and the Environmental Advisory Board was formed (with Stephan Schmidheiny, a major ABB shareholder, as its most prominent member).

Getting the house in order was the first job. In addition, life cycle assessments were performed for all its products, because ABB was convinced that the environmental impact of its products was greater than any similar production process (for example, a 1% improvement in the energy efficiency of an electric motor for industrial use generated more than 30 times the savings in energy needed for its production throughout the complete value chain).

The environmental organization was closely aligned with the ABB organization in general: local environmental controllers were appointed at every site, for every country a country environmental controller and – reflecting the matrix structure – each business area had its own environmental controller, too. Altogether, approximately 600 people were at least part-time on duty as environmental professionals. But this was just the tip of the iceberg – raising the company's environmental performance was every leader's duty and was integrated into business-planning and operation.

The headquarter staff were few, but powerful. Up to 2001 they were headed by Jan Strömblad who had earned his reputation before in very senior operational and manufacturing positions. The Swedish engineer had a reputation for straight-talking and getting things done. "Jan knows ABB so well," one country controller said with a sigh, "there is no place to hide. He seems to smell non-performers around the globe – and then he is in your office. So you had better get your homework done."

As an example of "lean environmental management", instead of writing lengthy corporate manuals, the decision was taken to expect every site to be certified as satisfying ISO 14001. Together with a pilot phase in 1995, a "train-the-trainer" programme was started to develop the necessary internal audit competence. Similar to the way that Life Cycle Assessments (LCAs) form the basis for environmental declarations about products, an environmental design software tool was offered to all business units.

In 1996, 50 sites were ISO 14001 certified globally by one centrally chosen certification company (one site was even in China). In 1997 the number jumped to 123 and in 1998 to 449 sites in 32 countries. In 1999, 96% of all sites (535 altogether) in 49 countries were certified (and in between, the railroad and power divisions were sold off and new plants – for example, in automation – came on board, so that the number of certified sites "bred by ABB" is probably above 600 – but, given the dramatic change in the portfolio of businesses, it will be almost impossible to reach exactly 100%).

However, environmental management systems are only tools to reach goals. These environmental goals were first formulated in 1995, with a second generation introduced in 1997 – all were reached by

2000. Now ABB reports on 39 operational performance indicators, from energy use to nonylphenolethoxylate (a de-greasing agent).

## The Bakun Dam – a defining moment for ABB

Just as progress toward world-class environmental performance was smoothly running its course, the Bakun controversy hit. In early 1996 the ABB-led consortia won the bid for constructing the Bakun Hydro Power Dam, whose 2,600-MW turbines were to produce 15% of Malaysia's energy, transported by a 1,300-km cable from Borneo to the Malaysian peninsula. Costing US$5 billion, it was ABB's largest project ever.

However, in September 1996, 205 NGOs – among them Greenpeace, Friends of the Earth, the International River Network, the Rainforest Action Network, the Berne Declaration – quickly followed by 35 members of the European Parliament wrote to ABB to request that it withdraw from the project, because it was "dumping an outdated, inefficient, uneconomic and environmental and social destructive technology" on the Malaysian people and displacing 10,000 indigenous people from sacred ancient ground.

Whereas the protest in Asia was limited – except for a brief occupation of one of ABB's offices – in Sweden and Switzerland, its home countries, ABB found itself at the centre of a storm of criticism, including the Protestant Bishop of Sweden. Percy Barnevik, the celebrated "Jack Welch of Europe", was personally criticized. Pressure was also exerted on two prominent members of the Environmental Advisory Board, Stephan Schmidheiny and Martin Holdgate, a prominent British conservationist.

It helped little for ABB to point out that the dam was an energy policy decision by the Malaysian government and that it would conduct the construction in the least harmful way (for example, certifying the construction site according to ISO 14001). The protesters attempted to link deficits in the process to ABB (for example, the environmental impact assessment or the peculiarities of Malaysian politics – the Chief Minister of Sarawak is the largest shareholder in a Malaysian company that would benefit not only from the construction but also from the concessions).

In the aftermath, the opponents admitted that they had chosen ABB as the "soft spot" – no other player had such a global, visible brand or was so vulnerable in its reputation. On further investigation, it became evident that the biggest environmental risk was not the dam itself, but new access to so-far-untouched rainforest for logging and potentially even palm oil plantations, which could also lead to earlier sedimentation of the dam basin.

Despite the protest and a lot of political and legal manoeuvring, construction of a tunnel to divert the river commenced in May 1997. However, the project was halted in September – not for environmental reasons, but because the Asian Economic Crisis had altered the investment landscape dramatically.

### Continue the dialogue

ABB continued the dialogue with NGOs and contributed to efforts by the World Bank and the semi-governmental International Union for the Conservation of Nature (IUCN) to develop some clear rules and criteria for large dams. The World Commission on Dams (WCD) was founded with the respected South African Minister of Agriculture and Water, Professor Kadar Asmal as Chairman. Göran Lindahl, ABB's CEO, served as the only representative from the industry on that Commission (all others were either from NGOs, water regulators or academics) and ABB supported the work of the WCD through fund-raising efforts in industry (although most of the funds were from public sources). In November 2000 the WCD presented its report. Although the WCD included some outspoken critics of dams as well as supporters, the Commission came to a unanimous conclusion, because they focused on clear rules for the development of dams and defined a transparent, multi-stakeholder process with operational standards (for example, involvement of all parties concerned, review of alternatives, environmental and social impact assessment, compensation for displaced people). It is expected that this report will be used by international development and finance organizations (for example, World Bank, UNDP) as well as private financiers as a benchmark for future large dam projects to live up to.

## Moving toward sustainable development

Within ABB, the Bakun experience accelerated the development of a broader perspective. Not that the environmental dimension became unimportant. This is an ongoing activity driven by ambitious goals, covering more and more main product lines with environmental product declarations (and commitments to further reduce energy use and environmental impact), reduction of ABB's own greenhouse gas emissions by 1% per year and so on. But the social dimension was added to in various ways.

First, the sharing of technology received greater attention. The expression "sharing" was deliberately preferred over that of "transfer". Through its tremendous investment in developing countries, where every unit has access to ABB's global technology base, its wide range of co-operation with academia and government institutions (for example, the China Energy Technology Program), which in turn influenced technology development and the use of modern technology in developing countries, was much more an interactive process than a one-way flow. Second, its involvement in multilateral and private initiatives was stepped up (for example, WBCSD, WCD, UN Global Compact, etc.)

The "role model" for these kinds of efforts was the voluntary Greenhouse Gas Reduction Project, which ABB's CEO initiated at the World Energy Congress in 1998. Pushed by ABB's funds and man-hours, a database was set up in collaboration with the World Energy Council (WEC). It was to set an example (or even better, hundreds of examples) as to how, with new technologies, smart planning and dedication, greenhouse gases could be curbed in industry by 1 gt per annum by 2005.

The database documents more than 500 different projects (approximately 100 in developing countries) in 80 countries and calculates greenhouse gas reduction according to standardized methodology. The possible aggregate reduction already stands at above the target of 1 gt, so the target has been recently raised to 2 gt per annum by 2005. But the real challenge now is to raise public awareness about what is achievable, and to push other sectors (for example, agriculture, transportation, construction) to set similar goals. However, ABB executives admit privately that these kinds of collective initiatives are a heavy burden on ABB managers' time – especially when the UN is involved, since co-ordination and consensus-building are very laborious.

So, why is ABB doing this? The answer is not clear-cut. In one way, it is a feeling of responsibility, values and necessity to contribute to the common good. These views are widely shared not only in the top leadership but also among many managers, especially those from northern Europe. Additionally, the "carbon-restrained world" offered huge business opportunities for ABB – once it had shed the nuclear and large power plant business – in electricity generation and energy supply. ABB now focuses on regenerative energies (for example, with technological breakthroughs in wind energy, where the "Windformer" eliminated gear boxes and transformers in wind turbines, leading to higher energy efficiency and an approximate 20% cost reduction), micro-turbines and fuel cells for a much more decentralized (and therefore less capital-intensive) supply of heat and electricity, and its low-loss power transmission cable, to name but a few examples.

## Pioneering corporate social policy

The social dimension is mainly about the working conditions and its contribution to communities in the various locations throughout the world that ABB employs people. If global environmental standards are sometimes difficult to implement, they are dwarfed by the huge differences in social dimensions.

Some of these differences are due to the wide gap in economic development, reflected in different per capita income and thus different wages. Others are due to differences in political systems, culture, religion, family structures, etc. To get to grips with this complex task, ABB conducted case studies on the social dimensions of its activities in Brazil, China, Egypt, Poland, South Africa, Switzerland and the UK.

Local teams, supported by a local social scientist, were asked to write case studies that listed all social impacts, community activities, voluntary services or benefits to workers, etc. (Details are published in ABB's 2000 Sustainability Report.) The cases were reviewed by an internal corporate group and the (external) Advisory Board.

The case studies yielded a variety of activities that were sometimes more than imaginative: in Egypt, support for a Mecca pilgrimage was regarded as an important benefit; in Brazil it was education for children in slums – to give an example that shows ABB is tackling the North–South divide.

ABB used a "pyramid" model to cluster the different activities and make sense of the wide range of activities (see Figure 9.1).

As it turned out, there were only a few philanthropic initiatives for good causes and charity, most of them carried out by employees themselves. Many social activities were business-driven, combining employee motivation and retention through education and development, improving complementary services and operational requirements in the community, so that both sides benefit (the "win–win" situation). But many initiatives go beyond a defined business relationship and are classified as long-term social investments. Improving the local educational system (as compared with investing in the "human capital" of employees directly) is the most visible example.

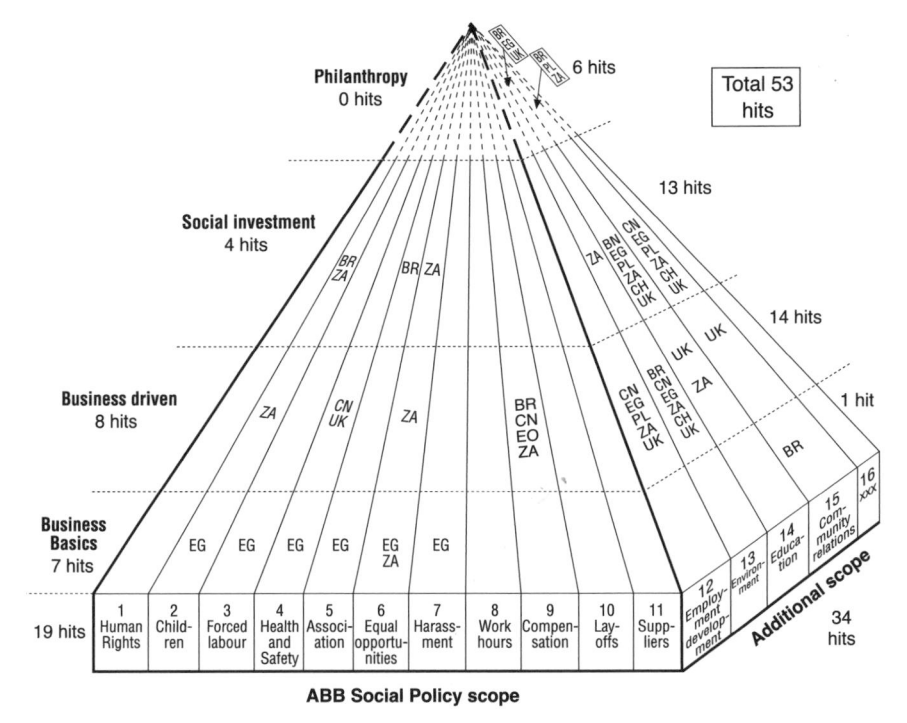

**Figure 9.1** ABB's social policy (reproduced by permission of ABB).

## Where to set priorities?

Some deficiencies were identified: systematic interactions with stakeholders were often lacking, running the risk that important shifts in the broader market, business environment and technology development could well be missed. Other cases revealed insufficient salaries and social welfare for unskilled workers and a lack of appropriate mechanisms to deal with long working hours in certain business situations.

ABB drew two conclusions from these case studies: first, to formulate a corporate social policy and, second, to intensify stakeholder dialogue. To formulate a social policy that is applicable in over 100 countries, yet satisfies each individual country, seems to be a job too far. "What leads you into a US jail for not having done something, brings you into a Malaysian prison for trying," remarked an ABB executive.

The potential conflicts are too great to be enumerated. Here are just a couple for starters: non-discrimination of gender and sexual orientation as part of equality of opportunity seems a "no-brainer" in developed countries. However, the Islamic religion does not tolerate homosexuality (often it is also legally forbidden) and in many Islamic countries there are cultural and legal restrictions on the employment of women. Elsewhere, to "join trade unions of their choice" is not an easy task (for example, in Argentina only one union per branch of work is legally accepted). Nor is it easy to talk about collective bargaining in dictatorships or autocratic regimes.

In Thailand, education ends at 12 years of age, which falls three years short of the "official" ILO entrance age for employment. And the controversy about human rights in China needs no further explanation. An earlier draft – to add an ironic twist – contained a firm commitment to limiting work to 48 hours per week – but it was unclear whether this also applied to ABB's senior executives ...

The way out was to formulate a social policy in just those areas that ABB can exert direct influence (all the above examples are from this area), either in its own operation or along the supply chain. International treaties can also help to establish a "base line".

The most important thing for ABB was to position social policy as a starting point for a stakeholder dialogue, commit to continuous improvements and develop a set of key social performance indicators, against which progress could be reported (ABB's social policy is also documented in the Sustainability Report 2000).

In early 2001 a pilot project in which 40 countries had participated was commenced, with a view to conducting stakeholder dialogue, mainly on social policy. NGOs, unions, (local) officials, customers, etc. were invited and partly surprised about ABB's proactive dynamic. It is too early to anticipate where this stakeholder dialogue will eventually lead – except that it will increase the pressure for implementation. But the "early wins" were encouraging: it supports business development and helps to recruit and retain motivated employees.

### Is ABB's development typical?

ABB's journey along the path toward higher sustainability has been told here because it contains several "typical" ingredients that are needed in order to ensure progress:

- A strong commitment from top management, in line with shared values and a supporting culture.
- The ability to professionally implement an ambitious but realistic policy, supported by efficient management systems and reporting transparency.
- The ability to creatively build a business case for sustainable development in the operational business – and control the results.

But it is clear that every company has its own specific history, its way of doing things and its obstacles to deal with. As in nature, the variety is overwhelming – but there is a pattern.

## 9.2 DAIMLERCHRYSLER: RESPONSIVENESS AND DETERMINATION

Christoph Walther, Head of Communication at DaimlerChrysler, expounds: "The key to success when dealing with a broad range of stakeholders lays in managing a double tension: first, to have a set of clear messages on issues and on your corporate values, but to be responsive to the questions with which you are confronted, and secondly, to decentralize all stakeholder activities as far as possible, but make sure that all who are communicating externally use the same song book."

At the company's 2001 General Assembly, clearly the disappointment with the share price was at the top of the agenda. But, as on similar occasions, pressure groups used the platform to voice their concern: DaimlerChrysler's "Dodge" supports bullfights in Mexico; there are no female managers in top positions; DaimlerChrysler subsidiaries are still producing landmines, etc. One seasoned journalist commented: "In comparison to other controversies, for example, those faced by the oil companies, this is really peanuts." But it should be stressed that to achieve these results more efforts than "peanuts" are needed.

Automotive engineers, who dominate the management of Daimler-Chrysler, are known for their systematic approach, analytical skills, persistence and attention to detail. You can observe this sort of culture wherever you look at management of the business environment.

Since November 1998, after the merger euphoria faded and now exacerbated by heavy losses in the Chrysler Group and Freightliner, DaimlerChrysler came under criticism by financial analysts due to an underperforming share price. But otherwise you have to go back many years to find DaimlerChrysler in negative headlines: being the first to implement a new, but controversial law for sick payment brought massive protests from the metal-workers' union, workers' council and ordinary employees. Discovering that (at that time) Daimler–Benz were pretty much alone in doing this in German industry, the CEO Jürgen Schrempp backed off and negotiated a solution with the workers' council.

### Successful crisis management

The "moose test", an extreme and controversial test by a Swedish journalist in autumn 1997, toppled the newly launched "A-Class" car and was brought to a "happy end" with an apology and costly measures to resolve the problem. It now serves as a good example for crisis management. Apart from this and despite the dissatisfied financial community, DaimlerChrysler enjoyed years of positive media coverage.

This had not always been the case: in 1991 the new Mercedes S-Class was the focus of a broad coalition of critics as being an irresponsible product, neglecting environmental concerns and resource conservation, and increasing traffic jams due to its sheer size. Greenpeace staged a major demonstration at the door of the Frankfurt Automotive Fair, piling up all the barrels of oil that an S-Class car would consume during its life cycle. After the unsuccessful, but ambitious strategy to transform the car company into a technology concern, Daimler–Benz, like the S-Class, were considered the dinosaurs of German industry.

Chrysler was faced with another situation with regard to its business environment, different from that of the high-profile Daimler–Benz subsidiary. Being the smallest of the "Big 3" in Detroit, Chrysler tended more to follow the industry mainstream and was less visible – and risk-exposed – than were the more global General Motors and Ford. But, it had a long tradition in promoting diversity and minority business as well as a more philanthropic fund that was based on the philosophy of "hands-up not hand-outs" for community and cultural initiatives.

Surely, the successful economic turnaround since 1991 for Chrysler and since 1995 for Daimler–Benz laid new ground work. "Only an economically successful company can be a good corporate citizen environmentally and socially," is one of the strong beliefs of Jürgen Schrempp, DaimlerChrysler CEO, in this regard. But even with economic success, the rest does not fall into place ... It all starts with a broader analysis of stakeholder expectations and trend evaluation.

"The Corporate Communication Group is one of the truly merged parts of the company, and the issue management process is driven from Auburn Hills globally," explained Terri Houtman, Director Global Communications Strategy.

### Detect the pattern

The system is based on the assumption that there is a pattern in the dynamic of issues and that you can detect it early. You then have to respond differently, depending on how the escalation has worked out (see Figure 9.2). Therefore, extensive scanning of leading media companies in Europe and the US (approximately 60, plus their online offspring), based on a set of criteria, is an ongoing activity. In addition,

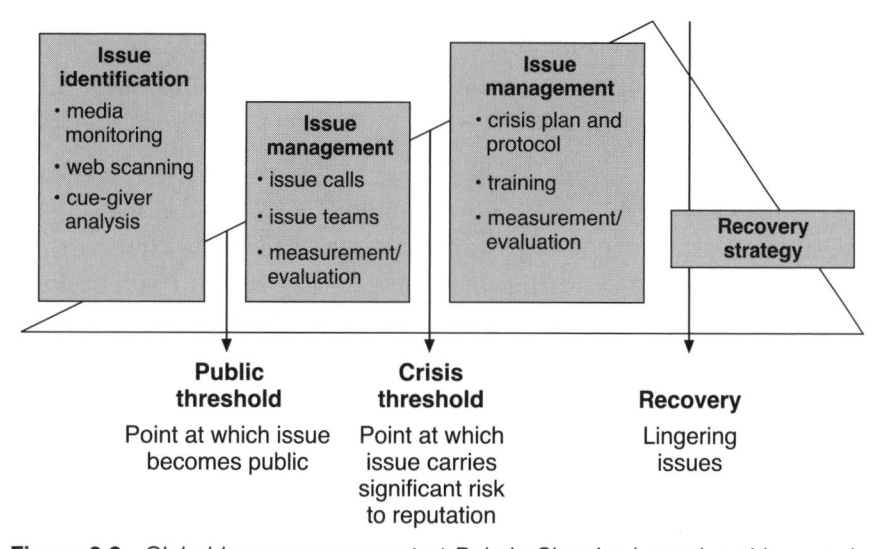

**Figure 9.2** Global issue management at DaimlerChrysler (reproduced by permission of DaimlerChrysler Corporation).

relevant chat rooms are visited – the themes raised there often serve as an early warning system too. From this regular scanning, a list of pertinent issues is developed weekly, covering issues ranging from product-related (for example, a recall), corporate themes (for example, financial reports) to general, political, social or environmental trends relevant to DaimlerChrysler.

On these issues, a large number of communications professionals and other observers provide their input weekly, and at the end of the week the CEO and the management board receive a "key issue briefing" of not more than three pages.

"The CEO and his team should never be surprised by media reports – he should know before," Terri Houtman defined the goal of this process. The amount of processed information should not be underestimated: 20,000 quotes on DaimlerChrysler per month is not extraordinary, as Michael Kuhn, Head of Media Monitoring, observed. Sophisticated IT equipment in the "war room" makes this possible. Financial analysts increasingly dominate the reports in business newspapers with their quotes, whereas environmental and social issues are driven by NGO activities. And through the online editions there are no longer "deadlines as in the good old days – the print media's race for the 'hottest' information is a permanent one."

## Matching internal and external expertise

But to understand, evaluate and privatize the input from the external world, you need in-house competence that can process the information, make sense out of it and put it into a framework that allows management conclusions for strategy, products and organization. At Daimler-Chrysler, an interdisciplinary internal research group "Society and Technology" is fulfilling this role. Based in Berlin, Palo Alto and Kyoto, the research group focuses on the future-oriented identification of societal "needs", using scenarios to understand upcoming "bottlenecks" and to complement market research with a better understanding of context factors (for example, ageing), trends (for example, multicultural societies), individuality and environmental values (for example, leisure time).

This work complements the existing research and technology departments, so that newly developed technology can address these needs and issues and contribute to the solution of problems (see Figure 9.2 for the basic process).

With its approximately 25 multi-disciplinary teams, however, it is not only shaping new technologies in the DaimlerChrysler Group. An important product is the annual "Delta Report", which documents research into the socio-economic environment as a basis for decision-making in all business units.

It is heavily used in the annual planning process, called "strategic-economic discussions". In addition, the group supports the innovation process and internal organizational learning with "laboratories of the future", where decision-makers from all disciplines learn to understand the complexity of the business environment, conflicting views and expectations – and test the available contributions in different scenarios (the group is known in the scientific communities for its competence in scenario technique and methodology in technology assessment).

Commented Eckhard Minx, head of the "Society and Technology" group: "But next to an intensive communication with our internal stakeholders, where we have to constantly prove the benefit we bring to the company in various inputs and projects, it is key to have a wide network in all walks of life, and even to deal sometimes with seemingly obtrusive ideas. But never forget: all of the powerful ideas which rule today's world were developed yesterday in a minority opinion. With this sensitivity, we cannot foresee the future, but we can better prepare for the uncertainties to come."

### From information to action

To monitor information is one thing, to act on it is another. When one issue is identified (for example, the Kerkonian legal attack against the merger in late 2000), a master plan is developed. In the case of issues that are expected to be around for a longer period of time (for example, slave labour compensation payments for slave labour in Nazi camps), an IT-based platform is the focal point of all activities.

All members of the project team centring around this issue have to report their activities and observations so that everybody has access to "up-to-the-minute" information and an understanding of the direction. If needed, a "dark website" is developed in advance and brought online when a broader audience needs to be informed immediately.

The underlying infrastructure for all these activities is the "Global News Bureau" where all DaimlerChrysler results and positions on specific issues are documented. Only internal PR people have access to this database – but every senior manager is obliged to consult his or her related PR staff and be coached on the relevant issues before an interview. "This gives real power to the PR function," observed Marc Lemcke, DaimlerChrysler's communication controller. "Nobody can ignore them and you hear a consistent message from DaimlerChrysler around the world." And consistency is one of the key ingredients for credibility. The Global News Bureau also integrates the different communication units that either focus on a brand, a subsidiary (for example, DaimlerChrysler Services) or corporate issues.

## Positive rulings

The success of these efforts are visible in many image studies around the world, and all results are published on the corporate website. In the *Wall Street Journal*'s Global Corporate Reputation Survey 2000, measuring everything from products to financial solidity to environmental policies, DaimlerChrysler came 11th overall, but was the best automotive company (General Motors came 17th; Ford, suffering from the tyre recall, came in 38th; Honda and Toyota are ranked in-between them). In the corporate responsibility section, DaimlerChrysler ranked 8th. In the *Financial Times* rating of the "World's Most Respected Companies", DaimlerChrysler came in overall as 12th, but as best German, second-best European and second-best car manufacturer.

One might argue that such feedback instruments as image analyses matter little when it comes to sales, where product features and price matter. But Wolfgang Inhester, director of Mercedes' press office, disagrees with this view: "The corporate image is a very decisive factor in whether or not potential customers will buy their vehicles from DaimlerChrysler or from a competitor – after all, you want to earn respect from your family and friends with your purchase – not disdain."

Based on this common framework, the brands and subsidiaries focus on their own tasks. But it is important that "for every new model launched, you review the social and ecological framework as a communicative bed in which you place the car," notes Inhester. And great efforts are undertaken to link brand values to corporate messages globally in all their facets. Leading innovation in safety easily relates to responsibility; quality has a strong environmental dimension. And design depends on the mood and values of the time, reflecting whether the company is attuned to the development of society – or not.

This applies to every brand DaimlerChrysler owns. The logic beyond this is that a tarnished corporate image can easily spoil the product brands – and vice versa. So if something goes wrong (and in a global company it is nearly impossible for nothing to go wrong ...), it is important to contain the damage in the first place. If, for example, DaimlerChrysler's former subsidiary Adtranz had quality problems with its tilting trains, this should not reflect on the car brands. Especially if certain issues "smoulder" for a longer time (for example, in the case of the economic difficulties at the Chrysler Group), it is important to prevent contagion. But everybody understands that this is in the long run (and in today's world this means six to nine months) not possible, unless the business unit fixes the problem rapidly – be it technical (for example, as with the A-Class), economic (for example, Chrysler) or in other important stakeholder areas (for example, slave labour).

### Who is an important stakeholder?

Two stakeholder groups are currently of special importance – the work-force and investment communities. Whereas the US media jumped enthusiastically at the chance of "German-bashing" – when economic problems hit Chrysler – the European media like to ridicule the quality of Chrysler cars. To prevent a deep division between "them" and "us", internal communication has become even more important. "Our DaimlerChrysler Business TV has clearly helped to create a shared understanding of us as a global company," noted Ulrike Becker, Director for Internal Communications. She has built a system of communication channels, aimed at specific target groups and time-frames. Whereas DaimlerChrysler Business TV is most attuned to actual events, the annual employee journal (also for company pensioners) wraps up the year and provides educational information in an entertaining manner. "Credibility, relevant, topical. These are the three ingredients which you must ensure are heard by your own people, not only in times like this."

But the toughest communication job currently falls probably to Elisabeth Wade, Head of Investor Relations. Following initial enthusiastic praise for the merger, it fell out of favour when the first bumps in the road were felt and the stock price remained static. The public investment community is shaped by hundreds of financial analysts, all competing for prominence and advertising their advice. "A common rule for analysts and journalists is: they write you down as long as they have written you up," commented an experienced observer of cyclical tendencies. Elisabeth Wade, being a former investment banker herself, sees only one way out: "We have to cut through the noise and speak to the investors themselves."

Having established a process to do this, top management can bypass middle-men and outside advisors, creating space for face-to-face meetings with institutional investors, major shareholders and rating agencies. "These tougher times are a learning process for all involved. It forces us to be meaningful, consistent, timely and systematic in addressing our shareholders." But there are, too, important audiences beyond the stock market.

A special unit copes with non-brand-specific corporate themes and sponsoring. They maintain good relations with environmental groups or NGOs, and conduct regular dialogue. Sponsoring has a philanthropic dimension, which builds mainly on the Chrysler tradition of community involvement and promoting opportunities for minorities and disadvantaged people. To be credible, you have to do it inside and outside the company. Senior executives serve therefore as sponsors of internal interest groups (for example, Afro-Americans), and purchasing rules ease access for small- and medium-sized businesses, especially when these are owned by minorities. As everybody could imagine, this was especially tough when Chrysler hit a downturn. So, by adhering to their values in tough times, their credibility increases, acting as a buffer when everything is not perfect.

## Beyond philanthropy

In addition, the DaimlerChrysler Corporation recently concluded an agreement with labor representatives to promote the employment of women and remove barriers to their career development. Continuing along these lines, in 2000 the DaimlerChrysler Fund sponsored, for an amount of US$32 million, a wide variety of education, community development and cultural groups across the world – from the Society of Women Engineers in Michigan, Nelson Mandela's Children's Charity fund to the Charities Aid Foundation in the UK. In Germany, the Daimler–Benz Foundation, founded on the 100th anniversary of the company, has become an innovative sponsor of interdisciplinary, cutting-edge research, centred around the theme "man – technology – environment".

Beyond the philanthropic dimension, corporate-sponsoring is also related to leveraging DaimlerChrysler's core competence for the solution of ecological, social and scientific problems. Uli Kostenbader, Head of Corporate Sponsoring, has therefore set up projects that relate to the key corporate goals and help to establish the image of a "troubleshooter": for example, satellites from the aerospace division collect data for an environmental project, researchers in sophisticated transportation simulation models receive support from DaimlerChrysler engineers, as do road safety education programmes.

In addition, corporate-sponsoring has enabled the building of platforms for communication with a wide variety of opinion leaders – be it a UN conference of young scientists or the Berlin Seminar. This brings together leading scientists who present their research without any "translators", to enable interaction with decision-makers in corporations and administration.

## Leverage communication

In any case, communication is an important by-product of all activities in the non-market domain. "As a big global company, we normally keep a low profile on specific political issues. This allows us to keep the lines of communication open to everybody, including our adversaries and critics," explained Dieter Spöri, a former economic minister in the state government of Baden-Württemberg and now Corporate Representative in Germany. "Yes, we have our interest as a company, but we are ready to listen to every argument."

Except for Germany and the US, which have full-time professional concern representatives, in all other 36 countries in which Daimler-Chrysler maintains production facilities, the head of the company country is the "face" seen by the public, politicians and the media. Those who run the business should also be involved in public affairs.

But sometimes DaimlerChrysler has also taken the lead. In the delicate issue of slave labour compensation from the Nazi era, Manfred Gentz, DaimlerChrysler CFO, was a leading figure on the German industry side. Although less damaged by the past than companies that were founded by the Nazis (for example, Salzgitter or Volkswagen), DaimlerChrysler thought that, as a predominantly German–American company, it had a special responsibility and – if things had gone wrong – a special risk exposure to justify this extraordinary engagement. But, as a close observer to the top management noted: "Beyond business logic, this has something to do with values, compassion and an understanding of history."

An honest approach can be seen across all activities. "No hope, no expectations beyond delivery, but consistency and clearly structured implementation" is the basic gospel of Christoph Walther. Good corporate citizenship is part of the business. Nothing more, nothing less. But all this would not be credible if it was not long term (the Chrysler Fund started in 1953) and if it was not permanently on the issue list of the CEO.

## Bringing in the CEO

Although Schrempp earned an image as a "Rambo" and shareholder value advocate, when he turned Daimler–Benz around in the mid-1990s, few of his speeches did not touch on the above themes. A good example is his speech to the Detroit Auto Fair, 15 January 2001, where he had to address a gathering of 1,500 mostly executives at the peak of the Chrysler crisis. He defined four key challenges for Daimler-Chrysler and global automotive companies. Number 4 was: "Successful automotive companies today have to be culturally diversified and socially responsible." He fought against the notion of a "footloose" enterprise, arguing that DaimlerChrysler only has a bright future if the communities the company works for and invests in have this too. In this speech, as in many others: consistency starts at the top.

But Christoph Walther is far from complacent: "We can do better in our early warning system, being more comprehensive and detecting not only business risks, but also opportunities. And probably we can be a bit more proactive. Currently, we struggle to raise an issue before anybody else does it. But we are reacting too much to themes others are driving: journalists, analysts, NGOs, what have you ... My ideal would be that we have an authentic set of messages which we communicate as our contribution to the debate."

## 9.3  SHELL: WHAT DOES IT MEAN TO BE A SUSTAINABLE ENERGY COMPANY?

*Sometimes a crisis helps*

In 1995, Shell was in the midst of an organizational change and policy review process, when the Brent Spar and Nigeria crises hit – events that were still being described in mid-2001 by the then chairman Sir Mark Moody-Stuart as "shaking" and "which struck deep at our own self-esteem, basically".

Being defeated by Greenpeace at the gas pump (having lost the "hearts and minds" battle to Greenpeace) and branded as a ruthless collaborator with a brutal dictator in Nigeria, the years 1996 and 1997 brought much soul-searching and looking for a right way forward at Shell.

Those times are now gone. Brent Spar is a widely quoted case in academia, but of no practical business relevance any longer – the sliced pieces of the huge oil storage buoy serve unobtrusively as a quay foundation in Norway. On the Nigeria issue, Shell is facing an ongoing court battle – among others – in a US court, but with much less blame and finger-pointing than in the mid-1990s. The brand has more than recovered.

In taxing times for the energy industry – due to the roller coaster of oil prices – Shell has embarked on a huge transformation. The experiences of 1995 and 1996 clearly helped in that the momentum did not get lost in all the cost-cutting, restructuring, etc. and in that the new pledge to move toward sustainability was upheld in all the short-term turbulences.

Now, as Robin Aram, Vice President, External Relations and Policy Development, observes, "We are more confident and have to be careful not to become boastful. The Number 1 task is: what does sustainable development mean for the operational business? How to integrate this? And what are the results to be delivered?"

Phil Watts of Shell now easily admits that "corporate responsibility has widened ... society is demanding solutions." But what are the issues that need to be dealt with, taking Shell as an example? What are the expectations? And most importantly: What can a company like Shell really deliver?

### Identifying the issues

I believe that Shell has – in addition to normal business challenges – one big issue to deal with: climate change. As mid-sized issues, I choose two: Nigeria as a symbol of how to conduct business under difficult political circumstances, and biodiversity as the "lead indicator" for minimizing environmental impacts (besides climate change) of fossil fuels.

In addition, there are – in my estimate – between 100 and 150 smaller issues that have to be dealt with: from pipeline leaks in Bolivia, piracy in the Malaysian Strait, religious-motivated protests against sales of girlie magazines at Shell stations in the US to violation of competition laws in Sweden. "If you are not careful, each of them easily can flare up," Shell's Environmental Adviser, Richard Sykes, states, speaking from experience.

In this chapter I have analysed these large- and mid-sized issues first, and then proceeded to future deliverables, preconditions for public acceptance and management implications.

### Climate change: a make it or break it?

Since the "Earth Summit" in 1992, the debate on the "warming up" of the Earth's climate has climbed dramatically on the international agenda – now even a source of political tension between the US government and its European partners. Regularly, international conferences, starting with the Climate Convention in 1992, have paralleled the mounting evidence that the release of "greenhouse gases" might change the climate with unpredictable impacts. The resulting agreement was the "Kyoto Protocol" in late 1997. This, however, has not yet been enacted due to a lack of ratification by member states. And, after the Bush administration renounced the Protocol, public attention is again on the increase – only interrupted by the events of 11 September 2001.

The Bonn Conference in summer 1992 agreed on more flexibility and outvoted the US 171:1. But any global reduction of greenhouse gases without the US – the country representing approximately 25% of the global problem – will be difficult.

The science behind all of this is more than complex, and there are clearly gaps in our knowledge. But the bottom line is simple: if we put all the carbon that has been "stored" as coal, oil or gas deposits over millions of years in the Earth's crust back into the air, we get a similar climate to that which the Earth had before the formation of the present energy resources. That is, much hotter, with higher sea levels, different vegetation – in short, more suited to dinosaurs than mankind.

Clearly, burned fossil fuel is only one of the major sources (between 50% and 60%) of the problem. Other emissions come from methane (especially in cattle raised for beef production or increased rice production) or special chlorinated hydrocarbons. Due to the many interacting variables, it is hard to predict exactly what could happen, and when.

But once the process has started, it will be difficult to stop. Whereas a dwindling minority – centred around the Texan oil industry – argue for more scientific research, most agree that it is time to act now. Even economists, normally not a profession for environmental scaremongering, support this, because decision theory has taught that in decisions under uncertainty, risk-aversion is a rational attitude. The higher the potential loss, decision theory teaches, the more one should be risk-averse.

The EU, as with many nations, has set reduction targets for the emission of $CO_2$ and other greenhouse gases, leading to slower growth of $CO_2$ accumulation in the atmosphere. Targets could be achieved by a change in lifestyle and consumption pattern and more efficient use of energy or "carbon-free" energy sources, from nuclear to renewable sources of energy (with most public opinion supporting the latter). Governments, wary of upsetting the voter, prefer the latter two policies and have started to act along these lines (for example, eco-taxes).

In all this confusing controversy, the public is looking for the "villains" of the piece. By failing to take on their own responsibilities as consumers, it is easy for the public to identify those big companies that are extracting fossil fuel from the Earth's crust. And Exxon Mobil seems to be happy to take on the "villain" role, whereas the European "Majors" – namely Shell and BP – have pledged to lead the world into a sustainable energy future.

*Reducing CO$_2$*

A first move is the "dash for gas", which means using gas instead of coal in power generation. The greenhouse potential of natural gas is approximately 25% lower than coal and can better combine with more efficient technologies (for example, micro-turbines). For Shell, as the biggest gas producer worldwide, this fits nicely into its business strategy, especially after it sold off its coal business – more for commercial reasons than anything else.

A second move is a 10% reduction of Shell's own CO$_2$ emissions by 2002 (related to 1990 as a reference year), despite ambitious growth targets. Although the set target for 2001 was missed, Shell's management is confident that it will reach the overall goal. Internally, CO$_2$ reduction is supported by an exploratory internal emissions trading system, mimicking an emergency market-based scheme for greenhouse gas reduction (basically, units that can cost-efficiently overexceed their targets can sell it to units that have difficulties or face much higher cost than the price of a certificate).

A third move is that every investment project is now calculated under the assumption that between 2005 and 2010 a "carbon tax" of US$5 per tonne of carbon is levied, and thereafter US$10 per tonne.

Critics point out, however, that the emissions by Shell (as with any other oil company) are minor ("peanuts") relative to the emissions of the products sold. They accept the reduction as a gesture of goodwill, but object that this could be used to disguise the bigger environmental impact. So, in all conflicts surrounding new exploration and production sites, environmentalists call for the end of fossil fuel extraction to be replaced by investment in renewables.

*Making renewables commercial*

Shell claims that it is doing what it can in renewables. "If it is commercial, we are serious about it. But we have to make it commercial. And this takes time," insists the former chairman Sir Mark Moody-Stuart.

"But make no mistake about it, hydrocarbons, liquid and gaseous, are going to be absolutely fundamental for decades." Only after 2020 does Shell foresee a real commercial pick-up in renewables, leading to an approximate 30% share of energy supply in 2050 (according to new long-term energy scenarios, the variation is between 30% and 37%, including hydro).

Shell is working on renewables continuously: it has elevated renewables to the fifth business division (next to exploration and production, oil products, chemicals, gas and power). The strategy covers: cultivating sustainable, commercial hardwood forest; converting wood fuel into marketable energy products; implementing rural electrification projects in developing countries; manufacturing and marketing solar panels plus complementary electrical systems; and developing wind energy projects. However, Shell rejects demands to internally cross-subsidize the renewables as it would violate the principle that every division has to self-sustain its revenues.

Another indication of the commitment to transformation of the energy supply toward sustainability was the foundation of Shell Hydrogen in 1999. The vision was that, by 2010, Shell Hydrogen would have led the way to the hydrogen economy. Those were the heady days of fuel cell euphoria, based on technical breakthroughs that brought fuel cells much closer to being commercially viable. In 2000 car manufacturers announced mass-fabrication by about 2005, but have considerably scaled back their projections since then.

By 2010, the consensus assumes there will be 50,000 hydrogen cars, buses or trucks on the streets worldwide – which is approximately 0.000 02% of the total fleet population, probably centred in California and Northern Europe.

This assumption indicates a typical "chicken-and-egg" problem: no hydrogen cars on the street, no fuel infrastructure; no filling infrastructure, no cars on the street. To make things worse, different players will go different ways to generate hydrogen: Japan's project will be based on reforming petrol; the US and Europe are considering either compressed hydrogen gas or liquid, with mainly natural gas as the fuel source. The "wonderland" stage, where cheap electricity is produced from photovoltaics is decades away.

"So you are looking for stepping stones to survive a long winter," a Shell executive described the situation of the company, which has made a couple of – cautious – technology portfolio investments. These intended to learn about market development, gain competence in the new area and observe further developments. Ironically, Shell did own hydrogen know-how in its refinery and chemical plants. This along with other supplies was outsourced for cost reasons – and with it the know-how.

It is of little help to Shell Hydrogen that the market for fuel cells will pick up eventually. Decentralized power production using fuel cells has gained considerable attraction. Companies as diverse as the Swiss engineering company Sulzer and the US giant General Motors now mass-fabricate fuel cells for the building market, which is less demanding than that of the motor industry. But the power supply of the future will come mostly from the existing gas supply and not from hydrogen delivery.

In addition, the Shell Foundation is working with US$30 million in capital to support sustainable energy supply in the framework of community projects (for example, in Bolivia).

But critics are unmoved. Thilo Bode, former head of Greenpeace International, sees far too much inertia and "old thinking" in the oil industry – including Shell – and doubts that the Shell companies are "happily cannibalizing" their business as they claim. "The litmus test for the talks on sustainable development will be how rapidly they will move into renewables. And we will confront their rhetoric on every occasion with their deals."

This determination taught BP the hard way, when they translated their logo into "Beyond Petroleum". Critics saw much higher expectations raised and rushed to bash the "Greenwashing", pointing to BP's ongoing predominance in fossil fuel activities. The company was put in the position of having to withdraw its advertising and PR campaign.

## Nigeria: The long way to normality

Historians, ethnologists and sociologists could argue endlessly as to why a country like Nigeria is blessed with natural resources yet is still one of the poorest countries in Africa and is perceived as one of the worst managed in the world.

For Shell, the question goes beyond any academic deliberation – it is the largest oil and gas producer in Nigeria, although mostly in the position of a minority shareholder relative to the Nigerian National Oil Petroleum Corporation. Here, as in other politically difficult areas, Shell has to either make it work – or get out. Having been in Nigeria for more than 60 years, Shell has always decided to stay ... but today – as a web search reveals – it is no longer the public whipping boy, a greedy multinational, only interested in profits, a picture often painted in the mid-1980s.

The new democratic government in Nigeria faces a number of mind-boggling challenges: out-of-control inflation, crumbling infrastructure, including that of power generation and telephones, epidemic corruption, unimaginable levels of crime and tribal violence. These are but a few of its problems, although a decline in both sabotage and hostage-taking gives some hope for a more positive development.

Despite not having been in Ogoniland since 1993, even today Shell feels unable to return to properly decommission its oil wells, out of concern for the safety of its employees or contractors.

Nonetheless, Shell has changed its approach, how it operates and conducts itself in the business environment. "Proper management of the operation and some hand-outs to dependent communities" would be a pointed, but not unfair, description of the traditional approach. Now, as Heinz Rothermund, former Managing Director of Shell Exploration and Production International and now retired explains, the company's commitment has three pillars:

1 Leveraging the experience in Nigeria by contributing productively to the further development of the energy industry (for example, high-tech development in deep water, liquefying natural gas).

**2** Stimulating the Nigerian economy beyond its involvement in the oil and gas industry (for example, by investing in power plants to mitigate the notorious electricity cuts or by development of contractors).

**3** Stimulating local economies around the locations where Shell is operating.

Whereas the first two pillars are easy to understand as part of a sensitive business strategy, community activities are definitely not. It covers a wide range of actions: micro-credit-financing, income-generating projects for co-operatives and small businesses such as fish-farming or market-gardening; a youth enterprise programme; supporting hospitals, health centres and schools (including adult literacy), building up the rural electricity supply; running training programmes, from catering to secretarial services – to name just some of the most visible.

But it even goes beyond this: "Women have also demonstrated a strong ability to intervene and mediate effectively to avert the escalation of crises in communities. We support ongoing training in peace-making and conflict resolution, and are working with our hosts to establish a critical mass of skilled women's peace groups throughout the (Niger) Delta," reports Shell.

### Stakeholder dialogue in Nigeria

As Rothermund explained – after five workshops with over 500 participants from local communities, NGOs, government departments at all levels, experts and Shell executives, where Shell's social and environmental performance was reviewed and the priorities for further progress were discussed – "We come from an environment where fingers were pointed and blame was laid, for a situation where, over the years, we have all come to know each other and understand each other better. We have begun to build a platform of trust on which we can work together."

The analysis for this book indicates that the new Nigerian government is ready and willing to channel money received from oil revenues, plus development aid from UNDP and European governments, into those regions where oil is produced. But it definitely lacks, as yet, the administrative infrastructure to make the funds work – whereas Shell claims that it is already using government funds in a "transparent and co-ordinated way". So Shell has stepped in to help the national government to do this. But the real question is: Where do you draw the line under such an engagement?

Advocates of "the business of business is business" would clearly argue that all this is going too far. After all, they point out, societies developed governmental institutions to build physical, legal and executional infrastructures and frames, within which businesses can operate. That is true – but what can be done if a government is not living up to its obligations? After the blame it got in the first round, obviously Shell decided to offer to take over some functions that are not normally the core competence for corporations (and let's face it, it is easier to live with mostly academic critics than tolerate the previous outrage). But there are limits to what companies can or should do.

After all, corporations are more efficient than political organizations, because they have a focused, measurable goal: satisfying market demands and earning money out of this. As numerous examples of "politicized" enterprises reveal, companies tend to lose efficiency if they have to follow broader, hard-to-measure and often conflicting political goals.

Putting the reasoning about principles to one side, the Nigeria example contains some interesting lessons about the social dimension of Shell's activities in developing countries. New exploration licences often contain the provision to pay a certain amount as "compensation". Instead of just considering this a cost, Shell is now working with the money and investing it in local capacity-building – not daily needs. By doing that, Shell gets involved – directly or indirectly – in social performance management. This risks technocratic or paternalistic flaws, if it is not balanced by strong engagement with local communities and other stakeholders. This is a slow, laborious and sometimes frustrating process – but there is no alternative.

Shell executives stress that the criticism of its activities in Nigeria has faded and that the lessons learnt have been transferred to other areas, for example, the oil sand project in Athabasca, Canada. "The chances that we are the preferred partner in such projects are increasing with our track record on how to deal sensitively with indigenous people and the environmental concern," argued Tom Delfgaauw, formerly Vice President Sustainable Development (now retired) about the business merit of Shell's new approach.

### Biodiversity: exploration in harmony with nature?

"You Can Be Sure of Shell: Huge Profits Fund Destruction Abroad," headlined a Friends of the Earth press release in February 2001, listing two controversial exploration projects in "some of the world's most environmentally sensitive areas": the exploration in Pakistan's Kirthar National Park (a joint venture with British Premier Oil) and in the Sundarbans mangrove wetland in Bangladesh (home of the Bengal tiger).

Oil and gas reserves, of course, do not only cluster in politically sensitive areas but also in environmentally protected areas. Environmentalists demand "a cast iron guarantee to stay out of protected areas and invest the money in renewables, instead", whereas Shell believes it can operate in these areas with such minimal damage that – balancing all sustainability criteria – it can justify exploitation.

Shell's confidence stems from what was learned in the Camisea project. This took place in an environmentally sensitive area in the upper Amazon region of Peru, bordering the Manu National Park and home to indigenous people. Shell not only received awards for its innovative "inclusive stakeholder" approach but also praise for the new standards of environmental analysis and sensitivity it demonstrated. Previous projects were notorious for disrupting local physical and social environments, leading to deforestation, pollution of rivers and – through the road infrastructure – to an influx of settlers whose "slash and burn" agricultural methods were known to destroy large parts of the rainforest.

### Camisea: the role model

Based on international guidelines (for example, those of the World Bank) and standards, Shell developed an "adaptive" approach to monitor biodiversity and wildlife habits in detail, not just at the start of the project with its environmental impact assessment but continuing througout the entire life cycle of the Camisea project. This approach had to cover not only the exploration and production facilities on site but also the pipeline to the coast. The conclusions drawn from these studies included, for example, electrical power generation needed for the project should not be generated in the rainforest (although this made it more expensive), facilities had to be located far from the indigenous tribe, no roads should be built – instead the Amazon was used, utilizing modified hovercraft. Independent experts were involved and extensive dialogue with more than 40 groups of stakeholders provided feedback.

Throughout the project, it was vital to reach consensus with the operation and construction consortium, notably with Bechtel and Mobil. There was also strong involvement from headquarters, which set the standards and made resources available for the project. However, at the end of 1998 Shell decided not to pursue the project, for commercial reasons, and gave the licence back to the Peruvian government, who sold it to another gas prospector. Since then, environmental concerns for oil activities in the rainforest have increased. For example, in June 2001 a landslide ruptured Ecuador's transnational pipeline – the 14th burst since 1998 – leading not only to widespread spills but also fires in the Andean forest.

### The difficult road to consensus

Although Shell is clearly at loggerheads with some groups on consensus, with others it is trying to find common ground along a defined set of criteria. The organization "Conservation International", an NGO that focuses on biodiversity issues in 32 countries and combines a science-based approach with community involvement and dialogues, is facilitating the discussions. Meanwhile, the Shell Foundation gave a US$2.8 million grant to the Smithsonian Institute, one of the most respected science institutions in the US, to "establish a biodiversity baseline" on which to monitor the impact of human activities. In addition, the Smithsonian is to help to build local capacity in countries that as yet have not been able to meet their obligations under the Biodiversity Convention.

Furthermore, Shell has pledged to pay special attention to biodiversity in environmental assessments that have to be carried out in all new exploration and production projects. In addition, it accepts the need to manage activities in internationally recognized "hot spots" and – if needed – develop conservation plans in co-operation with local stakeholders, where compensation measures are defined or other restrictions imposed. Shell, too, has set up an "early warning system" to inform stakeholders when it intends to work in sensitive environmental areas.

"For business reasons", as Shell maintained, it swapped its stake in the Kirthar National Park for another project in Pakistan. But Friends of the Earth, who led an alliance with local environmentalists and challenged Shell in a Pakistani court, nevertheless claimed victory. With regard to the Sundarbans, Shell declared that it had no intention of moving into this mangrove wetland. Although Shell's authorized bloc covers the area, the promising geology is elsewhere. This, however, might not provide much relief to the pressure on the ecologically stressed Sundarbans. Due to population growth in Bangladesh, 3.5 million people have already moved into the area and now depend on agriculture, fishing and logging – legally and illegally.

### Can Shell build a business case?

Without any doubt, Shell's new approach toward sustainability has been a great success in PR terms. Today, the harder part of implementing these ideas, criteria and sometimes restrictions into operational processes in countries and businesses is in full swing. Shell thinks that it has a powerful process in place to ensure integration of sustainability into its day-to-day business:

- A sustainable development committee has been formed, presided over by the new Chairman of the Committee of Managing Directors (the executive power centre of Shell), and comprises very senior business representatives and senior corporate staff.
- Corporate governance principles stress stronger transparency and dialogue, part of which is Shell's extensive reporting on sustainable development issues.
- The group planning process and, in future, performance assessment and enumeration, will also depend on criteria beyond the bottom line (balanced scorecard approach).
- Key performance indicators for measuring progress are currently identified and verified with stakeholders, so that progress toward sustainable development can be measured.
- Each of Shell's country heads is required to submit an annual "letter of assurance" indicating whether and how he or she has complied with the Shell General Business Principles, which include a commitment to contribute to sustainable development.

However, the desired change – to reach into every corner of the global Shell empire – will only happen if there are positive incentives for operational managers to actively pursue a strategy for sustainable development. So far the upside of the corporate strategy can be seen in the following:

- Negative exposure in the media and public opinion of Shell has been dramatically reduced, the "Fight Shell" individuals and organizations are marginalized. To quote from just one survey of global opinion leaders: in 1999 approximately 65% had a favourable opinion of Shell (compared with 48% in 1997), only 8% had a negative opinion (compared with 12% in 1997). This is no small benefit for a company that sells through 46,000 petrol stations around the globe to millions of customers, not to mention the many customers using heating oil, gas and chemicals, including many public institutions. Although Shell is – compared with its competitors – the most sympathetic brand, it is unclear how this translates into buying decisions. If it could be proven that Shell's strategy for sustainable development attracts more customers to the pumps, the business case would be compelling. But nobody has as yet given proof of this consumer behaviour.

- Shell learns more – and earlier – (for example, than Exxon) about emerging issues: from social trends that shape the markets to potentially disruptive technologies for the fossil fuel business (for example, hydrogen in fuel cells). The option value of this potential first-mover advantage is hard to quantify in ways that hard-nosed "bean-counters" like to be convinced, but it clearly diminishes the risk of being surprised by developments that could jeopardize the business. The available lead time for reaction in such a heavy asset business is a critical factor for long-term success.

- In the "war for talent", the Shell strategy is attractive. Obviously, many employees like what they read in the *Shell Report* (which again indicates that the internal repercussions of environmental and social reporting are more immediate than the external). Potential staff with high qualifications and many other options scrutinize the values of a corporation with particular care. For example, HR managers in Shell offices say that they get more job requests today over and above usual recruiting (however, they emphasize that commitment to sustainability cannot serve as a substitute for professional qualifications). It is plausible that Shell values are – at least in Europe – more in line with the values of most individuals (or as one Exxon manager admitted: "You probably have to be a Mormon to fully identify with our culture").

- Additionally, Shell hopes to become a "preferred partner" for oil and gas exploration or new infrastructure profits (for example, hydrogen stations in publicly funded fuel cell demonstration projects) due to its track record in stakeholder dialogue and environmental responsiveness. Governments all over the world do not want to generate additional trouble. They prefer to choose partners who do not lead to public outrage. Again, this advantage is hard to measure – but nevertheless relevant.

As far as the downside of Shell's strategy is concerned, the following evidence is also relevant:

- Even in sheer monetary terms, the additional cost that might occur – for example, through more intensive stakeholder consultation or investment in environmental technologies – appears to be minor (especially compared with the impact of volatile energy prices). One might argue that this only indicates that Shell has not truly implemented a strategy for sustainable development, but examples so far show that, with creativity, commitment and good management, long-term goals can be balanced with short-term goals (especially profit targets). And it should be noted that the sustainability trinity of economic, environmental and social goals does not necessarily imply that companies are acting in an economically unsound manner.
- There is a "certain transparency paradox": the more a company like Shell reports the less interested the public might become, because a sensational discovery of hidden "dirty laundry" is no longer likely. This is especially true of media reports: nothing ruins a headline more than the fact that this has already been reported by the company itself.
- For NGOs, however, the opposite might be true: the more Shell presents itself as a "force of good" the higher the scrutiny might become. In all conflicts, Shell has been confronted with its own rhetoric on sustainable development and has been accused of not

having applied it, especially in a few specific cases. But this indicates the importance of prudent and cautious communication, not raising expectations that one cannot meet and focusing more on achieved results than intentions. So far, this NGO scrutiny has not posed any serious problem for Shell.

# Appendix I – Business Case vs. Business Ethics

When religion dominated life in the mediaeval ages, businessmen's souls were regarded as being especially at risk, so the Catholic Church charged the Jesuits to take special care of merchants (the Catholic business schools in Spain are today some of the few reminders of this approach).

In Calvinist countries, during the Age of Enlightenment, circumstances changed slightly: now businessmen hired religious advisers to judge the morality of their ventures (it is not known how many were ultimately skipped through).

Over 200 years ago, Adam Smith tried to persuade his fellows, with the famous example that they did not owe their daily bread to the benevolence of their baker, but rather to his pursuit of profit. Since then, the debate of business versus ethics has raged on. Over the centuries, the cyclical discussion has increased in philosophical sophistication, but not in practical relevance. On the one hand are those who believe in the interpretations of Adam Smith, Milton Friedmann or Friedrich V. Hayek, that the only social responsibility of business is to make as much profit as possible (of course "within the rules").

## A fundamental controversy

On the other hand are those advocates – religious or adherents of Kant, among other philosophers – who want to hold businessmen accountable for high moral standards (sometimes higher than they themselves practise: it turned out that several US colleges, boycotting Nike for not paying decent "living wages" to workers in their Asian contract suppliers, failed to pay such a wage to their own workers on campus!).

In addition to the controversy, there is the issue of the comprehension of the word "ethics": which has such different meanings in different cultures. Whereas in the US – according to the definition of the Ethical Officer of the United Technology Corporation, Pat Gnazzo – it means: "Don't lie, don't cheat, don't steal", in Europe people will probably think deeply about deontology (the study of the nature of duty and obligation) versus utilitarianism (the doctrine that actions are right if they are useful or for the benefit of a majority). And what is referred to in the US as an "ethical issue" (for example, equal opportunity regardless of gender or race) is in Germany a normal negotiation between management and the workers' council (as described earlier in the DaimlerChrysler case).

But clearly the issue of business ethics is on the rise again. One measure in the US is the Ethical Officer Association, which was founded in 1992 with 12 members, and is now approaching a membership of 1,000 managers – albeit for very worldly reasons. The rise can be charted from when the US Defense Department began to clean up its supplies industry in the mid-1980s, when the business was awash with kickbacks for the famous "US$500 screwdrivers". Companies with "ethical compliance" programmes could get lower fines than those without. An additional boost was provided in that such programmes could keep a company's board of directors free from legal entanglements, once their managers ran into conflict with the law.

## Lessons from the environmental debate

But is the compliance with legal provisions the core of ethics? Most of the 246 codes of conduct recently counted by the OECD go beyond a specific legal framework, but are often more due to the practical reason that it is difficult for a multinational company to define its relevant legal framework (as has been visible in the case studies in Chapter 8). But most codes are not operational enough to guide daily, or even strategic, business decisions. And, as argued throughout this book, management is more about balancing legitimate but conflicting goals than about "right or wrong".

The environmental debate of the late 1980s and early 1990s is a telling example. Much was said about the clashes between economics and ecology. Although all companies in the Western world have become much cleaner, one is still hard-pushed to find a company that has been driven out of business mainly due to environmental reasons (however, environmentalists would argue that this only indicates that governments have not been tough enough with their regulations).

Once the issues were on the corporate radar screen, companies found many ways to reconcile environmental and economic goals (at least in the opinion of a reasonable majority of citizens). Shareholder advocates might argue that profits could have been higher, but this is a very hypothetical debate without any meaningful standard of reference (for example, the catalytic converter not only led to a cost increase in manufacture and price but also to higher sales due to the accelerated renewal of the car fleet).

### The instrumental view

To take such an instrumental view is trying to build conceptual grounds that accept companies as economic entities, but stresses the empirical evidence that, within economic restrictions, companies can achieve environmental and social goals as well – as outlined throughout this book. The shortcomings of business ethics and shareholder value/ profit maximization arguments should be analysed more closely. The concept of business ethics, regardless of the detailed conclusion, suffers five basic shortcomings. They are discussed below:

1 There is sufficient empirical evidence to demonstrate that individual beliefs or moral obligations do not change organizations, especially when incentives or sanctions point in another direction. A typical example is the subsidiaries of a multinational company such as ABB. Although an ABB plant in India might differ somewhat from one in the US (within the same business unit), the real

difference lies between the Indian ABB and a domestically owned plant, although in personal values the ABB employees might be closer to their Indian than their US colleagues. And ethics is foremost about personal, not organizational, values (can a legal entity have an ethic?).

2  Imposing one ethic on a multicultural, multi-religious, multi-professional workforce might violate basic constitutional rights. Even in the US, the question of privacy has become "big-time", where emails are scanned or Internet access is controlled to ensure "ethical behaviour".

3  Many advocates of ethical behaviour assume that corporations enjoy a degree of autonomy in actions and decision-making. This assumption is unrealistic. For good reason, competitors, customers, regulations, etc. limit the space companies have, even for pursuing their own ethical judgment. And, in addition, different ethical frameworks lead easily to different conclusions. In the debate over the risks of climate change, you can clearly see how the deontologists clash with the utilitarians.

4  An ethical concept that helps managers in their daily, even strategic, decisions has yet to be developed. Often such decisions are highly contextual (for example, can a company be a "force for good" under a dictatorship?). And most ethical frameworks are of a "love-thy-neighbour" variety: they relate, as a rule, to consequences that can be attributed to and observed directly by communities of close proximity, rather than for complex, interlinked, global and generational problems rife with uncertainties and diffuse outcomes, with no single decision/outcome relation.

5  Last but not least, as has been argued before, ethics concepts rarely help the legitimate goals conflict – a situation managers often face. Therefore, it is often easier to come to an agreement as to what is *not* ethical (often of the "don't steal, don't lie, don't cheat" type) than to formulate a comprehensive ethical code of conduct.

The worst thing that can happen to any company is for it to come up with a pompous "Code of Ethics" that is then not lived up to within the company – a fact that will soon be noticed not only by employees but also by customers and other business partners as well as stakeholders. The decline in trust will overcompensate any results of good intentions.

Shareholder value/profit maximization advocates have their short-comings in the way they view the company, that is, basically as a black box. Even assuming that an organization follows only one goal (and everybody is working altruistically in the best interests of the shareholders), given the many uncertainties in business it is rarely self-evident what maximizes profit – mostly one sees the outcome in hind-sight. And one never knows whether this is the maximum profit or whether an alternative strategy or decision would have led to even better results.

Alfred Rappaport, the founding father of the Shareholder Value Concept, was more realistic. His shareholder value is linked by "value drivers" to operational management decisions. These value drivers include value growth duration, sales growth, operating profit margin, investments, cost of capital, etc. – all factors that in turn can be influenced by the way a company manages its non-market environment. The implicit assumption of the profit maximization advocates, there-fore, is that regulators, NGOs and brand image do not matter, that they do not influence the value drivers. In an ideal, neoclassical market economy this might be true – but the empirical evidence of the real world suggests otherwise.

In addition, research on long-lasting companies has pointed out that they follow more a strategy of "optimization" rather than "maximiza-tion" (often by continuous improvement rather than revolutionary leaps). At the time of the dotcom hype, however, this strategy was re-garded as a disadvantage; now it is more in tune with investors.

And this raises the question: What do shareholders really expect from companies? Continuous, sustainable growth (as more pension funds would probably prefer), or a rapid rise, but with high volatility (which investment bankers seem to prefer). Shareholder value is obviously not as clear as its advocates assume.

# Appendix II – Relevant IMD Case Studies

| Case Study | Topic |
|---|---|
| Steger, U. (2002) Embarking on the Journey to Sustainability | Driving sustainability in a (disguised) European metal-recycling company |
| Steger, U. (2002) Hindustan Lever – Leaping a Millennium | Partnership between Hindustan Lever and rural self-help groups illustrating corporate social responsibility |
| Steger, U. (2001) Uniliver Indonesia: Linking Business Strategy to Job Creation | Unilever's business model links business to wealth creation and social responsibility |
| Steger, U. (2001) Under the Spotlight: "It's Always Coca-Cola" | Stakeholder relation and crisis management at Coca-Cola |
| Steger, U. (2001) Monsanto's Genetically Modified Organisms: The Battle for Hearts and Shopping Aisles | Issue and crisis management at Monsanto related to GMOs |
| Steger, U. (2001) Rabobank – Making Sustainability the Norm, Making the Norm Sustainable | Rabobank's efforts to convince customers (i.e. farmers) and staff of organic pig farming |
| Steger, U. (2001) Cleaning up the Supply Chain: Rolling out the Safechem Model | Supply chain management at a Dow subsidiary introducing a closed-loop system to the market |
| Steger, U. (2000) Tetra Pak: Freedom with Accountability | Tetra Pak balances its global environmental strategy with flexibility on regional level |
| Steger, U. (2000) Marine Stewardship Council (A, B) | Unilever and WWF set up certification scheme for sustainable fishing |
| Steger, U. (2000) Transrapid Maglev Train | Stakeholder management and role of the media with regards to a planned high-speed train link |

| Case Study | Topic |
| --- | --- |
| Morosini, P. and Steger, U. (2000) San Patrignano Community (A, B, C) | Leadership, organizational structure and management of an Italian community managed by rehabilitating heroin addicts |
| Steger, U. (1999) Xerox and the Waste-free Office (A, B) | Internal discussion and rollout of Xerox's take-back policy |
| Steger, U. (1999) Better Now than Later | Pros and cons of introducing environmental management systems |
| Steger, U. (1999) Rohner Textil AG: Surviving the Impossible (A), Leveraging Sustainability (B) | Eco-innovation, creation and expansion of a niche market |
| Steger, U. (1998) To Eat or Not to Eat: Mampf Foods and the Biotechnology Question (A, B) | Policy formulation regarding GMOs and crisis management |
| Steger, U. (1998) Murphy's Law and the Crisis at Jurassic Oil Company | Crisis management at fictitious oil company |
| Steger, U. (1997) Schoeller Plast Industries and Returnable Transport Systems (A, Abridged, B) | Business situation, strategy formulation and innovation process at German producer of returnable plastic bottles |
| Steger, U. (1997) Phasing out the Jumbos: Henkel and the Problems of Voluntary Environmental Agreements | Dilemma on if and how to participate in a voluntary agreement |
| Steger, U. (1997) Wetzel GmbH: The Fight against the Rubber Smell | Conflict management between medium-sized company and the local community |
| Steger, U. and Killing, P. (1996) Brent Spar Platform Controversy (A, B, C) | Stakeholder and crisis management at Shell |
| Steger, U. (1996) Tupperware and the BUND | Business–NGO co-operation and environmental marketing |

# Further Reading

Collins, J. C. and Porras, J. I. (1996) *Built to Last: Successful Habits of Visionary Companies.* London: Century.

Curtin, T. (2000) *Green Issues.* Houndmills, UK: Macmillan Press.

SustainAbility (2002) *Good News & Bad: The Media, Corporate Social Responsibility and Sustainable Development.*

Elkington, J. (2001) *The Chrysalis economy: How Citizen CEOs and Corporations can Abuse Values and Value Creation.* Oxford: Capstone.

Fussler, C. and James, P. (1996) *Driving Eco-innovation: A Breakthrough Discipline for Innovation and Sustainability.* London: Pitman.

Rheinhard, F. (1999) Bringing the environment down to earth. *Harvard Business Review,* **77**(4): 149–158.

Steger, U. (1998) *The Strategic Dimensions of Environmental Management: Sustaining the Corporation during the Age of Ecological Discovery.* Houndmills, UK: Macmillan Press.

Steger, U. (1998) *Discovering the New Pattern of Globalization.* Ladenburg, Germany: Daimler–Benz Foundation.

Winter, M. and Steger, U. (1998) *Managing Outside Pressure: Strategies for Preventing Corporate Disasters.* Chichester, UK: John Wiley & Sons.

Zadek, S. (2001) *The Civil Corporation: The New Economy of Corporate Citizenship.* London: Earthscan.

Kong, N., Salzmann, O., Steger, U. and Ionescu-Somers, A. (2002) Moving business/industry towards sustainable consumption: The role of NGOs. *European Management Journal,* **20**(2): 109–127.

# Index